SELF

ACTUALIZATION

PSYCHOLOGY

The Positive Psychology

of Human Nature's Bright Side

Meta-Coaching Volume IV

L. Michael Hall, Ph.D.

Published by: **NSP —*Neuro-Semantics Publications***
P.O. Box 8
Clifton, CO. 81520-0008 USA
(970) 523-7877

Printed by: **Action Printing**
Jerry Kucera, Owner
516 Fruitvale Court, Unit C
Grand Junction, CO. 81504
(970) 434-7701

Neuro-Semantics® is the trademark name for the model, patterns, and society of Neuro-Semantics. ISNS stands for the International Society of Neuro-Semantics. For more than 4000 pages of free information, see the web sites:

www.neurosemantics.com
www.neuro-semantics-trainings.com
www.meta-coaching.org
www.self-actualizing.org
www.nlp-video.com

Self-Actualization Psychology

Dedicated to

Abraham H. Maslow

the first psychologist to pioneer

exploration into the bright side of human nature

which launched Third Force Psychology

and the first Human Potential Movement

PREFACE

*"What lies behind us and what lies before us
are tiny matters
compared to what lies within us."*
Ralph Waldo Emerson

W hen I wrote my first book on self-actualization, *Unleashed: A Guide to Your Ultimate Self-Actualization* I used *Self-Actualization Psychology* as my assumptive theory. Yet as I did that, I also made a mistake.

The mistake was that I put too much of the theory in the book. Well, at least I attempted to. In the original text I included five chapters on the heart and essence of *Self-Actualization Psychology*. I thought it was needed there. Yet my larger goal was to write to a broad general audience. And given that those chapters were more academic, they just did not make the cut. Conversations with several editors made me realize that I needed to eliminate those chapters and to use them for a separate book. And that's how I gave birth to this book.

The book *Unleashed* focuses on *the how* of self-actualization. *How* do we actualize our highest and best? And of course, my inspiration for it all was the vision Abraham Maslow set forth:
> "Every baby has possibilities for self-actualization but most get it knocked out of them. I think of the self-actualizing man not as an ordinary man with something added but rather as the ordinary man with nothing taken away. The average man is a human being with dampened and inhibited powers." (Edward Hoffman's biography of Maslow, *The right to be human, 1988,* p. 174)

What is self-actualization? *It is being fully human.* It is being an *ordinary person with nothing taken away.* It is experiencing our innate and fundamental powers in their purity of strength and focus— not dampened or inhibited. How about that? It is getting over, and releasing, anything and everything that interferes with growing to full maturity. It is releasing everything that *dampens* and *inhibits* your powers. It is, as Carl Rogers put it, being a "fully functioning human being" or "becoming a person."

This vision of self-actualization by Maslow and Rogers was not about becoming extraordinary. The vision is rather to become everything that you already have the latent potential to become. And that is very different. That's why it is not about adding things as much as it is about *reclaiming* all that you already have within as your heritage as a human being.

What is Self-Actualization Psychology? It is the kind of psychology that undergirds the unleashing processes which enable us to actualize our highest and best. It is this psychology which provides the theoretical foundations and frameworks for *Unleashed*. And it is this kind of psychology that speaks about the bright side of human nature —the psychology of healthy men and women.

While researching the background for this book I discovered that Abraham Maslow wanted to write this book. Well, not this particular book. He did want to write a book on Self-Actualization Psychology. He spent his whole life in preparation for it. He created the foundations for it. Then tragically, he died before he could do that. Having studied self-actualizers from the 1940s through the 1960s, Maslow wrote five primary books about self-actualization. As a tremendous pioneer on the bright-side of human nature, Maslow caught a vision of studying and detailing the characteristics of people at their best, fully-functioning, and making real their highest possibilities.

That's the heart and soul of *Self-Actualization Psychology*. And for anyone working with psychologically healthy people, this is the kind of psychology that's needed today more than ever. It is for coaches, trainers, consultants, leaders, managers, business owners, marketers, entrepreneurs, sales people, parents, teachers, etc. It is the kind of psychology that's needed for changing our world. It is needed for self-actualizing companies, businesses, groups, churches, and countries. And that's why this book is also in the series of Meta-Coaching—this is also the Psychology of Self-Actualization Coaching.

Self-Actualization Psychology radically departs from traditional psychology. As a paradigm shift, it will be a shock to those trained in abnormal psychology who have spent years learning about human nature based on studying neurotics, people suffering from parenting errors, traumas, etc.

The focus in *Self-Actualization Psychology* shifts to a new concern. Its focus is on how good life, society, and business human nature allows us. It focuses on how to be our best and to bring out the best in others. It is based on a belief in the goodness of human nature, and that every form of human "evil" is a derived from frustrating human nature (deficiency) or hurting it conceptually (through distorting or diminishing our nature).

The foundations for *Self-Actualization Psychology* arose in the middle of the twentieth century as the third force in psychology after Behaviorism (Learning theory) as the first force and Psychoanalysis as the second force. Self-Actualization Psychology arose to offer corrections to these earlier psychologies. It is the psychology that inspired the movement that Maslow, Rogers, and many others created—the *Human Potential Movement.*

This book takes a new look at the first Human Potential Movement to explore what it was and what happened to it. After exploring the collapse of the first movement, I make a case for the need to launch a new twenty-first century movement. My intention is to pick up where Maslow left off and launch a new Human Potential Movement for explicitly focusing on actualizing human potentials.

Also within this book I have presented an exposition of a model of Self-Actualization. I've written one chapter on *the process of modeling* to identify what's involved in the creating of new models and what was missing in the original models by Maslow. In another chapter, I describe how I have extended the self-actualization models of Maslow to actualize his work and make explicit how self-actualization works.

If *Self-Actualization Psychology* offers a new kind of psychology and a new discipline that's focused on the self-actualizing process itself, then who will be the persons presenting and facilitating this kind of psychology? To address that, I've written a chapter on the emerging field of *coaching* and how its focus on psychologically healthy people makes it an excellent discipline for this kind of psychology. In other words, as coaches work with the population who has either graduated from therapy or who never needed it—they need a new kind of psychology, one that maps how healthy people actualize their best skills and expressions.

The paradigm shift that Maslow created exposed the inadequacy of the old theories of human motivation. He revolutionized psychology as he showed the biological basis of our higher needs, that our self-actualization drives originated in our instinctoid impulses. This means that it is human nature to *need* work to be meaningful, to be creative, to live in a world were we strive for fairness and justice, to want order, beauty, significance, preferring to do things well, etc.

If you want a developmental psychology that takes people to ever new and ever higher levels of experience and development, then *Self-Actualization Psychology* explores the farther reaches of human nature and the tools for actualizing generative change.

In this new Neuro-Semantic approach to self-actualization, we begin by revisiting the genius of Abraham Maslow. That will then allow us to stand firmly on his shoulders and the shoulders of the other giants who first explored the bright side of human nature. And that will allow us to see farther, to extend and expand their models, and to begin to push the boundaries of where we have mapped the unleashing of human possibilities and potentials.

A special acknowledgments to the following:

> *Michelle Duval* (Australia)
> > For her partnership in co-developing Meta-Coaching and encouraging me to explore Self-Actualization.

> *Cheryle Rayson* (Australia)
> > For her editing and proof-reading of the text.

> *Adrian Beardsley* (Australia)
> > For his insights and diagrams.

> *Shane Steward* (Australia)
> > For his proof-reading and provocative notes.

PART I:

THE

PSYCHOLOGY

Chapter 1

INTRODUCING

THE PSYCHOLOGY

The Psychology of the Bright Side
of Human Potentials

*"Man is asked to make of himself
what he is supposed to become to fulfill his destiny."*
Paul Tillich

"A person is both actuality and potentiality."
Abraham Maslow (1968, 10)

*S*elf-Actualization Psychology is the psychology that's specifically designed to focus on the farther reaches of human nature, rather than on remedial change and therapeutic issues. And it has a specific object—to *enable people to unleash their highest potentials*. This is the bright-side of psychology. It is the positive psychology of human growth and development. And involved in discovering this new kind of psychology is specifying the factors that limit, and have limited, traditional psychology from mapping the pathway of self-actualization.

As a discipline, psychology is the study of our inner life. To the extent that we speak about the mind-body-emotion system, we are speaking about human "psychology." This term simply refers to our *ideas* and *feelings* about ourselves and others, our beliefs and theories about human nature, and how we work. It includes our understandings when things go wrong, and how to correct them. It is a study of our psyche in all of its dimensions.

Yet to get into *the heart of unleashing,* we have to deal with a problem. Actually it is one of the biggest obstacles that stops and interferes with the kind of generative change needed for actualizing human potential. And that problem is the very psychology models which we have historically used to understand ourselves, our needs, and our potentials. The problem is trying to use psychological models about abnormality, trauma, how people become wounded, or even normality, for facilitating the process of functioning at our best.

Once upon a time, I took it for granted that "psychology" had a lot to say about people at their best, people experiencing the richest of thoughts and feelings, and people performing optimally. Then I was surprised, even shocked, to discover that it does not. In the history of psychology, stunningly little has actually been explored or written regarding all of the incredible potentials within human nature. Instead, the field historically has been focused almost entirely on hurt, trauma, brokenness, problems, abnormality, etc.[1]

This explains why the self-actualization of psychologically healthy people requires a paradigm shift and a whole new psychology. Now I am certainly not the first one to note this or the first one to forge in this direction. Not by a long shot. The shift began to occur in the middle of the twentieth century with the launching of "the third force" in psychology. Those who pioneered that movement recognized the need in the field of psychology for a focus on *people at their best,* people enjoying life and thriving, where they find themselves "in the zone," and people in *flow* states of self-actualization who are able to take their performances to new and exciting levels and regularly experiencing peak experiences.

The Dark Side of Human Nature

For those exposed or trained in *abnormal* psychology, and even in the normal psychology of the typical developmental stages, those who pioneered *the psychology of human potential* were the Christopher Columbuses of a new psychology, madly envisioning a brave new world.

To a great extent it is a *new* world because it is based on a whole set of premises that differ from those who started the first of modern psychology by studying the dark side of human nature—the *abnormal* psychology of human pathology. Now, it is not so much that the old premises are wrong as it is that they are limited. They are limited to describing people who are hurt and damaged and this approach limited psychology from exploring the highest of human potentials. Abnormal psychology describes people hurt, traumatized, threatened, arrested at various stages of development, and coping as best they can with both the external and internal factors that threaten to de-humanize them. Yet studying how people think, feel, and cope when they are battered and wounded isn't exactly the foundation for exploring "the farther reaches of human nature."

The psychology of pathology focuses on seeing the multiple ways that people in pain and suffering attempt to cope in maintaining their humanity, and even their sanity. Now if that hurt occurred early in life so that one began life with distorted understandings and mental maps, and then used those distorted mental maps during the formative years of the imprint experiences, then the ways that life can go wrong, become self-destructive, and sabotage one's own best interests seem almost infinite. There's so many ways for things to get into a muddle.[2]

Obviously, abnormal psychology has been helpful for those so unfortunate to go through living hells as children, or quiet de-humanizing contexts (dysfunctional homes run by people who didn't go to Parenting 101). Yet all of that is about *a psychology of human nature gone wrong.* It's not the norm of human experience, let alone of people thriving with passion and commitment. That's why only studying human limitations, traumas, and distortions has, to a large extent, led us astray. It has seduced us to "sell human nature short" as Maslow frequently commented. For many, it has even undermined faith in people and human nature and it has blinded our understanding of what's possible under the best of circumstances. Abnormal psychology has itself become one of the *prisons of the mind* that continues to keep people leashed to small ideas about personality change and the possibilities of human transformation.[3]

By inventing the category of "mental illness," psychology and psychiatry have created an entire domain on the classification and diagnosis of mental illness. How helpful this has been has actually been questioned even by many trained in psychiatry.[4]

The focus of abnormal psychology is like studying wrecked cars in a junkyard that have been crashed, blown up, driven off bridges or mountains, exploded in head-on collisions. It is like examining those wrecks and concluding, "This is the nature of automobiles." Imagine what we would build if our understanding of automobiles were based on that study. Wouldn't that be exciting! That would kill anyone's excitement in automobile design and construction. If car designers assumed that the cars are especially vulnerable, then metal plated square-boxes (military Humvees) would become the ideal.

Beyond the Dark Side
The good news is that there's more to our nature than hurts and pains. That we have both *dark* and *bright* sides says something significant about our nature. It says something about human adaptability. Our nature as human beings is not solely written into our genes, *we participate significantly in the development of our own nature.* Any particular human expression is *not* the whole story. We can move in directions that are diametrically opposite to our well-being. Because we have choice, we are not fated to either the dark or the bright side. Human nature is rich and varied. It can be grossly distorted as it can be incredibly inspirational and sacred.

To unleash potentials and to facilitate self-actualization, we obviously have to first heal our wounds, get over our traumas, and bring an end to whatever "unfinished" business we may still be carrying around. These things are foundational for moving to a higher psychology. Once regular psychology can get us "up to average" so that we are "okay," we are then ready for another kind of psychology. We are ready to turn to the bright side of human nature, to *self-actualization psychology.*

Traditional psychology has been almost entirely *remedial*—seeking to remedy the errors, distortions, and hurts that occur in the adventure of living. Later, as psychology itself matured, it began looking at the prescriptive side of things, identifying the normative, the way things are when all goes well.

It was not until the middle of the twentieth century that psychologists began to catch a vision of *generative* psychology. This meant going beyond what is normative, in terms of averages and probabilities, to what can be, to the farther reaches of human possibilities. As this exciting new idea took root in the minds of numerous people it gave birth to a great many new psychologies from Logotherapy, Reality

ıl-Emotive Therapy, Ericksonian, Psycho-Synthesis,
tive Therapy, NLP, Positive Psychology, etc.[5]

ın Psychology

psychology, psycho-pathology, and even normal
f-Actualization Psychology. The focus and heart
ın psychology is to explore the bright side of
...ıman nature by examining the best specimens and extrapolating
what else is possible. Self-actualization is making our talents,
passions, and potentials *actual* or *real*. Carl Rogers describes self-
actualization as becoming a "fully functioning" human being.

The verb *actualization* is a holistic one speaking of a mind-body
synergy. Such synergy arises from connecting and unifying the best
meanings, passions, and understandings on the inside world of mind
with the best responses that translate those ideas into everyday life.
It *makes actual* the inner game of our highest ideals, dreams,
meanings, hopes, and understandings giving expression in our outer
game of performance.

This gives Self-Actualization Psychology a practical orientation, one
away from theorizing to *implementing and making actual what is
possible.* It pushes the boundaries, provokes us to stretch beyond our
current experiences, and challenges us to even higher levels of
experience. It is particularly this pushing, stretching, and challenging
that makes this psychology different from the psychologies that have
governed and directed therapy which have been more focused on
nurturing, re-parenting, validating, supporting, and comforting.

What do we call this new psychology? Maslow called it Growth
Psychology, *Being* Psychology, Third Force Psychology, Self-
Actualization Psychology, Positive Psychology, Becoming
Psychology rather than deficiency psychology (1968, vii), and the
Study of Human Potentialities.

A New Profession for a New Psychology
If the psychology of abnormality and trauma spawned the
professional modality of psycho-*therapy,* what would be the
profession and professionals of this new psychology? What is the
profession of psycho-*actualizing*?

Professionals in this new psychology will not work to build up a person's ego-strength in order to face reality—that's the goal of traditional psychology. They will rather *challenge* people to take their experiences and performances to new levels by questioning

> *The psychology of human potential* is the Christopher Columbus of psychology, madly describing a compelling *brave new world*.

conventionality and releasing fears and taboos. They will use their knowledge about the *unleashing process,* and the psychology of self-actualization, to question, probe, test, provoke, co-create, celebrate and test people and the transformations they desire. They will initiate fierce dialogues to generate a crucible wherein they will "hold the space" for new kinds of experiences to emerge.[6]

Today one profession that seems to be coming close to doing this is the emerging field of coaching. At least the kind of coaching that clearly distinguishes itself from therapy, such as Meta-Coaching, which I'll describe in a later chapter. Because coaching psychologically healthy people requires a lot of ego-strength, it is not for the faint of heart. Nor is it for those who easily feel assaulted, criticized, offended, or hurt. People who are inwardly hurt and wounded first need the healing of therapy to prepare and ready them for the challenging nature of coaching.

What's unique about these professionals that goes beyond consulting, mentoring, and training? It is that those who facilitate self-actualization uniquely focus on *actualizing* a person's potentials use a *generative psychology* that brings forth the bright side of human nature.

Whatever we call this new profession, the self-actualizing process involves a rough and tumble of challenge, stretching, and confrontation. Via this approach a facilitator challenges beliefs, performances, achievements, the lack of achievement, etc. Believing in the resilience and the ego-strength of the client, the facilitator pulls no punches. He or she does *not* operate as a parent, expert, or even a teacher, but primarily as an awakener, challenger, prober, provoker—believing in the client (typically believing in the client more than the client believes in him or herself) and constantly challenging and evoking the client to not sell him or herself short from the potential possibilities that can be realized.

Abnormal/ Normal Psychology	Self-Actualization Psychology
Lower needs	Higher needs
Deficiency	Abundance
Remedial	Generative
Ego-defenses	Ego-expressions
Transference	Ownership of responsibility
Develop ego-strength	Challenge ego-strength
Get person up to average	Become the best one can become
Feel OK about self	Become self-forgetful
	Express oneself as full as possible
Feel safe	actualize, challenge, stretch
Coping	Mastering
Analyze and heal	Awaken and push
Develop responsibility	Assume and express responsibility
Re-parent errors of parenting	Give and nurture others

As a modality about change, it is especially for people who see and experience themselves as *change-embracers*. By contrast, while therapy also involves change, it aims primarily at *remedial* change. Typically, therapy approaches change more indirectly, often having to be very gentle, because the client can't handle too much "reality." This is *not* the case for people who are ready for self-actualization. Being excited by challenge, they embrace change.

Beyond Therapy to Actualizing
In the process of psychotherapy, and especially psychoanalysis, the great barrier in the beginning and throughout the process is *resistance*. The person wants to change and yet, at the same time, fears change, and so resists it. What explains this ambivalence? It goes to two things—the lack of safety and strength to change. The ego is typically not strong enough to fully face and embrace the change. The ego easily feels threatened and endangered and so activates various ego-defenses to fend off the possibility of the very changes so desperately desired.

What's a therapist to do given this? The first task is to create a sense of safety and a relationship of safety for the client. Therapists primarily develop skills for nurturing and comforting clients in order to make the change seem non-threatening. The therapist must also calmly and patiently listen, and seek to understand, the client on his or her own terms in order to be experienced as non-threatening.

Why all of this? Because therapists essentially work to *re-parent* clients, empathically giving support, care, love, and validation. And the reason for this is because generally the opposite of those ingredients were or are missing in the client's life and so often created at least some damage or deficiency in the first place. This explains why *transference* (the transferring of feelings from parents to the therapist) so readily occurs in therapy and has to be anticipated, dealt with, and utilized for the therapeutic process.

In *Self-Actualization Psychology,* the unleashing of potentials for self-actualization works in an entirely different way and so appeals to an entirely different population. It appeals to those who have successfully completed the developmental stages and who are not living a wounded life. It appeals to those who have the ego-strength to face change and those who actually enjoy, hunger for, and embrace challenge. The idea and feeling of change not only settles well with them, it is recognized and felt as the very heart of being alive. They enjoy change. No wonder *generative* change is viewed as a positive thing—something to move toward. No wonder it is embraced as something that brings pleasure and reward.

Self-Actualization Psychology does not deny or discount the psychologies that deal with hurt, trauma, and other disorderings of personality. Not at all! These are valid approaches to human nature and especially to those who have been hurt, violated, and who have tried to cope by using various ego-defenses. Having worked as a psychotherapist for two-decades, I know this area well and know how difficult and challenging it can be. I also deeply admire those who have developed the expertise and aptitude to work in this area that can be tremendously unnerving and frustrating at times.

However the approach here fits another context. It is for those ready, even hungry, for a challenge. *Self-Actualization Psychology* is for those who have successfully pushed through the hurt and trauma and have learned to cope with life and deal with the cards life has dealt them. They have moved beyond just coping and getting by to the place where they want to master life. They have developed the ego-strength to first accept reality for what it is to then fully appreciate it as they use it creatively for fully living the human adventure.

The vision here is that of going beyond the normative to living and becoming *fully human, fully alive.* It is a vision of passion, creativity, love, investment, responsibility, being innovative, contributing, and making a difference.

The Key Points in this Chapter
- *Self-Actualization Psychology,* building on the older psychologies, focuses on the next developmental stages of relatively healthy people. It focuses on those whose lower needs are basically taken care of and who are ready to move up to the higher or meta-needs.

- *Self-Actualization Psychology,* focusing on the bright side of human nature, addresses the highest potentials and developments in human possibility. Its aim is to *model the brightest and best,* those who have set a higher benchmark for what's possible in human nature.

- *Self-Actualization Psychology* is currently giving birth to entirely new professions—to the men and women who work with those who are ready for the adventure of embracing generative change. These psycho-actualizers are coaches and facilitators who focus on enabling known and unknown potentials to unleash so that a whole new world of possibilities opens up.

End Notes:

1. It makes perfect sense that the study of psychology and the practice of psychotherapy originally arose to deal with hurt, pain, trauma, etc. rather than human excellence. It arose originally to explain the problems that arise when people are violated or hurt. It arose to explain mental illness, hysteria, "craziness," dysfunction, etc. As such, it was *remedial* in nature—seeking *remedies* to fix things.

2. See Bateson, *Step to an Ecology of Mind,* Part I, Metalogues, "When things get Muddled."

3. In *Unleashed: A Guide to Your Ultimate Self-Actualization* (2007) I wrote about numerous "prisons of the mind" that create leashes.

4. See Thomas Szasz classic about this, *The Manufacture of Madness* (1970). Also see *The Structure of Personality* (2001, Hall, Bodenhamer, Bolstad, etc.).

5. The Cognitive Movement was launched in 1956 with George Miller and Noam Chomsky's work. Maslow and Roger's work began in the 1940s and extended into the 1970s. NLP began in 1975 as Bandler and Grinder modeled Satir, Perls, and Erickson. Positive Psychology began in 1999 Martin Seligman, Mihaly Csikszentmihalyi, Aaron Antonovsky, George Valliant, Suzanne Ouellette Kobasa.

6. The "crucible" space of transformation is described in the book, *Unleashed.*

Chapter 2

THE CORE IDEA

The Psychology of Realizing Possibilities

"My investigations on self-actualization ... started out as an effort
of a young intellectual to try to understand two of his teachers
whom he loved, adored, and admired
and who were very, very wonderful people . . .
I tried to see whether [their] pattern could be found elsewhere,
and I did find it elsewhere, in one person after another. . . .
My generalizations grew out of *my* selection of certain kinds of people
. . . whom [I] liked or admired very much
and thought were wonderful people."
Abraham Maslow

Given that the field of Psychology began by focusing on trauma and hurts, on things that interfere with normal growth and development, the entire focus of traditional psychology zoomed in on problems, dysfunction, neuroses, psychosis, and damage. As a result, the focus did not include people realizing their highest possibilities.

Yet the idea of self-actualization kept popping up over the years. It popped up momentarily in various ways in the writings of numerous people in the 1920s and 1930s and so set the stage for Abraham Maslow and the Human Potential Movement.

The story of Abraham Maslow is a story of a man who caught a vision and who pursued that vision to such an extent that he ended up creating an entire *paradigm shift* in the field of Psychology. In doing this *he led the way in changing psychology from the dark side to the bright side of human nature.* Amazing, wouldn't you say? And due to his commitment in modeling self-actualizers and peak experiencers, he established a human and scientific basis for the vision of people having far more potential than we ever dared to imagine and the mission of discovering how to unleash human potentials.

Precursors of Maslow

Alfred Adler broke away from Freud's negative and deterministic psychology to create Individual Psychology wherein he put a strong emphasis on the social dimension, life scripts, and the importance of the drive of striving for superiority. Adler also spoke about the emergence of the creative self which arises as our way of shaping our own personality. Realizing that our biological drives alone do not explain our psychology, but that there is a teleological pull forward for meaning, Adler focused on the importance of meaningful goals in our psychological life.

Adler was also one of Maslow's mentors and Colin Wilson (1972) in his biography of Maslow speaks about 1935 to 1940 as his Adlerian years. During that time he researched the idea of dominance in the sexual behavior of monkeys, he drew the conclusion that sexual behavior was used for the drive for dominance. Later in his studies of female sexuality he evolved a new theory with dominance playing a central role rather than sexual selection (1972, pp. 149-157).

Carl Jung, also broke from Freud, contributed to self-actualization with his concept of *individuation*. This refers to the developmental process that's directed toward achieving wholeness. For him, the self is the archetypal tendency of the personality to seek wholeness in its development as it works for order, unification, and harmony. Jung also contended that the mind lives by *aims,* that people can only be completely understood in terms of their *goals.*

Jung also contributed to self-actualization by identifying four factors that defines how we experience ourselves in relationship to information and to the world. He used Sensor/Intuitor distinction to differentiate the ways we relate to knowledge— do we tend to get data from the outside (sensory based information) or the inside from our constructs (Intuitive). He also differentiated those who move through life just observing and perceiving in order to adapt to it (Perceiver) and those who move through life with ideas about how it ought to be and so adapt the world to themselves (Judgers).

Years later these distinctions were used to create two important meta-programs in the field of NLP.[1]

Otto Rank was the last of the major disciples of Freud to brake away. His interest went beyond pathology as seen in his book, *The Artist*, in which he dealt with his lifelong preoccupation, the psychology of the artist.   It was Rank who rediscovered *the will* (conation) in psychology and who took a revolutionary step away from Freud as he talked about the will-to-health as a key ingredient in psychological well-being.

Kurt Goldstein, a psychiatrist, working with brain-damaged soldiers from the First World War, developed a personality theory using the term "self-actualization."   He described self-actualization as the inner process of the body and mind to fulfill its innate needs and potentials. He said that self-actualization is "doing the best with his capacities that the world permits." All other characteristics are in the service of this sovereign tendency toward self-actualization.

For him, the human organism is driven for self-actualization.
> ". . . the drive which sets the organism going is nothing but the forces which arise from its tendency to actualize itself as full as possible in terms of its potentialities." (1963, p. 172)

Karen Horney and *Erich Fromm*, psychoanalysts, contributed to the new psychology with their focus on the inner personal development of human freedom and responsibility. Malsow learned from each and found in Horney yet another mentor.

These were some of the first theorists who began asking questions about human nature beyond trauma and dysfunction.   Then, as Developmental Psychology began to emerge, others began asking the questions that continued to create a new space for self-actualization:
- What does it mean to be fully human?
- What are the stages after recovery from trauma?
- What is a mature, fully developed human being like?
- What are the highest potentialities for a person who continues to grow and develop?
- What needs, drives, and urges emerge in a person after the gratification of all of the basic biological needs?
- What does psychological health and maturity consist of?

Abraham Maslow's Quest

Maslow didn't begin with self-actualization, that arose and emerged over the years of his studies and experiences. In terms of his studies, he began with monkeys. In fact, he was part of the original research of Harry Harlow's work with chimpanzees. Here he worked with gentle animals with many social needs and the ability to learn and create for the pleasure of creating. This began to provoke many questions about the old evolutionary idea current at that time that based "human nature" on the paradigm of "bad" animals — mean, vicious, competitive, aggressive, red tooth and claw, etc.

Next, he moved into studying female sexuality. Yes, that's right. In fact, prior to Kinsey, Maslow had a reputation that surprised even him. He was recognized as a foremost expert on female sexuality. From today's perspective, it may seem funny. This came about as he was a post-graduate student working under the supervision of the famous Behaviorist psychologist, E.L. Thorndike, in his lab. Working on sex and dominance, he designed a questionnaire and simply interviewed females in his office about their sex lives. "And everybody was scandalized." And that was it, he simply asked them questions about their sexuality. Yet at the time, he knew more about that subject than anyone—well, from the "scientific standpoint."

Next, he explored anthropology and worked under the guidance of Ruth Benedict with the Blackfoot Indians in Canada. There he found a social group that was not based on the "animal" nature of competition, but that operated by highly evolved principles of sharing, giving, contributing, respecting each other, etc. This challenged the idea that human nature is inherently aggressive and competitive. It planted the seeds in his mind about the higher nature.

From these studies, an event occurred that caught his fancy and stunned him regarding the deficiency of his knowledge. After his doctoral studies, he moved back to New York for post-graduate work and there he met two professors who struck him as exceptionally wonderful people. So wonderful and exceptional did he find them that he began taking notes on them as he began his own private study to figure them out. But that's when he hit a road block. For all of the models, premises, and laws that he had learned in the psychology at that time (Behaviorism and Psychoanalysis), he could not explain these people. The psychologies of that time were woefully inadequate to explain or provide any understanding of *Max Wertheimer* (a co-founder of Gestalt Psychology) and *Ruth Benedict* (a pioneering leader in Cultural Anthropology).

So he had a problem. Everything he knew from his doctoral level understanding of psychology and how people function provided almost nothing that helped him understand these two very "wonderful people." In observing them, the psychological paradigms at the time completely failed to explain their style of life, motivations, or their everyday functioning. Something was missing.

Of course, the difference was that Maslow was looking at two extremely healthy, growth-oriented, and self-actualizing persons and the psychological paradigms at the time were focused mostly on abnormality. Behaviorism was just beginning to explore normality, but nothing about human excellence or self-actualization. So Maslow launched his *"Good Humans Study"* which he eventually called self-actualization and those who were experiencing it, self-actualizers. Then, a short time after that, another event occurred which would set the focus for his studies for the rest of his life.

A Psychology for World Peace
During the late 1930s, Maslow had been paying attention to the disastrous events in Europe and the World War that Hitler initiated. During that time, Maslow's curiosity was being stimulated about it— about war and human conflict.

Then came the bombing of Pearl Harbor. So in December 1941, immediately after the bombing of Pearl Harbor when the United States entered the Second World War, Maslow had a peak experience, an *Aha!* that changed his life. The first thought that struck him was that he had to do something to help. But what? "I'm too old to join the army." (He was 33 at the time.) So what could he do? What could he contribute? That's when the *Aha!* occurred.

What he recognized was that what world leaders really needed to create peace was a comprehensive and accurate model of human motivation. That was it! So he set out to create a model of motivation that would explain how people could be motivated to follow a Hitler. What motivated a Hitler in the first place? If we could understand what creates that kind and quality of neurosis, we could do something about it, something to prevent it. It was Maslow's urge to do something, to contribute what he could, that initiated the project that consumed the rest of his life.

Since he had been studying motivation—animal motivation, dominance and submission in cultural groups, female sexual motivation, the cultural motivation of the Blackfoot Indians and their way of life, Maslow realized that what world leaders, politicians, and leaders at all levels need was *a motivation theory* that could both explain people. What drives them? What is normal for human motivation? What is abnormal? How can motivation go astray? What do people need to be motivated for the highest and best of human possibilities? What was needed was a motivation theory that could adequately explain and predict the motivated actions of people, and how to work with human motivation in a way that enables people to keep on developing rather than regressing and so falling back into conflict and war.

To create peace we have to really understand what people want, we have to be able to answer such questions as:

> Why do people do what they do? What do people really want? What do leaders offer and provide that plays into their motivation? How does mature motivation get interrupted? Why are some attracted to a Hitler, Stalin, and Mussilini? What structures personalities to create different motivational states? What is needed to facilitate people to become psychologically mature? Are people innately evil or does evil arise from another source?

So it was at that moment in time, December of 1941, that Maslow decided that the best he could do for the peace table was to provide an accurate and useful model of human motivation. And with that his mission began in earnest. By 1943 he had created his *levels of needs* and had published his first paper on *the hierarchy* of human motivations. Then, throughout the rest of the 1940s, he published scores and scores of articles on this new model. Then in 1954 his classic work was published, a work that changed the face of psychology.

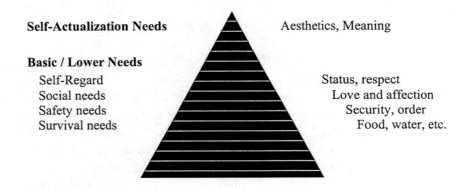

In *Motivation and Personality* Maslow presented a model of human motivation that classified needs in two categories: lower and higher needs or drives.

- *The lower needs* operate by deficiency and powerfully drive until the need that we lack is gratified. Then the drive dissipates and vanishes. This is the level of animal motivation and so governs "jungle life"—a phrase that Maslow later came to use for that dimension of life.
- *The higher needs* operate in a very different way. They are growth drives, drives for expression, development—for self-actualization. In these needs we are driven not by lack, but by a desire to be *all that we can be,* to more fully express ourselves and to contribute to the growth of others. When these drives are satisfied, we grow, become stronger, and become psychologically mature people so that we are more human, more civilized. We think more expansively and ethically about the whole of the human race.

Maslow introduced this model of motivation as *a hierarchy* with certain sets of needs giving rise to the next level of needs. The prepotency of the needs shows that all needs are not the same. At any given time, some needs would dominate, that is, they would be prepotent. They would dominate consciousness, emotions, and perception until gratified. Survival needs give rise to safety and security needs which then gives rise to social needs of love and affection which gives rise to self needs (self-esteem and self-regard). From these lower needs we then move up to *the self-actualization needs*—to the needs for knowing, organizing, creating beauty, order, truth, perfection, justice, spirituality, contribution, democracy, equality, collaboration, etc.

How does the Hierarchy of Needs help us understand people, groups, communities, and nations?   What does it offer leaders and politicians?

Because we are driven by *deficiency* for the lower needs, and the lower the need, the greater the desperation and the more likelihood people will ruthlessly compete with each other. So the first task is to create a society or community where all people are able to satisfy their needs for survival, safety, social connection (love and affection) and self-value (self-confidence, self-importance). If the structure and economics enable people to satisfy these lower needs, then no dictator-strongman will be able to attract or appeal to people in terms of rescuing them or "taking care" of them. There will not be the desperation of deficiency and lack creating a fearful desperation to survive. Nor will people need a scapegoat to blame for desperate times.

Then a society can move up the level of actualizing human possibilities for order, truth, discovery, beauty, knowledge, contribution, peace, etc. Maslow called these *higher* or *meta*-needs. It is here that we experience the meta-values and drives as well as *Being*-cognition.   Among the most radical aspects of Maslow's model was his demonstration that our higher needs or meta-drives were *biologically-based*—part of our instinctoid.[2] They are part of human nature—they are part and parcel of our animal and instinctual nature! This also is the bright-side of human nature.

Facilitating Self-Actualization

All of this raises critical questions: *How do we get there?* How do we facilitate individuals and groups, even nations, to move beyond the deficiency needs to the self-actualization needs? How do we facilitate the full development of people so that the majority can live at the truly human needs level?

The first step is obvious. We get there by adequately and accurately fulfilling our lower needs. As we gratify the first level, the next level arises, and then the next. In this, each level is prepotent to the next. As each of the lower needs is satisfied, it disappears from our consciousness and new higher needs emerge. In this way we move up the hierarchy and eventually rise up to the truly human needs. And at this higher level, there is no ultimate satisfaction.   The dynamics of need gratification changes at this level. The more we get of beauty, truth, contribution, meaning, value, love, etc., *the more we want, the more we have to give, and the more our appetite increases.* And it is here that we do things, not so much to get and attain, to make the drive go away, but to *express* ourselves, to *release the possibilities and potentials within.*

World peace— how does this model work for and facilitate peace on this planet? The model enabled Maslow to explore human motivations and how groups of people are structured to enable people to get their basic needs met. This lead to many other questions:

> "How good a society can we create given human nature?"
>
> "What do we need to do for the drives and needs of people so that we can create good people and a good society?"
>
> "What interferes with people getting their needs met and moving to the highest needs where they can move beyond the law of the jungle of the lower needs?"

In the 1940s when Maslow began his *Good Humans Study,* he started looking for people who were psychologically healthy and who had developed the full range of their potentialities. This is how he got into the area of modeling self-actualizers. By 1954 he published his paradigm-shifting model about human *Motivation and Personality* (the title of his book). The following comes from his 1956 paper to the American Association of Psychology.

> "Self-Actualizing people, those who have come to a high level of maturation, health, and self-fulfillment, have so much to teach us that sometimes they seem almost like a different breed of human beings. But because it is so new, the exploration of the highest reaches of human nature and of its ultimate possibilities . . . is a difficult and tortuous task."

This was absolutely revolutionary at that time. No one had studied psychologically healthy, productive, and actualizing people before. And because no one had explored *the bright side* of human nature, it was cutting-edge. Eventually it led Maslow to write his third book, *The Farther Reaches of Human Nature.*

What was so revolutionary about this? Namely that Maslow was asserting that there is a certain sense in which these extraordinary, whole, healthy people are actually *the only genuine representatives of human nature and psychology.* That is, the self-actualizing person is *not* an ordinary person with something added, but an ordinary person "with nothing taken away." In this way the self-actualizing person is a model or template for a new normality—a fully developed human being.   The self-actualization characteristics is then a description of the regular or ordinary person who has been *unleashed* from all of the man-made restraints of society, the human being without "dampened and inhibited powers and capacities."   For Maslow, this meant that the self-actualized person is synonymous with "human nature" in general.

Isn't this quite a vision?   Yet there is more to it.

> "But the truth which we can see more and more clearly is that man has infinite potentiality, which, properly used, could make his life very much like his fantasies of heaven.   In potentiality, he is the most awe-inspiring phenomenon in the universe, the most creative, the most ingenious."

For Maslow and the other pioneers of the human potential movement, being creative, authentic, unique, and self-directing was part and parcel of the farther reaches of human nature—this we already have within us.   It only needs to be unleashed.   No wonder that he constantly asserted that "human nature for centuries has been sold short!"   There is within all of us a tendency, an "instinct," and a predisposition to actualize our highest potentials.   In other words, the drive to self-actualize is a basic drive within all of us.

> "Even if all these needs are satisfied, we may still often expect that a new discontent and restless will soon develop, unless the individual is doing what *he*, individually, is fitted for.   A musician must make music, an artist must paint, a poet must write.   What a man *can* be, he *must* be.   He must be true to his own nature.   This need we call self-actualization."
> (1954, p. 46)

This has numerous consequences and implications.   It explains why we humans are never satisfied, and never can be, and why you may be surprised to discover that a restless discontent lies at the heart of self-actualization.   Trying to get rid of it only diminishes us.   Just as soon as we gratify one need, another emerges and we feel dissatisfied again.   *We are inherently restless.*   Have you noticed that? Restlessness is part of our nature.   It is not something to be despised or eliminated.   It is actually the basis of our full humanity and it leads to our creativity and to our never-ending innovations and ongoing development.

In this, restlessness, and its emotional component—anxiety, is to be embraced, welcomed, and enjoyed in the service of self-actualizing.

This is essential for unleashing our potentials. By embracing our nature, ambiguity, our never-ending restlessness we discover our true nature as self-aware existential beings.

In the studies of creativity, this is described as *embracing ambiguity* and being able to live with non-closure. If, however, somewhere along the way you "learned," or concluded, that you don't like non-closure, ambiguity, anxiety, restlessness or worse, then you create a belief that any feeling of insecurity is bad or unacceptable. That taboo frame then dampens and inhibits your full development as human being and so diminishes you.

The Core Idea of the Health Frame
From all of this, it's now easy to see that during the 1940s a paradigm shift was in the making as Maslow started *modeling self-actualizing people.* This was the unique synthesis that he created from his relationship with Alfred Adler, Ruth Benedict, Max Wertheimer, his studies of the Canadian Blackfoot Indians, etc. Then, with the outbreak of the Second World War Maslow felt called to his new vision which set his own life mission.

What resulted from all of this? Maslow created a new model of human motivation about human needs which changed the face of psychology as he focused on human possibilities rather than dysfunctions.

I first read Maslow's classic, *Motivation and Personality,* in the 1970s, but didn't realize just how radically transformative his work was. And there was a reason for that. By the 1970s, Maslow's hierarchy of needs, distinction between higher and lower needs, and exploration into the *bright side* of human personality, and into peak experiences and self-actualization had permeated psychology and society to a high degree and had already become fairly common knowledge. That's how quickly the Third Force of psychology penetrated American culture at least and had given humanistic or positive psychology a favorable hearing.

Maslow's challenging questions in his first works and speeches were these:

>"Have we not studied enough about how people become sick and neurotic? What do we know about how people grow, develop, become well, and transcend their problems and circumstances? What is possible for humans? What

distinguishes the healthiest humans, the most mature, and those who contribute the most?"

By these questions *Maslow set a health frame for the field of psychology* which began a revolution that has all but relegated Psychoanalysis and Behaviorism (the first and second forces) to a back seat as a hundred new therapies and psychologies have arisen to explore this area. From Logo-therapy, Client-Centered therapy, Reality Therapy, dozens of Cognitive therapies, Brief psychotherapy, Ericksonian, NLP, etc. up to Neuro-Semantics—there have been an explosion of therapies that now begin from an entirely new and different premise, from *the premise* that we are made to grow, develop, and self-actualize, that human nature is basically good and that given the right conditions, people will want to move beyond the lower needs to the higher needs.

None of this means that the disease frame and the medical model that Freud and others began with was wrong, *only that it was limited.* Indeed, it makes perfect sense that psychology began with an exploration into neurosis, disease, psychopathology, and mental ill-health. That was the first and most demanding need—to understand what was going on with those who were severely suffering, but whose suffering didn't seem to have any physiological source. So Freud began with hysterics.

But after the first fifty years of psychology, psychological knowledge of humans, human nature, growth and development, emotions, needs, etc. were based almost entirely upon *the disease model.* It was based upon the study of those hurt and traumatized. It was not based upon those who were the best specimens, the superior men and women in terms of mental and emotional health. That's the shift that Maslow introduced.

Studying chimpanzees under Harry Harlow, working with Karen Horney, mentored by Alfred Adler, studying the Blackfoot Indians, and meeting Ruth Benedict and Max Wertheimer—the presence of these two self-actualizing people launched his modeling project. So he set out to understand and model mentally and emotionally healthy individuals, self-actualizers whom he later called "peakers." In this way he set the growth frame in psychology and shifted the assumptions and premises of psychology from the "cruel or nasty animal" model of Freud to an uniquely human model.

This created *the new psychology of self-actualization* which exploded on the scene, and during the 1960s worked along with a lot of the cultural factors that created the counter-culture movement and the exploration into the farther reaches of human consciousness. Encounter-groups, growth groups, wild and crazy psychotherapies, etc. arose at that time. This, plus the untimely death of Maslow in June of 1970, caused the "Third Force" movement of Humanistic Psychology to never become a full-fledge "School of Psychology."

So here we are today, some 38 years later (1970–2008), and surprise of surprise—*there has been almost nothing written or developed upon Maslow's work in all of that time.* Without a single leader to step into Maslow's shoes, while the new paradigm of the *bright side* of human nature is well accepted and while there are many millions interested in self-actualization —the focus has been scattered into hundreds of competing camps, schools, models, and personalities.[3]

What's tragic about this is that during all this time, Maslow's models have not grown or developed. While there has been much confirming research on the Self-Actualization Psychology model that he created, the model has not been made explicit nor has it been expanded. In this, Maslow was *too successful* in getting people to step out of the old paradigm and imagining all kinds of new possibilities, and yet simultaneously, he was also entirely unsuccessful in leading that movement.

What's the next step? What is missing in the Maslow models? What can we add to the self-actualization psychology that Maslow initiated? The answer is, a great deal! First and foremost, we can add the one element that Maslow missed— *the role of meaning* in human growth psychology as a key of functioning of self-actualization. We can also rescue Maslow's work from the static and rigid implications of the metaphor that he used, that is, the Hierarchy of Needs. We can also give Maslow's impetus of self-actualization a fresh remake with a systemic model and integrate the work of Csikszentmihalyi on "flow." And that's just the beginning as you'll soon discover in the following chapters.

Key Points in this Chapter

- Given my high respect and honor of the pioneering efforts of Abraham Maslow, I hope by this work, as in the first (*Unleashed*), to build on the incredible contribution that he has made.

- *To be self-actualizing is to be creative.* When you are actualizing your highest and best potentials, you are becoming more creative not only in what you *do,* but more importantly, in who you *are,* that is, in your very *being.* That's why *creativity* is part and parcel of self-actualization —its core and its brightest expression.

- *We have sold human nature short.* And individually most of us have sold ourselves short of our possibilities. Have you sold yourself short? Are you living life having dampened and inhibited some of your best potentials? Are you ready to *unleash* new possibilities? Are you ready to awaken the self-actualizer within and learn how to step into the flow state of total engagement at will? Are you ready for the revolutionary advances that you can make in unleashing your potentials? We can now stop that and turn around to look for and appreciate the possibilities within.

- *To be self-actualizing is to embrace ambiguity,* to embrace the human condition of our existential lives of our inner restlessness. This isn't easy, yet it is the first sign of becoming fully human / fully alive.

End Notes:

1. Wyatt Woodsmall, Ph.D. contributed these distinctions to the NLP model of Meta-Programs. See his book *Time-Line Therapy and the Basis of Personality* (1989). In the first book on self-actualization, I used meta-programs to create *the Self-Actualization Quadrants* based on meaning and performance as the two key factors governing self-actualization. See *Unleashed,* Chapter 7.

2. Instinctoid needs. We do not have "instincts" in the way animals do. Their instincts contain content information about what to do and how to be the species that they are. As humans, we only have instinct-remnants at best—a general urge without content information. Maslow called these *instinctoids.* That's why we have to *learn* how to adequately and appropriately satisfy our needs.

3. Wayne Dyer tried to do so in his book *The Sky is the Limit,* Shostrum could have, Schutz also attempted to do so with his book, *Joy.*

Chapter 3

THE LEVELS OF

SELF-ACTUALIZATION

"The more one gets [of the higher self-actualization needs], the more one wants so that this kind of wanting is endless, and can never be attained or satisfied." (1968, p. 33)

"Human life will never be understood unless its highest aspirations are taken into account." (1970, p. xii)

Maslow's primary contribution to the Self-Actualization Psychology was his Hierarchy of Needs model. This model began mapping out the distinctions between the lower and the higher needs. Yet above and beyond that, it distinguished that there are *levels of needs* in the first place. At that time, that was brand new. It was revolutionary. Prior to Maslow, no one had identified a psychology that involves layers and levels of needs.

Our Lower Animal Needs
Life begins with the lower needs. It begins with our survival needs (food, water, shelter, sex), then safety, social (love and affection) and self (self-regard) needs. These biological instinct-like needs are similar for all of us as human beings. In fact, we share all of them with the higher or more intelligent animals.

These needs, driven by deficiency, are required for our foundational growth as persons in human communities. Here survival, safety, the social needs, and the self needs enable us to be good animals and healthy in our interactions with others.

What Maslow discovered was that our needs are not all the same and that self-actualization emerges via gratifying our lower needs. Some needs are more fundamental and basic than others. In fact, our needs operate hierarchically so that as we fulfilled those that are more basic and essential to our life, others emerge. Eventually, as our biological and animal needs are fulfilled, the higher human needs of our mind, heart, and spirit arise. These are our higher needs, our human needs, the needs that allow us to become truly human.

Because there are levels of needs, these levels relate to what we value and treat as important when we experience the need. Maslow distinguished our needs as operating at two fundamental levels, the lower and higher—needs which motivate us to strive to reach and fulfill them. The primary difference between our lower and higher needs is that the lower needs are driven by *deficiency* while the higher needs are driven by growth, *abundance, being-ness.*

Yet our human needs are in the end *needs*—necessities required for physical and psychological health. In this they are not moral or immoral, they are amoral. They are simply requirements for life. They are requirements for being well-adjusted to human reality. From them arise the motivation that drives us for growth, being, and becoming.

Maslow's most significant contribution was in stating that our needs are *hierarchical.* As we fulfill one need, the next level of need emerges. The lower need is *prepotent* to the next level—strong and dominating until it is gratified. Generally we move up the levels of needs through gratifying the previous needs. The lower needs are animals needs; the higher are the truly human needs—there we find and experience being fully alive/ fully human.

These levels of needs also develop over the life-span. That is, the needs themselves grow, develop, and expand as we develop in our sense of self.

> "Many of the principles of self-actualization are largely intra-personal, such as the making of plans, the discovery of self, the selection of potentialities to develop, the construction of a life-outlook." (1968, p. 38)

Your Level — Your Life
What I've learned from Maslow that makes these levels of needs and the hierarchy of needs so significant is that *the level we live at determines the nature and quality of our motivation and meanings. Deficiency* drives us in the lower needs, *abundance* drives us at the

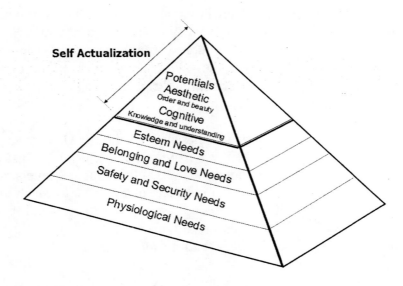

higher levels. We move up through the hierarchy of needs *innocently* and naively in childhood, *coping* with our first meanings and experiences as teenagers and young adults, and we move through them with *mastery* when we attain our full growth as adults.

In terms of the quality of our needs, our lower needs are inadequate for conveying the ultimate meaning of life. We cannot continually live at the lower needs only without doing damage to ourselves. Developmentally we are designed to keep unfolding so that we transcend the lower needs and actualize our inner potentials. We are designed to fulfill the meta-needs and meta-values.

Now Maslow began by asking, "Why is basic need-gratification a catastrophe for some people?" The answer is that for some people there are no higher meanings attached to the D-striving (D stands for *deficiency*). (1982, *The Journals of Abraham Maslow,* p. 337).

Each level of our needs has its strengths and weaknesses, its empowerment and its limiting traps. The biggest limiting trap involves the meanings that we give to the lower needs. If we give an inadequate or toxic meaning to the need, we then create and experience the need as a neurotic need. By over-loading it with limiting or toxic meanings, we undermine our effectiveness and happiness.

A need then can become healthy or sick (neurotic) depending on *the meanings* that we give it. In this, the health of the need is a critical concern. Is our experience of a need healthy and robust or is our development arrested with a particular need? Is it contaminated by a toxic idea?

From this Maslow identified that the basic pathologies arise from the frustration of the lower needs and that the meta-pathologies arise from the frustration of the higher self-actualizing needs. Here is a list of the *being*-needs of self-actualization and the meta-pathologies that can emerge when they are not fulfilled.

B-Values	**Meta-Pathologies**
Truth	Mistrust, cynicism, skepticism
Goodness	Hatred, repulsion, disgust, reliance only on self and for self
Beauty	Vulgarity, restlessness, loss of taste, bleakness
Unity; wholeness	Disintegration
Dichotomy-transcendence	Black / white thinking; either/or, simplistic view of life
Aliveness; process	Deadness, robotizing, feeling oneself to be totally determined, loss of emotion and zest in life, experiential emptiness
Uniqueness	Loss of feeling of self and individuality, feeling oneself interchangeable with anyone
Perfection	Hopelessness, nothing to work for
Necessity	Chaos, unpredictability
Order	Insecurity, cynicism, mistrust, lawlessness, total selfishness
Simplicity	Over-complexity, confusion, bewilderment, loss of orientation
Richness, totality, comprehensiveness	Depression, uneasiness, loss of interest in world
Effortlessness	Fatigue, strain, clumsiness, awkwardness, stiffness
Playfulness	Grimness, depression, paranoid, humorlessness, loss of zest, cheerlessness
Self-sufficiency	Responsibility given to others
Meaningfulness	Meaninglessness, despair, senseless of life

As adults, we experience our needs as defined and informed by our meanings. Maslow didn't say this and hardly recognized this. In fact, this is what he missed. Yet he was very close to this realization. as I will show in Chapter 8. Today we know that meaning conditions, colors, and filters our needs making them appropriate or inappropriate, healthy or neurotic. Therefore in *Self-Actualization Psychology*, meaning itself plays an extremely critical role.

Contrasting Lower and Higher Needs

Maslow seemed to have spent most of his early years mapping out the distinctions and differences between the lower animal needs and the higher human needs of our mind, heart, and spirit. In the following, I have sorted these out into various areas: gratification, pleasure, perception, goal-striving, experience, socially and interpersonally, self and ego, and love.

Gratification

> Lower Needs: Gratification avoids illness and fends off disease.
> Higher Needs: Gratification produces positive health and achieves triumphs of the human mind and spirit.

Pleasure

> Lower Needs: Scarcity pleasures seek for relief, ease, tension reduction. In pleasure at this level, the tension disappears.
> Higher Needs: Abundance pleasures lead to ecstasy, to increase tension that one finds pleasurable.

Goal Striving

> Lower Needs: Striving for goals here gratifies the need, reaches homeostasis, and reduces tension.
> Higher Needs: Striving for goals here gratifies the *being-needs* which then grow to expand our capacity as well as our desire to experience more of the goal.

Perception

> Lower Needs: Either/or perception is Aristotelian, we see A and non-A as mutually exclusive. This deficient-perception is ego-centric because it sees things in terms of its own needs.
> Higher Needs: Both/and and systemic thinking drives perception at this level. Here we see wholes or gestalts. As we see without judgment, we see with more appreciation and acceptance.

Experience

Lower Needs: Experience at this level is common to all, it is species-wide in nature. It peaks and then releases, and so is climatical and episodic, that is, it occurs as episodes.

Higher Needs: Experience at this level is continual—continual growth, development, improvement, and so is not climatical with peaks. It is more idiosyncratic with each individual.

Socially and Interpersonally

Lower Needs: We experience the social world as dependent on others to fulfill any basic needs. Here the dependent variable in getting our needs met is the other people who can provide for those needs, and so our need to please, to get along, and to placate others. This leads to being other-directed and emotionally anxious and afraid of others—their anger, aggression, withdrawal, rejection, criticism.

Higher Needs: At this level we experience the social world from a more independent position, more autonomous, more self-aware and more self-directed. Here we have more of a need for detachment and privacy, we are more determined by inner world rather than outer. We are also more resilience in adverse conditions. We have more psychological freedom from social constraints.

Self and Ego

Lower Needs: Here we are more dependent on others and outer-directed, more fearful and anxious, here we see others to use them. We have more of an inter-personal focus. A person's ego is weak and fragile as well as self-centered as we focus on ourself.

Higher Needs: Here we are more independent, more self-directed, we see others as wholes without a need for them or to use them. We are more disinterested and have an intra-personal focus. Our ego is strong and able to face reality for what it is, we are more able to transcend the ego, to become self-forgetful, more world centered and focused on problems to solve.

Love

Lower Needs: At this level we experience love as the needs of deficit-love, as a hole to be filled, an emptiness, and so as a love-hunger. Due to its dependency, this love is anxious and hostile. Love at this level is more likely to be blind. Higher Needs: In *being*-love we seek first to love, to give, to admire. This love is non-possessive, autonomous, and so sees reality clearly.

Nature	Motivation
Higher	
B-Needs: ultimate, more subliminal	Expression motivation
Easy to suppress, even deny.	Deficiency does not motivate Felt strongly as expression of growth
Less imperative for survival.	Memorable peak experiences
Governed by cognitive beliefs and understandings, felt in mind and spirit. Based in psychology and semantics	Gratification expands capacity Elicits passion for more. Can't be gratified to extinction.
Ongoing, open-ended process of development	Satisfied mostly indirectly Preconditions for gratification
Lower	
Based in biology and genetics Instinct-like; mostly determined by body and felt in the body	Deficiency motivation Deficiency states creates strongly felt states that are dominating states
D-Needs: more *immediate* Powerful and driving. Very dominating when lacking	Post-gratification forgetting *Disappear* when need is satisfied. Under-value it after gratification Boredom sets in when gratified. Satisfied directly with gratifications
	Few if any preconditions
Episodic, climatic, occurs periodically Distinct beginning and endings	

Tension / Pleasure	Social / Interpersonal

Higher

Non-purposeful: value in expressing self
Actions not aiming to *do* anything
except to *be* and to express oneself
Mechanism: *drive expression*
Desire disequilibrium
Embrace challenges and changes
Drives grows, expands, amplifies

Satisfied by oneself individually
Individualistic
More independent of others

Lower

Purpose: to reduce need, create
  homeostasis
Purposive behaviors designed to fulfil
specific goals: gratify hunger, quench
thirst, warm when cold, reduce pain, etc.
Mechanism: *drive reduction*
Desire homeostasis
Seek a relatively stable state of equilibrium
Removal of challenges and changes
Drive goes away, satisfied

Satisfied mostly in
relationships with others
Social, relational
Dependent on others,
especially via
communication

Key Points in this Chapter

- Self-actualization begins with the lower needs, but it does not end there. Nor is self-actualization fully possible with just the lower needs. Gratification of our biological needs facilitates the next level of need to arise and with that we are on the pathway to discover the human needs and to "grow forward."

- Our needs operate hierarchically so that with gratification, the next level of need emerges. The Hierarchy of Needs gives us a basic format for the arrangement of needs and highlights the needs to welcome the next level of restlessness.

- The level of our needs establishes our levels of values and self-actualization and speaks to the level of our experiencing of needs as we self-actualize.

- It is in the higher needs that we become fully human/ fully alive. Moving there enables us to begin to explore the full range of our humanness.

Chapter 4

PREMISES

BY MASLOW

"When the philosophy of man (his nature, his goals, his potentialities, his fulfillment) changes, then everything changes." "A new vision is emerging of the possibilities of man and of his destiny, and its implications are many ..."
                                    Toward a Psychology of Being

"It becomes more and more clear that the study of crippled, stunted, immature, and unhealthy specimens can yield only a cripple psychology and a cripple philosophy." (1970, p. 180)

Because there are always background assumptions in everything we say and do, it is wise, even essential, to acknowledge our assumed premises as we begin. So what are the implied frames that we are operating from?

- What are our starting premises for unleashing human potentials?
- What are our assumptions about human nature in Self-Actualization Psychology?
- What is best to *assume* about people, human development, human growth over the lifespan, the relationship between thoughts, emotions, and behaviors, change, learning, skill development, mastery, motivation, intentions, relationships, teamwork, collaboration, etc.?

Premises Behind *Unleashing Potentials*

Given that *Self-Actualization Psychology* significantly differs from those that govern traditional psychotherapy, I have devoted this chapter and the next one to examining the principles and premises of

Self-Actualization Psychology. But why two chapters? I first want to present the premises that Maslow offered in 1958 as his basic propositions for the new psychology that he was beginning to map out. These focus on his new paradigm about the inner core of human nature. From that I then want to focus on the premises of Self-Actualization Psychology as newly developed in the models presented in this book.

What follows here are the basic propositions that Maslow put together to summarize the paradigm shift from the older way of thinking about human nature and our "inner nature" or core. I have summarized Maslow's extensive paper and have re-written the points to maintain the theme of "our inner core." Maslow did not do that in his original paper. In fact, as you read these 43 premises, you'll probably note that many of these could be grouped together.

As you read these one or two lines of the premises, these are but very succinct summaries of what makes up *Self-Actualizing Psychology.* Even in Maslow's original paper, they were not developed much more than what you'll find here.[1]

The Basic Propositions

1) *We have an essential inner nature or core.* From this biological, instinctoid, and given core your natural inclinations, propensities, and inner voice arise.

2) *Our inner core is potentiality, but not final actualization.* Where you see and experience your actual, developmentally, is over your lifespan. That is where you actualize your potentials.

3) *Our inner core is weak biologically and it can be overwhelmed.* It can even be repressed. Authentic selfhood is being able to hear your impulse voices, to know what you really want and don't' want, what you are fit for and what you are not fit for.

4) *Our inner core has both species-wide and idiosyncratic characteristics.* We share many characteristics because we are human beings. You also have other characteristics due to your own unique history and choices.

5) *Our inner core can be studied scientifically and objectively.* It is not exclusively a subjective experience but shows up objectively as well.

6) *Aspects of our inner core can be repressed or ignored.* Yet while we can ignore our inner nature, we cannot kill these aspects of ourselves. While they can become unconscious drives and needs, they remain within you and continue to influence you.

7) *Our inner core,* though weak, *persists underground* (at an unconscious level) *with a "will to health,"* to grow, to self-actualization, and to quest for our identity. This is the drive inside your self-actualization impulse.

8) *Our inner core grows by both discovery and creation.* Because you are your own main determinant, life for you is a series of choices. To the extent that you are a real person, you are your own main determinant.

9) *If our inner nature is frustrated, we get sick and our full self-actualization is diminished.* Frustration of your basic human needs undermines your self-actualization so that you become less than you can be.

10) *Our inner core is good.* It is not evil. Uncovering techniques are required to release your love, creativeness, kindness, altruism, etc.

11) *Inner core guilt is a betrayal of self.* This differs from betrayal of society's rules which is extrinsic guilt. Intrinsic guilt, as an inner guide for growth, enables you to recognize when you are turning off the path to self-actualization so you can return to that path.

12) *A healthy anger in our inner core is self-affirmation, self-defense, and forcefulness.* Unwarranted hostility and destructiveness is a reactive response to bad treatment. "Evil" behavior comes from ignorance, misinterpretations, and reactions due to threatening frustrations.

13) *Our unconscious* (our inner core's depth) *is good, beautiful, and desirable.* This is a radical contrast to Freud's view of the unconscious.

14) *Psychological health becomes possible when our inner core is accepted, loved, and respected.* No growth toward self-actualization is even possible unless you accept and love your inner core. It all begins there.

15) *Our inner core needs to be brought out and encouraged,* not suppressed, repressed, or controlled. Fearing your psyche sets up neurotic or psychotic responses. For your inner core, you can experience and create either healthy and unhealthy controls.

16) *Our inner core can and will choose what is good for growth.* You need an environment that permits you to gratify your needs.

17) *A central path to health and self-fulfillment of our inner core is via basic need gratification.* Asceticism and self-denial, by way of contrast, will diminish you.

18) *Our inner nature needs frustration-tolerance.* It needs frustration -tolerance in order to discover your strengths and limits by overcoming difficulties. You profit from graded frustrations by becoming stronger. Conversely, over-protection will infantilize you.

19) *Inner core capacities need to be used and exercised.* Capacities, which are also "needs," clamor to be used, and used well. Unused, they atrophy your skills and diminish you as a person.

20) *Our inner nature deals with two worlds or realities*—the natural world and the psychic world. The psychic world is the world of wishes, hopes, fears, emotions. To be healthy is to live in both worlds at the same time.

21) *As our inner nature matures, we transcend our deficiency-needs.* This enables you to move to the place where you self-actualize and become meta-motivated. You are then able to be authentic, that is, to become a "person."

22) *With inner core maturing, our cognition changes.* You move from D-cognition to B-cognition. You grow beyond the cognitive diseases that stunt growth.

23) *With inner core maturing, we move from D-love to B-love.* And B-love is the basis of all good relations with other persons.

24) *In principle our inner core can easily self-actualize.* This rarely happens in practice due to the many human diminution forces including fear of self-actualization and the limiting belief in society that human nature is evil.

25) *Growth of our inner core forward requires courage, will, choice, and strength.* This is required in order to face the difficulties and fears of growth.

26) *Growth of our inner core is a dialectic.* It is a dialectic between growth-fostering forces and growth-discouraging forces and is empowered by enhancing all the advantages of growth forward.

27) *Our inner core has within it a naturalistic system of values.* And this naturalistic system of values enables you to identify what is good for you.

28) *Our inner core is not neurotic by nature.* Neurosis arises as a defense or evasion of your inner nature. Neuroticized needs, emotions, and actions is a loss of capacity, a diminishing of your person.

29) *Our inner core has needs*—like the need to understand and value. Your inner core needs a system of values; without such your values become psycho-pathogenic. You need a framework of values and a philosophy of life.

30) *Our inner core suffers when there is dichotomizing.* Conversely, you grow to self-actualization through the synergy of opposites and polarities. Work becomes play; maturity becomes childlike.

31) *Our inner core strives for integration.* In self-actualizing we integrate Freudian dichotomies such as id, ego, superego.

32) *Our inner core becomes more synergic in self-actualizing.* There you experience a synergy in all your capacities—thinking, feeling, choosing, and acting.

33) *Our inner core involves many kinds of cognition.* Among the kinds of cognition are verbal, non-verbal, metaphorical, ineffable, primary processes, concrete experiences, intuition. There is a healthy irrationality that promotes creativity.

34) *A healthy inner core enables us to regress at will.* When healthy, your inner core enables you to dip into primary processes and regress voluntarily—a main condition of creativity, play, having fun, etc.

35) *Our inner core is designed for peak-experiences.* It is designed

for esthetic perceiving and creating and esthetic peak-experiences which are integrative and life-validating of splits within your person.

36) *Our inner core transcend the neurotic problems via self-actualization.* By self-actualizing you face and address the real existential human problems. You move beyond the problems of *becoming* to the problem of *being.*

37) *Our inner core requires a healthy gender fulfillment for self-actualization.* That is, you fulfill your maleness or femaleness first, then your general humanness.

38) *Our inner core grows healthily into full-humanness by dropping the techniques used by the child.* You learn to gratify your own needs, you discover your own conscience, and you learn to enjoy being responsible for yourself.

39) *Our inner core requires culture.* For your inner core to move toward self-actualization you need a culture that gratifies the basic human needs and that fosters growth of full humanness. This gives us a comparative sociology.

40) *Our inner core can transcend self.* When your inner core self-actualizes, you are more able to transcend the self and paradoxically be more self-conscious and selfish in a way that serves the larger whole of your relationships and place in society which looks both unselfish and unself-consciousness.

41) *Our inner core gives us two worlds to live in and to integrate.* Self-actualizers are able to live in both and integrate both and can go back and forth voluntarily. This integrates EQ and IQ so you are not afraid of your inner psychic world but enjoy it as you do the more effortful responsible world of striving and coping.

42) *Our inner core moves us to two kinds of actions.* You move to goal-directed, striving action as you adapt to the world and also to "sheer expression" of yourself as you contemplate and enjoy life for itself.

43) *Our inner core enables us to experience both the past and the future.* And you experience the future in two ways, as now existing within you as ideals, hopes, and goals, and as here-now in peak experiences.

Maslow's Premises

As you read and examine these premises by Maslow, they cover a wide range of subjects within *Self-Actualization theory*. Some have to do with the nature of our inner core and some have to do with how we unleash our potentials (via discovery, creation, choices, acceptance, love, respect, gratifying needs, frustrating and testing, using capacities, courage, synergy, integration, creativity, differentiation, growing up, culture, etc.).

Some of them address facets of self-actualization: choice, responsibility, gratification, maturity, cognitions, love, the growth dialectic, values, peak experiences, the existential situation, gender, transcendence, experience of time. And some address the opposite of self-actualization, when self-actualization fails, namely, neurosis, sickness, meta-pathology, and human diminition.

Key Points in this Chapter

- These are the premises of *Self-Actualization Psychology* and, as you can see, Maslow made most of them explicit in his writings. Doing so helps to define this new paradigm-shifting psychology and helps us to see the contrast with the older psychologies.

- The inner core of human nature is basically good (or neutral) and certainly not evil. Instead, our inner core is wired for growth, ongoing development, and full humanness. Yet it can be interfered with so that it fails. So while self-actualization is a potential, it is conditional upon good conditions, understanding, and choice.

- Out of our inner core needs and their hierarchical development our values emerge as does the never-ending restlessness that's built within us to keep learning and developing. Accepting this innate and inevitable restlessness helps with self-actualization.

End Notes:

1. Maslow originally wrote these propositions in 1958 as a paper that he presented to ASCD (Association for Supervision and Curriculum Development), Perceiving, Behaving, Becoming: A New Focus for Education, A.Combs, (ed.). It is now chapter 14 in *Toward a Psychology of Being* and is titled, "Some Basic Propositions of a Growth and Self-Actualization Psychology" (pages 189- 214).

Chapter 5

SELF-ACTUALIZATION

PSYCHOLOGY

PREMISES

"What a man can be, he must be.
This need we may call self-actualization."
Abraham Maslow

By starting with the premises by Maslow regarding the inner essence or core of human nature listed in chapter four, we are now able to create a more precise summary of the premises for *Self-Actualization Psychology.*

These are the principles that govern our understanding about how we unleash our potentials and mobilize our resources. The principles and premises of remedial and generative psychology differ primarily from the older psychologies in that each psychology deals with people at very different times and stages in their lives. Psychotherapy is designed for people in pain, for people who are hurting, and who are not okay within themselves. The immediate need there is to identify the source of the distress, get up to "Okay," stop the internal conflict that creates the pain, and change one's distorted maps of the world.

• But once "okay" and up to average, then what?

- Once you are able to meet your basic needs, what then?
- Once you have finished the business of getting over all the parenting errors and hurts of development, what's next?
- How do you then begin to actualize your highest potentials?

Here the original model of Abraham Maslow provides tremendous insight. His Hierarchy of Needs enables us to distinguish the level of needs and the different states of mind that each level evokes. Because the lower needs operate by deficiency, they express *deficiency motivation.* By way of contrast, the higher or self-actualization needs operate by abundance and insatiability and so lead to our growth needs and *expressive motivation.*

From Developmental Psychology and Maslow's research on the peak experiences of self-actualizers, the following premises are at the essence of *Self-Actualization Psychology.* These premises govern human nature regarding ongoing development of full potential.

1) *Innate Design Premise*
Our growth is developmental in nature; our inner core is designed for continuously developing throughout our lifespan.

When we are born, we are quite unfinished. So if there's anything genetic and biological about self-actualization, it is that we are predisposed and determined to develop, to grow, to self-actualize, and even to participate in our own development. *So we are born unfinished.* After birth there's a

> *Development 'R Us*
> Wired into our DNA is the self-actualization drive.

lot more to be developed in human personality. We are *not* born fully developed, but incomplete—very incomplete. The ongoing maturing of our mind-body system occurs throughout our entire lifespan. This development is natural and inevitable as we grow and mature through lifespan stages. Within all of us is a drive to develop, to learn more, feel more, contribute more, have more, and to be more. The bottom line is that we are a needy species. We are forever restless and never satisfied. Within us is an innate impulse forever moving us toward ever higher levels of development.

Yet we have within ourselves a real self, a constitutional self to realize. We are not *tabula rasa*, a blank slate and can be made into anything. We have dispositions, tendencies, temperaments, and talents that make up our unique voices (Maslow, 1971, p. 75)

**Core Premises of
Self-Actualization Psychology**

1. Our growth is developmental in nature; our inner core is designed for continuously developing throughout our lifespan.
2. We develop as persons and actualize through creating rich and vigorous meanings.
3. We have an inner core, a real self that develops via self-discovery, self-awareness, self-respect, and self-love.
4. We accelerate our development via assuming personal ownership and responsibility for our lives, we are diminished as persons when we don't.
5. Our development depends upon stepping up to recognizing and using our choice points.
6. Because we are driven by needs, our development occurs through adequate gratification of both *D*eficiency and *B*eing needs.
7. The height of self-actualization is moving into the realm of *Being* and the *Being*-needs.
8. We accelerate our development via rich relationships with and through others.
9. We self-actualize through existential awareness and anxiety.
10. The self-actualization process is inherently experiential in nature.
11. For self-actualization, we enjoy peak experiences as rewards along the way.
12. Sustained peak experiences lead to and create peak performances.
13. Self-actualization also entails plateau experiences.
14. We self-actualize via synergizing dichotomies.
15. We self-actualize best under "good conditions."

If human nature is innately *developmental,* then it's no surprise to discover that we are born with an innate urge and orientation to continually develop. No matter how far along we have come, there's always more. There's always the next step. All of this occurs naturally given the proper conditions. If we do not have the right conditions, however, our development can be endangered.

If this is so, *how does our development become arrested?* It can be arrested by a trauma, an interference, a misuse of emotion, the lack of growth, the layering of defenses, etc. We become arrested in our growth as we stop our development through defense and escape mechanisms. Normally, the process of development involves continual changing, adapting, and transforming. Rather than being an alien experience, this is uniquely the human experience. We instinctively move beyond the deficiency needs toward the self-actualizing needs. So given the right conditions, self-actualizing is a potential within every one of us and is, in fact, our ultimate design as human beings.

2) *Constructed Premise*
We develop as persons and actualize through creating rich and vigorous meanings.
While our body is programmed to grow and develop via the instructions of our DNA, we are for the most part without "instincts." Left alone, we do *not* know how to be human. Being *human* involves language, symbolic reality, and the shared realities of culture to which we learn to adapt. If there's anything genetically programmed, it is our primary "instinct" to learn, to understand, to use our mind to find or create meaning. That's because it is by learning that we create the meanings which then shape our experience.

As for content programs, *we are without instincts.* This is the difference between us and animals. Animals instinctively "know" what to do and how to be who they are. We do not. At best, we only have what Maslow called "instinctoids."

> "As we go up the phyletic scale there is a steady trend toward disappearance of the instincts so defined." (1970, p. 27)

The "instinctoids" we have left are mere tendencies and dispositions, not detailed programs. For specific content, we have to turn to our culture. What *cultivates* our minds, emotions, values, actions, habits, etc. are the multiple layers of embedded cultures and cultural frames that we live within (family, education, religion, business, etc.). In these cultures, we are cultivated by the values and meanings within the meaning structures of those cultures.

Since meaning is not given to us by instinct, as it is given to animals, *it is up to us to find and create meaning.* This is the human adventure par excellence. We do not have it within our DNA. It is not in our biology. In fact, we do not have any inherent knowledge about how to be human. Several things fall out from this. First and foremost *is the vast openness of possibilities within us.* We can develop our humanness in so many ways.

This also calls upon us to create meanings that are realistic enough so we can survive and exciting enough so that we care about surviving. In this, we are left without a choice—*we have to invent our own constructs of reality* and for this reason, we are *the meaning-makers.* The source of meaning is not our DNA, not our biological heritage, not even our cultural heritage. Each of us individually are the meaning-makers of our lives. This is so much so that our development is mostly conditioned by our meanings. This, by the way, is the key thing that Maslow missed— our nature as meaning-makers.

At the simplest level, we live by meaning because, before we can respond to anything, we have to know what it *is* (definition meaning). If we don't know

> Self-Actualization is primarily a function of meaning.

what it is, how to define it, what it means, its significance, or what it leads to, we will not be able to respond. The lack of programmed meanings create this *empty space* within us. Generated by the lack of programmed instincts, we have room *inside* for learning and constructing meaning. This is also the origin of human creativity.

If there is a human "instinct," it is *the instinct of constructing meaning* which we do via learning. We do this, in part, by accepting and absorbing the meanings of our multiple cultures. Yet in all of this, *all of our meanings are invented.* None exist "out there." It takes a human mind and nervous system to create "meaning"—to create values, purposes, understandings, decisions, directions, etc. For this reason, our meanings are neuro-semantic in nature— *neuro* (or neurological, a function of our nervous system and brain) and *semantic* (a function of our cognitive processes). Consequently, the quality and character of our development depends on the quality, accuracy, and richness of the meanings that we invent and embody.

Further, our constructing of meaning drives and organizes everything in our experience from our thinking and emoting to our skills and performances. In this, our very nature itself is invented by the meanings we attribute to things.

3) *Self-Awareness / Self-Discovery Premise*
We have an inner core, a real self that develops via self-discovery, self-awareness, self-respect, and self-love.
Without instincts and without innate programming for what to do,

how to be, and what things are, a grand adventure is set before us. It is the grand adventure of *discovering ourselves* and of giving ourselves sufficient meanings to make our life interesting and vital.

After all, when we started this adventure as infants, we didn't even know that we were a self. At first we are completely fused and identified with mother. It is only over the months of our first year that we differentiate enough to become a *self.* Then through

> It is this *empty space,* which lacking instincts has created, that gives us *room* inside ourselves to learn and to construct meaning.

the following years we develop a *sense of self,* a sense of identity, and begin to discover the richness of our inner world of self. This *self system*, in fact, is our first discovery and invention. It is the first meaning construct that we form and the most important one that we never leave home without.[1]

Of course, we mostly define ourselves in terms of the information given to us by others and our environment and yet we do so with a one-year old brain, a two-year old brain, etc. We

> The quality and character of our development depends on the quality, accuracy, and richness of the meanings that we invent.

create our first self-image as we see ourselves reflected in the eyes of those who cared for us. We create the meaning that we are loved and valued, precious and important, loveable and significant or the opposite—depending on the ability of our parents to parent effectively. What we then map as our meanings about *self* and about all of the multitude facets of self, become our *self-meanings.* Given this, isn't it absolutely incredible that we don't send all people to "Parenting 101" and license only those who have a clue about what's involved?

Because it is our nature to develop as persons, our sense of self grows and expands as we learn more about ourselves, and as we discover our interests, talents, and passions. By this learning we not only create richer meanings about life and self, but we

> It's the Self (the self content) that grows and self-actualizes.

also develop our skill in actualizing our best self. Then by receiving feedback, we evolve to our next stage of development. As our instinctual drive, learning enhances the unleashing of our potentials.

So as we nurture our innate craving for understanding, our self-knowledge expands.

All of this takes a special kind of intelligence—*intra-personal* or *psychological* intelligence as encapsulated in the ancient wisdom, "Know thyself." This process of learning more about ourselves progressively opens us up to new possibilities for self-actualization. It enables us to create ourselves, to invent and to reinvent ourselves in ways that create a meaningful and fulfilling life. No wonder emotional intelligence is as critical in living as our IQ of know-how knowledge.

Through the self-awareness of our growing self-knowledge we become authentic, real in our person, and true to our visions and passions. With self-awareness we find and create our uniqueness, and hence the integrity which frees us to become ourselves.

4) *Ownership of Powers Premise*
We accelerate our development via assuming personal ownership and responsibility for our lives, we are diminished as persons when we don't.

Lacking the content information that instincts give animals, for us there's a gap between stimulus and response, a gap for thinking and choosing. This is the basis for our sense of inner freedom. Within this gap we use our powers of thought, emotion, speech, and behavior to choose our responses. This frees us so that we are under no obligation to respond in any prescribed way. It is in this realm that we are free. Instead, our response depends on our meanings, and our meanings depend on both the content and quality of our thinking and evaluating.

It is the freedom of this gap that gives us the ability to control *our powers of response.* How much power do you have? How much more power do you want for this?

These response powers serve as the foundation for how we respond to others, to the world, and even to ourselves. In the early developmental

> The powers of self-actualization have to be owned and activated.

stages, we merely *react.* At that primitive level, a stimulus triggers a response and we do whatever unconscious programming we have in our body or have learned. Yet as we grow and develop we discover that there's a wonderful and magical and fantastic gap —*a gap that gives us a moment of choice* about what to think, what to feel, how to perceive, what to say, and how to act. And with that, we experience the birth of human *freedom*, the origin of choice, awareness, and awareness-of-our-awareness.

Having the power to respond, however, is only the first experience. As we develop our awareness of these powers, we are able to begin to take ownership of these powers. It is at that point that we truly become response-*able*—empowered to respond as we choose. The powers at our disposal are the two private powers of thinking and emoting and the two public powers of speaking and acting.

Yet this development of choice is not inevitable. We can default at this point of choosing, and of owning our choices. We can give in and give up. We can construct the meaning that we do not have these powers, and mis-believe that others *make* us think and feel as we do. Paradoxically, it is our power to create this kind of dis-empowerment that we then experience ourselves as a victim of the forces and choices of others. Of course, to frame things in this way only diminishes our most basic powers. *If we default at the choice point we will develop no further.* We will be induced into a world of powerlessness, victimhood, blame, and passivity—meanings which imprison the human spirit and put our possibilities in shackles.

Conversely, when we joyfully take complete ownership of our *response-powers*, we propel ourselves into a very different world of meaning. Then we live in a world of empowerment, choice, proactivity, and initiative. This generates the sense of being in control of your responses. Obviously, these are the foundational states and frames of mind for the self-actualizing of unleashing potentials. This differs from trying to control the responses of others and all of the sick and toxic games we play to do that. The empowered person knows and respects that others equally have their own response-powers. We are not made less by the empowerment of others. In fact, seeing the response powers of others often unleashes more potential in us as we observe what's possible and view the other person as an exemplar.

5) *Choice Point Premise*
Our development depends upon stepping up to recognizing and using our choice points.

From our response-powers arise our sense of *choice*. In this, our growth, learning, self-actualization, and even consciousness are all choices.

> Ultimately, self-actualization is chosen as a free choice.

These choices emerge as we use our personal response-powers. We have such power that we can avoid learning, growing, and developing our potentials. We can even avoid consciousness. Yes, even consciousness is a choice since we can avoid awareness and defend ourselves against it. If these are all choices, and if being personally responsible is not inevitable, then a key factor in self-actualizing is accepting, owning, and developing this conative power of consciousness—of choosing and deciding.

At the core of the ongoing process of actualizing our potentials is being present and taking ownership of our basic powers for responding. Doing so is how we develop the proactivity and self-regulation that's required to author our own life. Unlike the lower needs or the instinctual needs of animals, *self-actualization development involves making mindful choices.* We have such freedom that we can resist the innate development that would otherwise move us to the level of self-actualization. We can choose to live at a lower level. We can make choices that create interferences to self-actualization that get us stuck at lower levels.

Why would anyone deny consciousness or repress awareness? Why would anyone not openly welcome awareness of whatever *is* and just get on to deal with it? The answer is simple, and simple in a profound way—low ego-strength and a lack of safety. The ego-strength required refers to the ability to look reality in the face without being overwhelmed or engaging in defensive knee-jerk reactions.

Yet because we don't even have a sense of self (ego) at birth, it takes many years of learning and growing to develop a strong sense of one's self as we cope and master the challenges of life. Eventually, with sufficient love and support, we learn to accept and love ourselves and others, advance past the magical and egocentric thinking stages of childhood, and welcome awareness of our fallibilities, limitations, and the constraints of our existence. Doing this enables us to own our powers and step back and step up to the choice point.

6) Need-Driven Premise
Because we are driven by needs, our development occurs through adequate gratification of both *Deficiency* and *Being* needs.

Though we lack instincts as such, and only have instinctoids, we have lots of needs at multiple levels. And these give us clues as to our nature as well as the direction for our highest growth and development.

As Maslow distinguished two basic kind of needs he identified two different kinds of motivations. D-needs

> It is our human needs that drive us to self-actualization.

operate via *deficiency* and B-needs operate through *growth, expressive,* and *being-ness.* His short-hand for this was D and B. The lower of *deficiency* needs—D-needs, the higher *being* needs—B-needs.

Our *D-needs* are truly "needs" in that they are absolute necessities. When we lack them, the experience of lack and the feeling of deficiency drive us. Hunger and thirst are prototypical of the D-needs. When we lack these necessities, life itself is in danger and so our whole body and organism becomes activated, and sometimes desperately activated to satisfy these needs. We become highly motivated. At that point all we can think about is food and water. The feeling of being desperate makes our D-needs incredibly intense and all-consuming.

We also experience the lower D-needs hierarchically. Our lower needs are hierarchical in that we move from survival to security to love to self-regard. And generally speaking, we have to gratify one level of needs, at least to some degree, before the driving power of the next level emerges. While this occurs in our first innocent experience of our needs, as we give meaning to them, the meanings we attribute to these driving impulses rearrange their importance and alter our experience of them.

When we move to *the level of the B-needs,* we enter a domain where our meaning attributions entirely define and govern them. In this, our

B-needs are highly conditioned by our semantics. Our drives for beauty, contribution, connection, honor, spirit, justice, compassion, music, knowledge, mathematics, curiosity, etc. arise as an expression of how we construct meanings about these things. When we reach this level, we are living in the dimension of meaning which colors our needs with these meanings.

At this level, we are able to transform our deficiency needs so deficiency as such no longer motivates us. We can change them so much that we no longer experience them as mere deficiency needs. Our meanings can over-ride the biological needs so that we exaggerate them and over-load them with meaning, or we degrade them so that they become under-loaded with meaning and lose all significance to us.

In this way the *psycho-logics*[2] of our meanings govern *how* we experience our needs. This creates disasters in human personality like psycho-eating, psycho-shopping, psycho-sexing, psycho-spending, etc. This loading of meaning onto things and experiences can also create such flow zone states that it can take our talents and turn them into gifts and competencies that advance the cause of humanity itself.

7) Being and Becoming Premise
The height of self-actualization is moving into the realm of *Being* and the *Being*-needs.

While there is a certain degree of unleashing of potentials through the stages of the D-needs, we really begin unleashing human potentials for self-actualization when we move to the level of the self-actualization needs. Only at this level are we driven by our need to *be*, to become, and to fully *express* ourselves.

Understanding the design of how we move from the D-needs and motivation to the B-level, enables us to appreciate our kind of life as human beings. We are

> Self-actualization is all about *Being-ness.*

a kind of life that naturally keeps moving *beyond doingness to beingness* to the B-values, B-love, and B-motivation. *In this, transcendence is built into our nature and mind.* The space left open by the lack of instincts creates an area wherein we can invent our own style of how to be and to function. We then fill this space with all sorts of meanings and layers of meanings which make for the incredible range of human cultures. This opens up yet more space for *becoming* and for transcending our current development.

What's the goal or objective of self-actualization? If self-actualization refers to "making real or actual" our innate talents, gifts, and potentials, then we become a "fully functioning person" as we discover, own, and develop our talents and as we become mindful of the range of our choices. Then we can transcend where we are as we move toward generating more "flow" and "peak experiences" in our everyday lives.

Self-actualization requires that we find and follow our passions so that the meaning of our lives reaches a peak of meaningfulness. Then peak performances result. When we reach this level, we move into the zone where we ideally optimize challenges and competency. Then it is all about *being*—being all we can be.

8) *Social and Conversational Premise*
We accelerate our development via rich relationships with and through others.

Given all of the open space within us for our own input and influence into our development as we construct meaning, there is simultaneously a lot of room for influence from others. Our openness for meaning simultaneously makes us tremendously receptive and vulnerable to the influences of others—to their meanings (positive or negative), and so to relationships, contexts, and cultures.

As social beings, our growth, development, and self-actualization occurs *in* and *through* relationships. No wonder communicating and relating are central to the unleashing process. We need others. *The paradox of self-actualization is that we can't do it on our own.* Our development occurs in social contexts and via relationships. We develop by relating, communicating, loving, and caring, and by these experiences our highest potentials are unleashed.

It is within this social dimension that our self-actualization develops via *the kind and quality of our communications.* That's because it is the kind and

> Self-actualization is never solo, it is always social.

quality of *dialogue* that we enable meanings (*logos*) to flow through (*dia*) us into a pool of shared meanings. As these meanings move through us we discover and create meanings which expand our vision and facilitate our development. Through conversation we are questioned and challenged. Through dialogue our thinking, valuing, and meaning-making is exposed and expanded and via dialogue we access mental, emotional, and personal resources that others share or trigger in us.

9) Existential Premise
We self-actualize through existential awareness and anxiety.

Because our existence is unfinished and undetermined, it is open to continuous and unending development, to uncertainty, to continuous learning, and to anxiety. And all of this is good! It's good because anxiety stimulates our growth in awareness. We develop by embracing such anxiety, ambiguity, uncertainty, and open-endedness and conversely we relapse when we seek to escape from anxiety.

We can relate this to the subject of tension. Tension in our D-needs arouses and calls us to gratify those needs. When we do, the gratification creates a

> Anxiety always and inevitably drives self-actualization.

satisfaction moving us back to homeostasis. Typically we experience D-tension as an unpleasant motivation— as lack, need, deficiency, unhappiness, and pain so when we gratify the need, it negates the motivating drive. The motivation goes away.

In contrast, we experience B-tension as challenge and excitement. We experience it as a *call to stretch* to new levels of experience, growth, and development. Consequently, as we embrace the disequilibrium that B-tension creates, and we find it exciting we no longer seek to make it go away. Instead we harness it for our growth.

Maslow spoke about the difference between real problems and pseudo-problems. For self-actualizers, who perceive reality more clearly, pseudo-problems disappear and go "poof!", which then free them to move on to the real and unsolvable existential problems of life that can only be accepted and understood.

10) Experiential Premise
The self-actualization process is inherently experiential in nature.

The process of self-actualizing is not merely a mental exercise. Nor is it merely an emotional arousal. Rather it is a full mind-body-emotion experience that activates every aspect and function of being human. It activates our thinking, emoting, speaking, choosing, relating, and acting.

Self-actualization involves the way we reason, solve problems, connect to our families and communities, interact with the environment, and leave a legacy that makes a positive contribution. Because it is holistic, it requires experience in every dimension. It requires critical thinking skills, a higher evolved mindfulness, a richer and more robust emotional life and emotional intelligence, a more accurate and precise use of language, a more empathetic and compassionate way of relating to others, a more effective and empowered ability to execute and follow-through in performance.

As an experience, self-actualization is something experienced somatically. Reading about it won't do. You have to get in and get your hands dirty. You have to use your capabilities and functions as you act and relate.

11. The Peak Experience Premise
For self-actualization, we enjoy peak experiences as rewards along the way.

How do we know if we are self-actualizing? One very clear sign is the experience that Maslow labeled *peak experiences.* In *Unleashed* I have described the flow state as "the zone of self-actualization." This is the state where we are completely present in the here-and-now so that all of the meta-levels of the mind "go away" so to speak so that we are "all there." Here meaning in the sense of challenge and performance in terms of competence are optimally synergized. In this flow state we enter into "the zone" of experience and performance so that we are at our best.

In all of this, we see that in self-actualization, we transcend ourselves, we transcend time, and in fact, we transcend many other things culture, gender,

> Self-actualization is seen and experienced in peak experiences which then leads to peak performances.

race, and so on. In peak experiences, we more fully feel and experience our self-reflexive consciousness so that we keep transcending the constructs that we have previously created. On the subjective level, peak experiences feel other-worldly and mystical.

Conceptually, a peak experience is the optimal interaction of sufficient challenge so that it stretches our competency. That is, it is a function of some rich meanings (challenge) and performance (competency) so that we make it real. As we then experience that special synergy, things seem to just "flow."

12. The Peak Performance Premise
Sustained peak experiences lead to peak performances.

In self-actualizing, we develop greater skill and competency so that we are able to create performances that reflect our highest and best. Through the process of immediate sensory-based feedback, we keep refining our skills. And through a commitment to continuous improvement, we keep taking our skills to the next level of improvement. Peak performances occur as we persist in our focused engagement and resiliently bounce back after anything that knocks us down or sets us back.

13. The Plateau Premise
Self-actualization also entails plateau experiences.

One of the myths is that self-actualization is continuous in the sense that every day we experience Aha! insights, revelations, incredibe creative breakthroughs. To counterbalance that myth Maslow said that in the self-actualizing process we will plateau from time to time. In fact, hitting a plateau is part and parcel of self-actualizing. Experiencing a plateau gives us time for integration of our learnings so that our competencies become more fully embodied and part of our muscle memory. It is a gracious rest, a step for enjoyment before the next step upward. In plateau experience our B-cognitions are more serene and contemplative than climactic ones.

14. The Synergy Premise
We self-actualize via synergizing dichotomies.

If dichotomizing reality creates limitations and leashes, then framing things in terms of two extreme opposite poles and thinking of choices as *either/or* undermines self-actualization. So what's the alternative?

It is to *synergize* the opposite poles. It is to rise above the linear continuum of the two poles and move to a higher or meta-position wherein we can take both into consideration and utilize the strengths of each.

The third alternative offers a meta-solution to the old either-or contrasts. To describe this Maslow used a term he learned from Ruth Benedict, *synergy*. Synergizing opposites enable us to step out of the either-or world of choices and utilize a position that leads to the emergence of new choices. And the experience of self-actualization itself is a function of this kind of synergy.

15. The "Good Conditions" Premise
We self-actualize best under "good conditions."

To self-actualize, we need certain good conditions. These are the conditions that enable us to get our lower needs met and gratified in a healthy and proper way so that we can move to the higher human needs. These are the conditions that enable us to move through the natural growth states easily and without trauma. Good conditions speaks about the importance of early family life, parents, and society to provide the requirements that fit for human growth, learning, and development.

Yet while we self-actualize best under good conditions, in and of themselves, good conditions alone are not sufficient to guarantee self-actualization. People have, and do, self-actualize without them. That is a possibility. Yet we self-actualize best with the good conditions of loving and intelligent parents, a democratic and productive society, etc.

The Self-Actualization Model for Unleashing Potentials
These are the first premises of human development that govern human experience and functioning. As such, they influence how we unleash more and more of our innate drives and potentials. And as you can tell, these premises flesh out a psychology very different from the remedial psychology that focuses on fixing problems and curing mental illness.

As you move through this book, you'll notice that from these premises the *Self-Actualization Matrix* provides a tool for guiding how we unleash potentials in ourselves and others (Chapter 11).

The Key Points in this Chapter

*   As there are premises in every field, there are theoretical frameworks that govern how we can self-actualize and unleash our potentials. With these concepts, understandings, processes, and models, we have an informed pathway.

*   Making the premises of *Self-Actualization Psychology* explicit puts us in a position to test and measure them as we actualize ourselves. These premises help us create more accurate maps about our nature and the vast possibilities before us.

*   By making these premises explicit, we have a brief description of the heart and essence of *Self-Actualization Psychology.*

*   The premises highlight that we are all unique, that each has his or her own talents, and an inward drive to discover, develop, and express those talents and aptitudes and translate them into something exceptionally unique for ourselves.

*   We all want to live a good life, and will, if we are given the support, opportunity, and tools. If given the chance, we all want to believe in people, be on a winning learn, and become all we can become.

End Notes

1. "Self" as information content is the information we hold closest to ourselves. For this reason, in the Matrix Model (2002), we have put the *Self* matrix as the first and the one closest to ourselves. In this, the thing that develops over the life-span is the *self concept.*

2. The term *psycho-logics* originated with Alfred Korzybski and refers to the unique kind and quality of our reasoning (*logics*) which creates the layers of mental contexts in our mind as we think and reason. Whenever we entertain a thought and feeling *about* some idea, experience, emotion, etc., we set that thought-emotion as our frame. This then makes the first mind-body state a member of the class of the second. In this we are not logical, we are psycho-logical. And it leads to doing things for psycho-logical reasons. It leads to psycho-eating for example. For more about that, see *Games Fit and Slim People Play* (2001).

Chapter 6

THE SELF-ACTUALIZATION

MODEL

"Children do not have to be taught to be curious."
(1970, p. 50)

"The higher the need the more specifically human it is."
(1970, p. 98)

For a model of *Self-Actualization Psychology* to exist, it will have to have four distinct features. First, it will have a theoretical foundation comprised of various concepts and abstractions about self-actualization. Then from these foundational propositions we will be able to specify the components and elements that are the key variables of the Model. These are the pieces we will be working with, the pieces that make up the model. Third, we will need some basic guidelines for how to work with the variables given the theoretical understandings. This will include heuristic rules as "rules of thumb" about what to do, when, and with whom as we apply the Model. Finally, there will be some techniques or patterns by which we can activate the Model and do something with it.

I have used these distinctions in this chapter to sort out these four facets of a full description of a complete *Self-Actualization Model*. So following each premise you will find these four elements: theory, variables, guidelines, and patterns. This offers a way to summarize the model in a quick over-view and to trace from theory to variable to guideline to patterns. The design is to be able to present the Model fully in an easily summarized form.

1) Our growth is developmental in nature; our inner core is designed for developing throughout our lifespan.

Four Distinctive Features Required for a Model:

A) Theory
B) Variables
C) Guidelines
D) Patterns

If Self-Actualization is a natural and organic development, then the variables that we work with involve the cognitive, social, sexual, etc. stages of human growth. This development is also based upon the assumptive belief that human nature is "good," or at least neutral, and definitely not "evil" or "depraved." What hurt, pain, and evil that arises comes primarily from the interference of our development and the frustration of our needs.[1]

This premise also proposes that *there is an inner core that develops,* grows, and becomes more of what it can become over the lifespan. Within each of us is *a self* that will develop and grow so that we can become more and more our real self.[2]

From this arises the basic guidelines that Carl Rogers made explicit in how organic growth occurs and what's required. For him, anyone facilitating the growth needs in another needs to be authentic and congruent, able to attain and reflect an accurate empathy of understanding, and able to give unconditional positive regard. This area involves the practice of looking for and validating the positive intentions behind behaviors even those that are hurtful and "evil." And this distinction between person and behavior lies at the heart of all reframing models. Person and behavior are different phenomenon occurring at different levels.

A) Theory:

> Growth is organic and innate. Growth requires a proper environment and nurturing. We are born to develop and move through developmental stages to actualize our potentials. Human nature is good; human intentions are driven by positive intentions. We are born without content instincts about how to develop.

B) Variables:

> Innate talents that can become skills, aptitudes, and competencies.
> Development stages: social, sexual, cognitive, etc.

Information processing to represent and frame our understanding about how to survive, cope, thrive, and succeed as humans.

Support from others for development: our social context and relationships.

C) Guidelines:

Give unconditional positive regard (Rogers)

Trust natural processes as inherently good.

Look for and validate positive intentions.

Keep learning about how best to develop.

D) Patterns:

Elicit and prioritize values.

Finish unfinished business in stages of development.

Set high intentions to encourage ongoing development.

Eliminate interferences to growth.

Create safe environment.

Welcome *ecstasy* as the ability to "stand outside" oneself to get a larger view.

2) We develop as persons and actualize through creating rich and vigorous meanings.

In human nature, meaning is not given. In terms of what we know intuitively and innately when we are born, we have *no instincts* the way animals have content instincts about how to be what they are. In terms of knowing what things are, what leads to what, and how to live meaningfully, we have to invent it all. This describes the human task of meaning-making. And with what seems to be a "language acquisition device" within us (Noam Chomsky), we are wired to construct meaning and to hold representations constant as we invent a world of meaning within our minds. So we work with symbols in order to live in the symbolic world of language and abstractions.

Learning is the process that allows all of this—learning the frames of reference by which we create frames of meaning that we hold in mind to understand things. This also leads to the technologies that allow us to create meaning at multiple levels and to enrich our lives with what we consider significant and valuable (our "values").

A) Theory:

Without instincts we invent the meaning of life as well as the meaning of everything else. We strive for meaning, value, and purpose. These are not given, but must be discovered and created.

The lack of instincts creates a gap for human creativity and innovation. Not knowing how to be human instinctively, we have to learn to become human. Meaning doesn't exist "out there," it takes a meaning-maker to create meaning and to live in a world of meanings.

B) Variables:

Thinking and feeling which we use to frame, reframe, deframe, outframe.
The gap between S-R Learning (Stimulus—Response).
Intention and attention.
Levels of meaning in our self-reflexive consciousness.
Kinds of meaning.
Scale of meaning.

C) Guidelines:

Reduce interferences to natural development.
Challenge to evoke awareness (Perls).
Use counter-intuitive or paradoxical processes (Frankl)
Build up enhancing frames for the games of life.
Quality control meanings to insure they are healthy and ecological meanings.

D) Patterns:

Framing and reframing.
Accepting Ambiguity pattern.
Frame Game or Inner Game Analysis.
Matrix Detection Pattern.
Meaning Enhancement Pattern.
Quality Controlling Pattern.
Clearing out Cognitive Distortions.

3) We have an inner core, a real self that develops via self-discovery, self-awareness, self-respect, and self-love.

What develops over the lifespan? What is it that develops in Developmental Psychology? What do we actualize as we find and develop our potentials? The answer is as simple as it is profoundly fascinating—it is our self. It is *the self* that develops.

We discover our self—what we are capable of, our predispositions, temperament, likes and dislikes, weaknesses and strengths, etc.

Maslow repeatedly said that it is the "real self" that we are to get to know and our inner voice that we are to learn to hear— to hear that voice over and above the cultural voices that plead for conventionality and conformity.

The paradox is that it is through the discovery and development of self, and the strength of our ego to face reality, that we are able to get the ego out of the way and experience a self-forgetfulness. There are numerous patterns for this.

A) *Theory:*
> We develop by discovering ourselves—our talents, nature, mind, via learning and becoming more authentically ourselves.
> As we are born without a *self*, all of life involves developing and inventing a *self* construct that supports and enriches us. We are not born as a blank tablet, but are born with predispositions and talents that we can actualize if we are to fully develop.

B) *Variables:*
> Self-knowledge.
> Self-exploration.
> Strengths and Weaknesses.
> Aptitudes and Predispositions.
> Freedom of choice for discovering and creating our self.
> Experiencing and gratifying needs that move us up the hierarchy of prepotency.

C) *Guidelines:*
> Self-definition governs experiences.
> Distinguish self-esteem from self-confidence to create an unconditional sense of self-value as a human being.
> It takes a lot of self-esteem to be humble and modest.
> Develop self-efficacy to trust yourself in stepping out into the unknown and inventing yourself as you go.

D) *Patterns:*
> Self-esteeming.
> Self-accepting.
> Self-appreciating.
> Dis-identifying.
> Swishing to a Resourceful Self.

Owning your disowned parts (Perls).
Expressing resentment as an unfinished gestalt (Perls).

4) We accelerate our development via assuming personal ownership and responsibility for our lives, we are diminished as persons when we do not.

While self-actualization is a possibility for everybody, it is not an inevitability for anyone. The process of self-actualization requires choice, the personal responsibility to opt for it and so occurs through dozens if not scores of choices for awareness and responsibility every day.

A) Theory:

We develop by taking ownership of our powers of response and so become *responsible* persons.
We are not pawns of deterministic forces, but are able to choose our responses.
We have choice about developing and about the direction of our development.

B) Variables:

Sensory awareness.
Being in the moment, in the here-and-now.
Awareness of awareness, meta-cognitive awareness for expanded choice.
The core human powers for responding and choosing.
Implementation of what one knows to embody in actual behaviors.
Recognition of choice moments as they appear in life.

C) Guidelines:

Be fully present and learn to just notice what *is*.
"Lose your mind, come to your senses." (Perls)
Discover and develop your ability to choose.
Own your powers to respond (Frankl).
"They can't make me hate them." (Frankl)

D) Patterns:

Sensory Awareness.
Courage to be (May).
Power Zone: Ownership of Powers.
Distinguishing Responsibility To/For.
Mind-to-Muscle pattern.

Acceptance of Accountability.

5) *Development depends upon stepping up to recognize and use our choice points.*

Self-Actualization inevitably involves a highly developed sense of choice and responsibility. The reason for that, in part, is because every day we experience choice points for growth or regression, for honesty or deception, for effort or passivity, for other or self, and so on. And with each choice, we either make a choice for actualizing our highest and best or we make a choice that works against such.

A) *Theory:*
The lack of "instincts" leaves a gap within us about how to be human thereby requiring that we fill that gap via learning and choosing.
What we learn and choose are our "meanings"—what we understand that something is, how it works, its significance, what led to it, what it will lead to, what it is like, and scores of other conceptual understandings.

B) *Variables:*
Mentally and emotionally weighing alternatives of what to choose to think, feel, say, and do.
Criteria of our standards that we create for choosing.
Comparing pros and cons, advantages and disadvantages between two or more possibilities.

C) *Guidelines:*
Develop understanding about what criterion to use in any given context when making a choice.
Reality test the accuracy and appropriateness of the criterion as well as the choice.
Step back to gain perspective to other perceptual perspectives.
Step back to run a quality control of the choice in terms of all of the systems of interactions.\
Realize that to not choose is a choice. We cannot not choose.

D) *Patterns:*
The Step Back Skill of meta-stating.
A Well-Designed Decision Strategy.
Problem-Solving skills pattern.
The Power Zone pattern.

Responsibility To/ For pattern.

6) Because we are driven by needs, our development occurs through adequate gratification as both Deficiency and Being needs.

Self-actualization springs from our biology, from our instinctoid nature and so is wired into all of us as a *need.* It begins with the lower needs. Then through adequate and accurate gratification, we naturally move to the higher self-actualization needs.[3]   As this requires proper understanding of the needs, it is dependent upon the meanings that we give to our needs. If we over-load our needs with too much meaning, our psycho-logics can undermine and interfere with our self-actualization.

> "Man is a wanting animal . . .   As one desire is satisfied, another pops up in its place. . ." (1970, p. 24)

The three-faces of the pyramid enables us to view our experiencing of needs in terms of naive experiencing, coping experiencing (lack of effective coping, and so toxic experiencing), and mastery.

A) Theory:

We develop by discovering and fulfilling our D-needs and B-needs.

As a source of joy and fulfillment, our needs clamor to be satisfied.

Our needs are hierarchical with the lower needs prepotent to the higher needs.

Any need can become more important than any other via the meanings we give to it (this creates our psycho-logics).

Our nature develops and our self unfolds by need gratification.

We naturally move from the basic needs to the meta-needs.

Gratification releases us from one level of need for moving to the next level.

At the meta-levels we are forever restless and discontented which is the source of creativity and innovation.

As our deficiency needs become layered with meanings, they operate as holons within the holarchy of mind-body system.

While our needs are basically good, we can develop neurotic needs.

B) Variables:

Growth, movement.
Learning / Change.

Emergence.
Prepotency.
Moving through need stages.
Experimenting.
Actual gratifiers and not merely symbolic gratifiers.
Discontent and restlessness.
Frames of meaning within frames.
Embedded frames as the psycho-logics of our mind.
The classes and categories that define inner reality.
Values, desires, wants.
Fears, dislikes, aversions.

C) Guidelines:

Growth happens, so look for it, anticipate it, and structure for it.
Nurture your biological roots for a solid foundation.
Needs are neither moral nor immoral, but amoral.
D-needs must be adequately and accurately gratified if we are to move forward.
Because of the meanings given to needs, avoid over-loading needs with too much meaning (semantic loading).
Tease out the meta-levels of frames.
Detect your Matrix of meaning frames.
The quality of your meanings determines the quality of your life.
Identify the psycho-logics of any "need."
Discover the level you are attempting to gratify.

D) Patterns:

Discovering Passions pattern.
Develop talents into skills.
Access Personal Genius.
Accessing Respectful Humor.
Welcoming the mysteries and ambiguities of life.
Entering the Crucible pattern.
Matrix Detection pattern.
Meta-Questions for flushing out the meta-levels.
Meta-Stating Concepts.
Pleasuring and De-Pleasuring pattern.
Propulsion System.

7) The height of self-actualization is moving into the realm of Being and the Being-needs.

Being in Self-Actualization theory stands in contrast with *doing*. We *do* at the lower needs as an instrumental urge to achieve the gratification of needs. By way of contrast, in the self-actualization needs, our desire is to be and to express ourselves for no other purpose. This is true for our B-values, B-love, B-cognition, etc.

A) Theory:

In the level of self-actualization we learn to *be* who we are as human beings which transcends the instrumental drives of the lower needs.

In actualizing, there is *Being*-motivation, B-love, B-values, etc. Life moves beyond doing, achieving, accomplishing, stirring, and working to *being*.

As we develop our full potential we become fully functioning human beings.

B) Variables:

The self-actualizing, expressive needs.

Self-discovery; self-expression.

Beingness.

Functioning—operating effectively in various domains of interest.

Peak experiences and plateau experiences.

Non-instrumentality.

C) Guidelines:

Transcend your *deficiency* needs and move into a higher realm of *being*.

Find and follow your talents, passions, and visions.

Move beyond doing and instrumental striving to the *being* realm where the focus is on expressing your inner nature.

D) Patterns:

Self-Esteeming pattern.

Dis-Identification pattern.

Meta-Stating Love.

Stepping Back skill.

Living with Passion pattern.

Accessing Personal Genius pattern.

8) *We accelerate our development via rich relationships with and through others.*

As social animals we have needs for the lower needs of love and affection and for self-regard. Within the lower needs, we need others to help satisfy the needs whereas our higher self-actualization needs are mostly satisfied by ourselves as we find our individual uniqueness as well as our resourcefulness for self-support. Yet at the higher levels, rich relationships reward us in our passion for contribution. At the higher levels we relate to others non-purposefully and in a non-instrumental way. Here we need people in order to give, contribute, and support.

A) *Theory:*

As social beings, we derive our original identity from our interactions with others.

As we actualize our potentials we become more autonomous and so less dependent on others for need gratification.

In self-actualizing, we seek to give love to others and contribute our best expressions.

B) *Variables:*

Relationships.

Social connections.

Social emotions.

Individualizing, separating from groups.

Standing on one's own feet using one's own inner resources.

Internal referencing with an external check.

Attention to others.

C) *Guidelines:*

We are hurt and healed by people.

Love, understanding, empathy are healing social emotions for self-development.

Discover and be true to yourself—to your values and visions.

Shift your orientation from taking to giving.

Develop an internal reference with an external check.

Every act of kindness, love, compassion initiates a therapeutic influence into the world.

D) *Patterns:*

Communication dialogue.

Listening.

Forgiveness.

Giving and Receiving Feedback.
Magnanimity.
Caring.
Releasing Judgment.
Responsibility To/ For.

9) We self-actualize through existential awareness and anxiety.

Self-Actualization, involving our existential needs, is forever tinged by the existential anxiety which is part and parcel of the human condition. There is no ultimate escape from such anxiety, there is only the acceptance and management of anxiety. Anxiety creates an inner restlessness so that we are never ultimately satisfied, but always creatively engaged as we seek to understand more, contribute more, and find new and better ways to live.

A) Theory:

We develop by embracing the existential anxiety of human reality.
Anxiety is natural and normal, to be embraced along with uncertainty, mortality, and fallibility. Our existence is unfinished and undetermined and so open to uncertainty.
We seek to satisfy and reduce the tensions of lower needs while creating higher level tensions.

B) Variables:

The tension of anxiety as an emotion.
Positive and negative emotions.
Uniqueness of each self, fallibility.
Time awareness; morality.
Disequilibrium.
Tensions and stresses, meta-tension and eustress.
Gap between current and desired reality.

C) Guidelines:

Raise your frustration-tolerance level.
Expand awareness and acceptance of what *is*.
Frustrate the client to provoke him to develop his potential (Perls).
Welcome tension to discover the gap between current reality and what's potentiality.
Manage tension so that it is optimal for challenge.
Identify dichotomies and synergize to transcend them.

D) Patterns:
Meta-stating Emotions pattern.
Meta-stating Anxiety (as a stimulus for growth).
Centering Self pattern (for a strong sense of self).
Super-Charge Your Attitude pattern.
Ego-Strength Enhancement pattern.

10) The self-actualization process is inherently experiential in nature.
We self-actualize via encountering ourselves with a honesty about ourselves, others, and the world that set us free from delusions, illusions, and cognitive distortions. We actualize our potentials by speaking the truth to ourselves and others. This sets us free from "secrets" and "the unspeakable" which are factors that create sickness and dis-ease.

A) Theory:
Self-actualization emerges as we come to "know ourselves."
Self-awareness and growth is a life-long process of discovery and development of one's self.
Because knowing *about* differs from experientially *knowing,* we need both kinds of knowledge to self-actualize.

B) Variables:
The impulses of our needs, and drives.
Acceptance and appreciation.
Honesty with oneself without defenses.
Interpersonal contexts for encountering our reality.
Unconditional positive regard.

C) Guidelines:
Enter the crucible of unconditional positive regard so you can welcome your boiling needs and hot thoughts and emotions.
Human growth requires the safety created through acceptance and appreciation.
Step back to simply and purely witness your needs and their meanings without judgment or reaction.
Hold the space for another to explore and notice what *is*.
Give unconditional positive regard to persons above and beyond their behaviors.

D) Patterns:
The Step Back skill.

Releasing Judgment pattern.

Meta-stating self or other with acceptance, appreciation, honesty, etc.

Ruthless Honesty pattern.

Crucible Construction pattern.

The De-Contamination pattern.

11) In self-actualizing, we enjoy peak experiences as rewards along the way.

A peak experience is a transcendence experience that occurs at times when we are at our very best when the world, time, space, others vanish from our awareness. Within the experience itself there is no awareness of the experience itself since we are so totally engaged with the object of our commitment and fascination. It is only later when we reflect upon it that we realize that we were in an altered state, perhaps even what we call a mystical experience.

A) Theory:

We accelerate our development by moving into the zone of self-actualization where we are completely present, where we synergize our meanings (challenge) and performances (competence). This is the flow state or the zone.

Self-actualization enables us to transcend ourselves, time, culture, gender, and race.

B) Variables:

Focused sensory awareness.

Embodiment that closes the knowing-doing gap.

Lost in the moment in a compelling engagement.

Intention and attention.

Frames for getting lost in the moment.

Self-reflexivity.

C) Guidelines:

Access your highest executive frame and set conditions for total sensory awareness.

Align your attentions to your highest intentions to create a focused engagement state.

Give permission to let go of non-relevant attentions.

Set relevancy frames for the engagement experience.

D) Patterns:

Accessing Personal Genius pattern.

Sensory Awareness exercises.
Meta-Stating Intentionality pattern.
The Meta-Alignment pattern.

12) Sustained peak experiences lead to and create peak performances.

Actualizing our best skills and competencies consistently and persistently sets up the conditions for regularly experiencing peak experiences which gives us a taste of self-actualization and leads ultimately to peak performances. Sustaining regular peak experiences around a desired engagement facilitates increased competency and expertise.

A) Theory:

In self-actualizing, we develop greater skill and competency so that we are enabled to create performances that reflect our highest and best.

Developing mastery in an area requires persistence, discipline, patience, ongoing learning, feedback, shaping, resilience, etc.

B) Variables:

Behaviors and activities.
Talent developed into skills and competencies.
Learning, growing, and developing.
Feedback and accountability.
Patience and persistence.
Resilience.

C) Guidelines:

Keep learning and receiving feedback to improve your performance.
Use persistence to keep following your inner dreams and values.
Develop the resilience to bounce back from anything that causes a set-back to your long-term goals.
Make *kaizen* (continuous improvement) your everyday philosophy.
Keep refreshing your attitude and spirit to keep your highest intentions alive and fresh.

D) Patterns:

Continuous Improvement (Kaizen) pattern.

Benchmark specific skills for measurement.
Receiving Feedback pattern.
Peak Performance pattern.

13) Self-actualization entails plateau experiences as well as peak experiences.

As we develop we can expect to plateau at times. This is normal, to be expected, and to be taken with a graceful patience. It is not something out of the ordinary, but the way growth occurs. In the plateau experiences we have the opportunity to integrate and consolidate our learnings more thoroughly to make them fully a part of who we are and how we move through the world.

A) Theory:

When in the self-actualizing process we often and regularly hit plateaus. This is good and normal because it gives us time for integration of learnings and competencies.
Plateaus do not mean we have stopped developing, are stuck, or have reached our limits.

B) Variables:

Stages in the processes of growth and learning.
The time element in integrating new learnings and skills.
Integration time.
Acceptance and persistence of plateaus.
Understanding of the plateau, what it means, and how to use it effectively.

C) Guidelines:

Read plateaus as a developmental stage.
Expect to experience plateaus along the way and arise to consolidate your progress at such times.

D) Patterns:

Meta-stating Acceptance pattern.
Meta-Alignment pattern.
Super-Charging Attitude pattern.
Resilience pattern.

14. We self-actualize via synergizing dichotomies.

What undermines self-actualization is positing such things as mind *and* body, work *and* play, selfish *and* unselfish, etc. as polar opposites. This creates false-to-fact dichotomies and limiting *either-*

or choices. Yet when we examine the reality of these phenomena we find that we can more accurately and usefully view them as part of the same system. This allows for *both-and thinking* as well as the thinking of degrees, extent, and probability.

A) Theory:

Maslow's study of self-actualizing individuals indicated that a common sign of self-actualizing is synergizing opposites which thereby eliminates false choices and contrasts. The principle of synergy, as a higher level of awareness, integrates and resolves dichotomies.

B) Variables:

The polar ends or opposite ends of a continuum.
The process of synergizing.
The principle of synergy.
Logical levels.
Thinking patterns.
Framing.

C) Guidelines:

Step back from the either-or thinking that creates a black-or-white choice to gain a higher and more expansive perspective.
Identify the continuum of the polar opposites to recognize the unifying concept.
Integrate the opposites on a singular continuum by valuing each and setting frames that support the synergy.

D) Patterns:

The Unleashing Possibilities pattern.
Expanding Meta-Program pattern.
The Meta-Stating pattern.

15. We self-actualize best under "good conditions."

While it is not necessary or sufficient for self-actualization, good external conditions (e.g., a good home life, environment, economics, politics, etc.) support self-actualization making it more likely. While people have and can live a self-actualizing life under the most severe conditions as Nelson Mandela, Martin Luther King, Jr., etc., they are the exceptions. Most do not. Most people need the support of "good conditions."

A) Theory:

The Hierarchy of Needs is based upon the theory or principle of relative prepotency which means that gratifying the lower needs enables the next higher need to emerge. Maslow's studies of self-actualizers indicated that children who have their lower needs met accurately and adequately during childhood are more likely to move to the higher needs and are more resilient in handling the ups-and-downs of life.

B) Variables:

Human needs.
Levels of human needs.
Gratifying needs.
Deficiency needs and experience.
Growth needs and experience.
The emergence of needs through gratification.

C) Guidelines:

Gratify the lower needs with true satisfiers.
Give the lower needs appropriate meanings (understandings, beliefs, decision, etc.) to avoid semantically loading them and creating psycho-eating, sexing, etc.

D) Patterns:

The "patterns" for this is good parenting, good counseling, good education, good civics, good politics, etc.
New Behavior Generator pattern.
The Swish pattern for directionalizing the brain.
Modeling Excellence Strategy and competence.

Key Points in this Chapter

• The theory of self-actualization which Maslow discovered, developed, from studying and modeling self-actualizers offers a full model. It is the foundation for a *Self-Actualization Psychology* model.

• From the premises of self-actualization in the previous two chapters, we are now able to specify the theory, variables, guidelines, and patterns inherent in the Self-Actualization Model.

End Notes:

1. Evil also arises from physical sickness, mental pathology, ignorance, stupidity, from immaturity, bad social and institutional arrangements. (1970, p. 117).

2. How long does it take in order to self-actualize? Maslow found that it generally takes 50 years. So he wrote about confining the concept to older people and saying that by the criteria he used, it does not occur in young people. Why does it not occur in younger people? Because they have not had enough time to experience an enduring, loyal, post-romantic love relationship, find their calling, work out their own system of values, or experience enough of being responsible to others, tragedy, failure, achievement, success, etc. they have not had sufficient experiences that enable them to shed perfectionism, learn to be patient, or learn about evil in themselves and others to be compassionate (1970, p. 168). As a result he separated the concept of self-actualization into two areas: 1) Mature, fully-human self-actualizing people. 2) Good-growth-toward-self-actualization at any age.

3. Maslow wrote extensively about Gratification Theory in his chapter "The Role of Basic Need Gratification in Psychological Theory" as the theory he developed at the heart of Self-Actualization Psychology. He also based it upon six previous theories in psychology (1970, p. 60).

Maslow identified the trend toward a positive, growth psychology and named many people who had influenced his own thinking in this direction (1970, p. 78). The growing sense in psychology at that time was what we today call a strength-based or solution-focused approach.

Chapter 7

MASLOW

AND THE ROLE OF MEANING

> "... Self-actualizing people, even though all their basic needs have already been gratified, find life to be even *more* richly meaningful because they can live, so to speak, in the realm of Being."
> (1970, p. xv)

It was in the 1940s that Maslow set out to engage in his project of modeling psychologically healthy persons. His goal at that time was to model *self-actualizers* and, from that, *the process of self-actualization itself*. To achieve this he began identifying the features and qualities of self-actualizing people, he then began selecting people (both living and dead) who meet those qualifications. As he did, he also had to theorize about what motivated these people and how their motivational life and level differed from people who were not self-actualizing their potentials, but still living at "the level of the jungle," that is, at the level of the basic needs driven by deficiency.

The Meaning of Lower and Higher Needs
In the process of doing this, Maslow collected "needs, drives, instinctions, goals," etc. that move and motivate people and classified them. From that came his creative insight that differentiated lower and higher needs. He called the higher needs, *meta-needs*. In fact, he used the word *meta* abundantly during the 1940s and may have been the first to do so along with Bateson. He spoke about *meta-values, the meta-life, meta-motivation, meta-pathologies, meta-pay,* etc.[1] I don't know who began using the term first. Of course, given his work with Ruth Benedict and then his correspondence with Margaret Mead, he discovered and met Gregory Bateson, so the

question may be, which one influenced the other regarding the use of the term *meta*?

Out of this arose the only model that's been popularized which comes from Maslow and his pioneering efforts in *Self-Actualization Psychology,* namely, the Hierarchy of Needs. There was another model, the Growth Model, a lesser model that we will explore in a later chapter (Chapter 9). Yet this first model was so simple, useful, and insightful, that it very quickly, and I mean very quickly, began to permeate psychology, self-improvement, management, leadership, consulting, communication, motivation, learning, education, etc.

Prior to Maslow's work with the instinctual needs, there was *a War of the Instincts* in the field of psychology. This began about the first of the twentieth century and continued for decades. Every psychologist and theorist was trying to identify *the primary instinct,* the key instinct, the mother of all instincts, in their effort to understand and create a theory of human nature: Was it sex, aggression, growth, self-perfection, equilibrium, homeostasis, fear, power, dominance, self-esteem, love, food, death, meaning, etc.? One psychology textbook said that over 137 "instincts" were identified in that period.

What Maslow did in the morass of that confusion was to offer a model that brought all of the human instincts, drives, and needs together as he provided an unifying mechanism for conceptualizing and ordering the human "needs." And he put them together in a format that showed the prepotency of the lower needs, which explains why we feel them so strongly and why they are so biologically based, and how gratification bring into our awareness a new set of needs.

About this, biographer Colin Wilson (1972) wrote,
> "What was revolutionary about this theory was that it represented such a huge synthesis." (p. 143)

Wilson went on to say that Maslow essentially showed that, to some extent, everybody was right. And at the same time, he simultaneously showed that to the same extent, everybody was wrong about the so-called human "instincts."

The Meaning of the Lower Needs
We experience a similarity to the animals in our lower needs for

survival (food, water, air, sex, shelter, warmth, etc.) in that they are very strong and driving. The primary difference is that while animals have innate programs for knowing *what* will satisfy their needs and *how* to satisfy their needs, we humans do not. We have the urge, the need, and the impulse, but we are without the information content. Compared to the animals, we are program-less. Maslow said that we only have *instinctoids*—remnants of instincts.

This becomes more and more true as we move up the levels. We move first from the survival needs to the need for safety and security, the social needs for love and affection, the self-needs for feeling regarded by others in our community as important and valued. *How do we satisfy these inner drives*? What will satisfy them?

Insightfully Maslow recognized *deficiency* as the driving mechanism and nature in the lower needs. When we do not have them, we feel a powerful sense of *lack.* This induces feelings of desperateness. We want. We need. Yet something strange happens when we gratify the need. *Poof! The drives goes away!* It vanishes. Suddenly, we are no longer hungry, cold, insecure, etc. In fact, gratification not only makes the drive go away so that we do not want it any longer, but we typically even forget how driving the experience was. Maslow called this "post-gratification forgetting."

The Meaning of the Higher Needs
If the lower or deficiency needs arise from our biology and describes our connection with the animals, *it is the higher needs that differentiates us from them.* By gathering all of the other needs, the ones that make us uniquely human, Maslow created the category of *higher needs.* What we want at this level is meaning, purpose, direction, intention, beauty, order, contribution, truth, unity, integration, synergy, and all of the needs-wants-instincts that relate to our "spirit." The lack of these needs lead us humans to feel "dis-spirited." And the fulfillment causes us to feel "in-spirited."

> "So far as motivational status is concerned, healthy people have sufficiently gratified their basic needs for safety, belongingness, love, respect, and self-esteem so that they are motivated primarily by trends to self-actualization (defined as ongoing actualizing of potentials, capacities and talents, as fulfillment of mission (or call, fate, destiny, or vocation), as a fuller knowledge of, and acceptance of, the person's own intrinsic nature, as an unceasing trend toward unity, integration, or synergy within the person)." (1968, p. 25)

The higher needs do not operate by deficiency. We can live without them. Yet when we lack them, while we will not be desperate in the way we are when we lack the survival needs, yet something other than death occurs in us. Without them we will tend to live "quiet lives of desperation" (Thoreau). Nor is there any post-gratification relief. Satisfy these higher needs and instead of going away, they become stronger! We then want more and more of them. In fact, gratification will expand our very capacity. We develop more capacity for wanting and experiencing the higher needs—it stretches us for the need. In this, we cannot get too much truth, beauty, meaning, excellence, contribution, awe, art, etc.

> "The appetite for growth is whetted rather than allayed by gratification." (1968, p. 30)

When we live at the level of the meta-needs and meta-values, we live very differently. *It's a world of abundance* rather than deficiency. It's the uniquely human world of growth wherein we feel driven for self-expression—to *express* ourselves, rather than trying to get more of some external gratifier. Maslow struggled for the decades trying to find the right words to describe this very special experience. As an experience of *being*, we lose the doing or achieving motivation to *achieve* something as a means to some end. Instead we become *expressive* of ourselves and so non-instrumental in our striving. Our striving is no longer instrumental as it is with the lower needs. The value of the experience is the experience itself, so our striving is "non-purposive." This is the place for self-actualizing, *becoming* more and more all we can become, and the place of peak experiences.

Meaning as both Need and Mechanism

Yet in all of this, Maslow missed something.   While he acknowledged meaning as one of our meta-needs, he missed the central role that *meaning* and *meaning-making* plays in human personality. So in the process of updating and extending Maslow's work. I have put *meaning* into Self-Actualization Theory.

> *Maslow missed the role of meaning-making and specifically how meaning-attribution governs our experience of the lower needs. It is the construction and the quality of the meanings (messages) that we invent that determines how we cope or fail to cope, or perhaps master our needs.*

True enough, he was close to it. For example, he recognized that the Hierarchy of Needs was not a strict hierarchy. He realized and spoke about how any *need* can become so important that it dominates all other needs. He also wondered about why some needs can become so unimportant that they fail to drive us at all. But he didn't identify the mechanism of *meaning* as the mechanism that made that difference.

Failing to recognize this meant that Maslow didn't see how *the meanings we create in our mind* self-organize our entire mind-body system as an attractor frame creating a self-fulfilling process. Yet now that we know this, we can introduce a more *systemic understanding and images* into the old static hierarchy pyramid. To the static and rigid pyramid, we can add the information feedback loops to show how meaning influences and even governs how we experience our needs.

Via our self-reflexive consciousness, we are enabled to add layer upon layer of *meaning* to our experiences. And this describes the highest and most critical human "instinct" of all, how we invent and attribute meaning.

How Maslow Missed Meaning
In spite of recognizing meaning as a meta-need and at the heart of the *being*-needs, *Maslow missed meaning as the central mechanism of self-actualization*, and, indeed, of motivation and personality. So in spite of the exciting, and even revolutionary, insights that he achieved with the Hierarchy of Needs model, because Maslow overlooked the role of meaning in our experience his model became static and rigid as a triangle or pyramid. This now raises the question, How did he miss meaning?

Perhaps he missed meaning simply because he put *meaning* as one of the self-actualization needs and, having filled the category, he didn't see that it could have other functions as well (1954, 1970, p. 101). Perhaps he missed it because he used other words for it, and so many other words, in fact, that the very use of the synonyms blinded him from seeing the role of meaning as cognitive creation.

Actually I am surprised by the wide range of terms that he used as synonyms to "meaning." Maslow used value, significance, "for the sake of," "symbolic value," caring or not caring about it," "perceiving a situation," "cognitive capacity," "learning," etc.[2] Perhaps he was so focused on describing the higher states of self-actualization, modeling self-actualizers, and linking it to the lower biological needs that he just didn't think it was important.

And finally, perhaps that's why, toward the end of his life, his dissatisfaction with "the third force" in psychology (the growth or human potential movement), he began to pioneer an entirely new approach, his "fourth force" (transpersonal psychology).

Whatever caused it, Maslow missed the most dynamic factor in human personality and development. He missed the key factor that actually serves as the *leverage* within human experience for change, ongoing development, transformation, the quality of life, the content of development, and more.

The Meaning Maslow Missed

What is the meaning that Maslow missed? And how does it play such a critical role? The meaning that Maslow missed is the freedom we have as human beings for defining, representing, associating, framing, and evaluating things. There are *multiple levels of meaning* so that our ways of creating meaning and filling in the details that define our kind of life are many. We create emotional meaning, associative meaning, survival meaning, representational meaning, definition meaning, metaphorical meaning, linguistic meaning, contextual meaning, evaluative meaning, perceptual meaning, intentional meaning, social meaning, etc.[3]

So when we ask the question about any given experience or object, "What does that mean to you?" we have to listen to the many things that the person holds in mind about the reference, the many ways that the person encodes or represents his or her meanings and the levels or layers of meaning. In that way, we can identify and map out the person's entire meaning system or matrix.

The Meaning of Food

What does *food* mean to you? What does *eating* mean to you? Does it only mean fuel, energy, vitality, and health? Or does it mean love, reward, comfort, the good life, deserving, de-stressing, socializing, feeling full, enjoyment, fun, etc.? Whatever it means to you determines how you *experience* it, how you *feel* about it, how you *relate* to it, and it *relates* to you. The more meaning you endow it with, the more meaning it holds for you— positive or negative. If you over-load it with meaning, if you semantically load it with too much meaning—food can become dominating and controlling, even destructive to you.

To semantically load something with too much meaning creates a psychological frame of mind about it. The meaning as a belief, value, identity, decision, intention, understanding, etc., sets a psychological frame. We then see, hear, and feel it in terms of that frame of meaning. This is what we mean by saying that the meanings are the psycho-logics of that thing or experience. How we reason, think, and make sense of something (our psycho-logics) sets our meaning frames about it. We then see it, think about it, and experience it through those lens.

People who can't say *no* to food and to over-eating, may now have a habit that has them. And within and above the habitual way of handling food is a mental habit—a conceptual frame about what saying *no* to food *means* to them. So, for example, if it means deprivation, loss of joy, loss of love, loss of comfort, misery, etc., then the person will experience and feel that saying *no* to three extra helpings of dessert means "the loss of the good life" and that may be far too painful to endure. It would mean the loss of rich and rewarding meanings.

In this instance, the feeling of pain, loss, deprivation, dieting, giving up, etc. are *semantic reactions*. They are reactions from the *meanings* we attribute to food and eating. Give food and eating opposite meanings, "fat, ugly, undesirable, out-of-control," etc. and we over-load it with negative meanings that create other problems. We then create eating disorders. Then, our meanings about being fat, about the importance of being thin, etc. will even shift our perceptions distorting our body image.[4]

Meaning — the Critical Factor

Meaning is the most critical factor in human nature. There's nothing more essential or core to our nature and experiences. In the end, no experience and no event "makes" us feel anything. In itself, no experience means anything. Meaning is not inside events.

Meaning is what we create and attribute to those events and *it is meaning that creates our experiences and our emotions.* That's why every emotion is always right— right in relation to the meanings (the mental maps) out of which they arise. That's also why we cannot blindly trust our emotions. It is from our mappings of meaning that we derive our emotions. They reflect the *relationship* between the meanings we have mapped and our experiences of the territory they seek to help us navigate.

Knowing all of this now enables us to recognize the static nature of Maslow's hierarchy and how he missed the most *dynamic variable* of all in human motivation and personality—a dynamic that would energize the hierarchy and transform it into a more dynamic model.

Maslow even admitted such. In *The Farther Reaches of Human Nature* (1971), he wrote:

> "It is a great mystery to me why affluence releases some people for growth while permitting other people to stay fixated at a strictly materialistic level." (p. 316)

Today, we can answer the puzzle. The experience of affluence is just an event or experience. What it means to any given person determines how that person will regard and feel about affluence. Is it good or bad to the person? Is it a blessing or a curse? In his classic work, *Motivation and Personality* (1954) Maslow described meaning as a *cognitive capacity* and as a capacity that can itself be threatened.

> "If we remember that the cognitive capacities (perceptual, intellectual, learning) are a set of adjustive tools, which have, among other functions, that of satisfaction of our basic needs, then it is clear that any danger to them, any deprivation or blocking of their free use, must also be indirectly threatening to the basic needs themselves." (p. 47)

Yet he never follow up on this to indicate the relationship between our cognitive capacities for creating meaning and our experience of our needs. In the same work, about the search for meaning, he describes meaning as simply one of our higher needs:

> "This process is called by some, search for meaning. We shall then postulate a desire to understand, to systematize, to organize, to analyze, to look for relations and meanings, to construct a system of values." (1954, p. 50)

Maslow even wrote that an object that we desire may have two meanings. Its *intrinsic meaning* is what it *is*—an ice cream cone is a sweet and a treat (a definition meaning). Yet it could also have a secondary *symbolic value.*

> "A goal object may have two meanings for the individual. First it has its intrinsic meanings and secondly, it may have also a secondary, symbolic value." (1970, p. 106)

He then illustrates the difference in terms of the meanings given to an ice-cream cone. It can mean itself—a food item, a sensory gratification, a desert, a treat. Or it can mean a mother's love.

Maslow described meaning when he wrote the following about the distinction between an *external situation* and how an organism *perceives* it.

"Ultimately, only that is *psychologically* important which the organism perceives or reacts to, or by which it is affected in one way or another." (1970, p. 112)

Meaning Synonyms

So Maslow put meaning as a being-value and didn't see its other roles, especially that of defining and framing our needs. Yet Maslow came very close to recognizing the distinction between needs and the meanings we attribute to them:

"Eating may be partially *for the sake of* filling the stomach, and partially *for the sake of* comfort and amelioration of other needs. One may make love not only for pure sexual release, but also *to* convince oneself of one's masculinity, or *to* make a conquest, *to* feel powerful, *to* win more basic affection. (1954, p. 55, italics added)

In this insightful reference, he used the phrase "for the sake of" and the word "to" as synonyms for meaning. Perhaps that's what caused him to miss the significance of meaning. Who would have guessed that "for the sake of" or "to" could be synonyms of "meaning?"

In the following, Maslow used the phrase "symbolic value" for meaning and describes the role of meaning in experience. Here he even speaks about the levels of meaning although he doesn't describe them as levels.

"A goal object may have two meanings for the individual. First, it has its intrinsic meaning and secondly, it may have a secondary, *symbolic* value. A certain child deprived of an ice-cream cone that he wanted may have lost simply an ice cream cone. A second child, deprived of an ice cream cone, may have lost not only a sensory gratification, but may feel deprived of the love of his mother because she refused to buy it for him."

"For the second boy the ice-cream cone has an intrinsic value, but may also be *the carrier of psychological values*. First, carries the physiological value only [first level meaning], the second adds a psychological value to it [second or meta-level of meaning]. It's only when a goal object *represents* love, prestige, respect, or other basic needs that being deprived of it will have the bad effects ordinarily attributed to frustration in general." (1954, p. 106 italics added)

In this instance, Maslow was so close to seeing the intimate role of meaning and yet so far away. Maslow here recognized that the meaning one gives to food will fulfill different needs—either for food or for love. He recognize that an item could have symbolic value (meaning) in addition to its "intrinsic" or definition meaning. Ah, maybe that was the thing that tripped him up. There's no actual "intrinsic meaning" in anything. There is only the see-hear-feel, empirical description or definition meaning of an ice-cream cone. All meanings of an ice-cream cone are symbolic.

The Meaning of Sex
Regarding celibacy, he wrote:
> "It's now well known that many cases are found in which celibacy has no psychopathological effects. But if it felt to *represent* rejection by the opposite sex, inferiority, lack of worth, lack of respect, isolation, or other thwarting of basic needs – it is pathological."

Yes, neither sex nor the lack of sex damage people. It is rather what either experience means to a person. If a person interprets the lack of sex as meaning that he or she is undesirable, unlovable, missing out on life, etc., then these meanings do the person damage. It is *meaning* which can turn either experience into a trauma.

Maslow even recognized that the experience of deprivation differs from the meaning of a threat. "Deprivation is not psycho-pathogenic; threat is." (1970, p. 107; also page 23). In this he understood that, "Most neurotic symptoms or trends among basic-need gratification bent impulses that have got stymied or misdirected or confused." That is, distorted meanings and responses about needs—this is what creates distortions. Obviously, Maslow was so close to discovering meaning, and discovering the role of meaning for self-actualization, and yet he did not.

Maslow wrote that our potentialities must be seen developmentally because they are mostly actualized, shaped or stifled by culture, family, environment, and learning. Hidden in this is the realization that we *learn our meanings.*

"Very early in life these goalless urges and tendencies become attached to objects by canalization, but also by arbitrarily learned associations." (1968, p. 191)

Here he speaks about associative meanings, the associations that we learn about what things mean by attaching emotional states to objects. My sense is that because he used the psychoanalytic concept of canalization, he missed the critical role of meaning.

The Dynamic Nature of Meaning

Precisely because our construction and attribution of meaning is a *dynamic process*, what something means can, and does, change. It changes all the time. First we frame it one way, then we frame it another. This reframing of meaning creates transformation both helpful and hurtful.

Yet in missing this *dynamic variable,* Maslow's hierarchy ended up being rigid and static and that led to the pyramid metaphor and emblem. That is, *without putting into his model the ever-changing nature of meaning,* Maslow was left with a Hierarchy of Needs that could only define any given satisfier for what they were. Food is simply food, and not "love" in spite of Maslow's insight that it can hold a symbolic value for some people at times.

We now know one thing that we can do to make the Hierarchy of Needs more accurate and more dynamic. Namely, we can introduce the ever-changing nature of meaning into it. To address this, we need to introduce meaning into the pyramid, and dynamic meaning at that.

Recognizing and incorporating *the dynamic variable of meaning construction* into the picture will enable us to re-frame the old pyramid. In a later chapter I will show how meaning can turn the pyramid into a volcano with the spiraling, swirling reflexive thoughts-and-emotions of a human being within it creating all kinds of meanings about things (Chapter 19).

And if we can accept, embrace, and use our ego-strength to look this square in the face, we have a holding place for meaning-making, *a crucible.* So within the volcano of our driving needs we can put *the construct* of our meaning-making as we meta-state layers upon layers of meanings and when we construct meanings that work, that fit the territory, and that can enable us to navigate in our development, then it enables us to explode out of the pyramid into the higher self-actualization needs where we are in *the zone of self-actualization.*

These three facets (the construct, crucible, and the zone) describes one Neuro-Semantic approach to self-actualization, the one described in *Unleashed* (2007) and in the Self-Actualization Workshop.[5] As we are pushed by desires and pulled by meanings, as we take charge of our construct and establish the transformational holding place of a crucible, we are able to jet propel ourselves into the zone of self-actualizing—the zone of a total engagement. And all because we have recovered meaning in the self-actualizing process.

Key Points in this Chapter

- Maslow put meaning into his model, but only as one of the *being*-needs at the level of self-actualization. As such it operated as content rather than mechanism. And even though he briefly wrote about the role of meaning as a mechanism that dynamically alters our experience of our lower needs and governs the health or sickness of our needs, he missed this dynamic role of meaning and so did not incorporate it into the Hierarchy of Needs.

- In the Hierarchy of Needs, we experience the lower needs developmentally so that they are prepotent at every enfolding stage of development. The higher needs only emerge as lower needs are gratified. But when meaning enters the picture, the pyramid becomes dynamic and fluid.

- Our needs can become either steps toward self-actualization or leashes which hold us back and imprison us in an inescapable prison. It all depends on the meaning we give to our needs.

End Notes

1. The term *meta* was actually first used in mathematics. It was then brought into linguistics, psychology, cognition, and there are now even entire disciplines that contain the term, meta-cognition, meta-analysis, etc.

2. In his original paper, "A Theory of Human Motivation," published in *Psychological Review,* 1943, 50, pp. 370-396, Maslow made a list of seven sets of exceptions to the apparent fixity of the Hierarchy of basic needs.

3. For the levels of meaning, see *Unleashed* (2007), Chapter 5, "The Construct." Working with meanings and levels of meanings is a central focus in Neuro-Semantics.

4. The book *Games Fit and Slim People Play* explores this whole realm of the frame we give to both eating and exercising.

5. *The Construct, the Crucible, and the Zone* is the format used in my first book on self-actualization, *Unleashed* (2007) as well as the structure of the introductory workshop on Self-Actualization, "the Ultimate Self-Actualization Workshop."

Chapter 8

RECOVERING

MEANING:

THE MISSING ELEMENT

"Since we know also that our needs are not completely blind, that they are modified by culture, by reality, and by possibility, it follows that cognition plays a considerable role in their development." (1970, p. 101)

I have asserted that Maslow floundered with his model because he did not recognize meaning and its role in self-actualization except as a being-value. Yet at the same time there were several people who were on the verge of recognizing meaning and putting *meaning* into the self-actualization model. William Frick was one of those persons.

William Frick, a professor of psychology, was associated with Humanistic Psychology almost from the beginning. He was highly influenced by Clark Moustakas and in 1971, he published *Humanistic Psychology: Interviews with Maslow, Murphy, and Rogers*. In 1982 he wrote in *The Journal of Humanistic Psychology* an article with the title, *"Conceptual Foundations of Self-Actualization: A Contribution to Motivation Theory."* In this insightful and penetrating article he examined some of the problems with the Hierarchy of Needs model and offered some suggestions for making it more viable.

Within the article, Dr. Frick quoted an interview he conducted with Maslow about a theoretical problem with Maslow's self-actualization model at that time.

> "Dr. Maslow, you said 'meta-motivation now seems not to ensue automatically after basic-need gratification.' Now, it seems to me that this represents an important shift in your theoretical position. Is this true?"

Maslow:

> "Yes, it's a surprise. I'd always assumed . . . that if you cleared away the rubbish and the neuroses . . . then the person would blossom out, that he'd find his own way. I find that with young people that it just ain't so sometimes."
>
> "You get people who are in the . . . beautiful . . . need-gratifying situation and yet get kind of a *value* pathology. That is, it's possible to be loved and respect, etc., and even so, to feel cynical and nihilistic, and to feel there's nothing *worth* working for . . . It's sort of a loss of nerve . . . These are the basic need gratifications so far as safety and security is concerned. You know, they have enough glory and applause and appreciation and self-respect, and yet they look out on the world and on society and say, 'My God, what a shambles' and then feel hopeless." (Italics added)

Here Maslow speaks about meaning in the words that I've italized, "value" and "worth." He describes meaning in reference to life's meaning and the lack of meaningfulness in those who otherwise have the basic needs gratified. While he defines the problem as a "loss of nerve," he doesn't seem to explore what's behind it, namely, the loss of meaning.

Frick:

> "Even with all these basic gratifications, they don't move on into any self-actualizing kind of stage?"

Maslow:

> "Some do, and some don't."

Frick:

> "What does this mean theoretically, Dr. Maslow? What are

the implications here for theory? What are the variables here? Let's say we take two people and both are basically need-gratified and feeling safe, secure, comfortable, and operating within this framework. Yet one moves on toward something better, more self-actualizing, while the other stays put in a sense. Now, what makes the difference?"

Maslow responded to these questions, by saying that this is one of the things he was working on, but that he didn't know. He was making up "all sorts of words" about it, how a person could be satisfied and not pro-life at the same time. But he had not come upon the right words to formulate a theory so that he could take a position on this. When pushed about this he went back to biology, suggesting that maybe the source of this problem of a need-satisfied person not self-actualizing is genetic. Maybe it's due to constitutional differences. At this point Frick challenged Maslow about falling back on biology or genetics to explain the lack of self-actualization.

"Dr. Maslow, it seems to me that this calls for a reworking of your whole need-hierarchy theory. The implications are rather important here and I'm inclined to think that this is less instinctoid; that is, the moving over the hurdle, after basic need-gratification, I would like to think is less instinctoid than apparently you do."

Frick expresses his doubts about the biological option that Maslow was considering, and yet in that conversation, Maslow didn't know what else could explain it. He didn't seem to have much of a clue. Yet Dr. Frick did. And his idea is very much the same as what I've presented in this work and in *Unleashed* (2007).

What makes the difference in two well-gratified persons that determines whether one goes on to self-actualizing or not? *Meaning.* Meaning and choice. Here's how Frick expressed his thoughts.

"Self-actualization requires *conceptual* support. . . . I propose that as the power of biological controls decreases, the importance of the conceptual and symbolic powers of the organism increases and assumes more and more prominence in ordering, promoting, and directing personal growth in accord with the self-actualizing trends of personality development. In other words, the higher in the motivational hierarchy we move, *the more important a conceptual orientation becomes to our continued development.*" (p. 41)

The conceptual support and orientation that Frick describes refers to a cognitive frame that gives meaning to life at each level, and the higher the level, the more important the concept and meaning of growth. Frick speaks specifically about the importance of an individual believing in the possibility of renewal to achieve it.

> "We may say that an individual cannot achieve self-renewal if s/he does not have *some working concept of self-renewal.* I believe that such a conceptual support or orientation toward one's own development, in part this 'belief in the possibility of it' is one of the most neglected considerations in motivation theory."
> "*Concepts* lend structure to our perceptions but, more profoundly, *concepts are essential bearers of meaning.*" (p. 42, italics added)

Ah, there it is! It's not the impulse alone, nor the need, *it is the meaning-bearing concept.* Then quoting Rollo May, he writes, "I *cannot perceive* something until I can conceive it." . . . This principle holds true for any conceptual model.

> "It now appears important in self-actualization theory to establish some link of communication—some connecting structure—between preconceptual, unarticulated growth forces and . . . the more cognitive and conceptual powers of the organism. . . . Thus, *growth-enhancing concepts* become a strong motivational force for self-actualization in their own right." (p. 43)

> "In the literature of human motivation theory and among S-A theorists there has been little or no emphasis on conceptual orientations as they may guide and enhance one's self-actualizing potential."

Frick here ties together the self-actualization motivational forces with "growth-enhancing concepts." Yet for him, the concepts were specific to the belief of growth and self-development. He didn't seem to express that it might also refer to any and all enhancing meanings that we create from our "cognitive and conceptual powers."

> "The weakness or richness of our conceptual repertoire, therefore, serves to restrict or expand consciousness; it withholds or affirms meaning and value."

Regarding "our conceptual repertoire," Frick included the role of language and words. Quoting Hillman, he writes, "Words, like angels, are powers which have invisible power over us." He speaks about the vital participation of our conceptual powers in relation to images and symbols for creating an integrating center in our lives. He speaks about the fact that "a change of concept changes one's reality to some degree," and of the importance of a "conceptual framework to the process of personal growth."

From all of this, he then spoke about "the role of meaning" in goal-setting, the meaning of an interpreted life of some philosophical or belief system that provides structure and significance to one's life. He also described how the past is altered in meaning as we grow, learn, suffer, and change (p. 47).

As you can see in all of this, Frick was on the verge of recognizing *meaning* as the crux of the matter. Like Maslow, both were so close to discovering *meaning* and in a sense they did as they spoke about symbolism, conceptual frameworks, philosophy, and belief systems. Yet, in the end, they did not articulate *meaning* or precisely how it plays such a crucial role in self-actualization. So they did not incorporate it into the Needs-Hierarchy model as a "link of communication—some connecting structure—between preconceptual, unarticulated growth forces and in the more cognitive and conceptual powers of the organism."

William Frick even had some tentative ideas about what to include within a conceptual framework for the process of personal growth and self-actualization.

> "I would like to suggest five of the components I feel are essential to a growth-enhancing conceptual orientation."

Below you will find his five components and I have related them to the Matrix Model within which I've been using in modeling and detailing the Self-Actualization Matrix (chapter 11).

1) The ideal self.

> The ideal self consists of an image of wholeness and a concept of movement toward self-transcendence. It is a reality created, given form and meaning from our fictional ideal self-image as described by Alfred Adler.

> In the Matrix Model, we use the *Self* Matrix to bring together all of our meaning frames about our self-definition, self-value and worth, self-confidence, self-efficacy, our sexual self,

career self, recreational self, etc. This gives us an ideal *self* that gives a strong enough identity so that we can believe in our possibilities and become a self-actualizing person.

2) Autonomy.

The next component of a growth-enhancing concept is a sense of inner direction and control, a posture of freedom of choice, self-determination, and personal responsibility.

In the Matrix Model, the *Power* Matrix contains all of our meaning frames about our abilities, talents, skills, competencies (self-efficacy and self-confidence), our inner resources, problem-solving skills, etc. Here we experience our sense of power or capability to take effective action and to make a difference. Within this concept we have our ideas about our confidence to act using our skills (self-confidence) and our sense of power and efficiency in trusting our wits to figure things out (self-efficacy).

3) Life as process.

This factor involves a process conception of development, the sense of always evolving and undergoing change, never static, "life at its best is a flowing, changing process in which nothing is fixed" (Carl Rogers), and an ever-expanding consciousness.

In the Matrix Model, the *Time* and *World* Matrices define our meaning frames about time itself—past-present-and-future times and what it means, and where we are going. It also includes our ideas about progress and destiny, as well as our meaning frames about the larger world that we interact with at work and play. It is due to this emphasis that the Matrix Model is a developmental model that refers to the ongoing stages that we experience over our lifespan.

4) Interpersonal wholeness and community.

This factor is oriented toward the wholeness of the interpersonal and social realm, of other selves, of the social interest instinct (Adler), of interpersonal intimacy (Erickson). In the Matrix Model, the *Others* Matrix includes all of our meaning frames about people, human nature, friends, loved ones, social skills, interpersonal skills for getting along, etc. It highlights how we are hurt and healed by people within relationships.

5) The transpersonal realm.

This factor is oriented toward fulfilling our self-transcending potential, moving beyond ego-centered reality toward higher levels of consciousness, levels that transcend the personal in which we have an altered sense of reality.

In the Matrix Model, the *Meaning and Intention* matrices include our ability to construct meaning at multiple levels as well as our highest intentions by which we define our highest objectives, values, and goals. It is here also that our self-reflexive consciousness can, and does, enable us to keep transcending our current state and situations so that we create our beliefs and our realm of spirit or inspiration.

Key Points in this Chapter

• The lack of recognition of the role of meaning in the self-actualization process led, even in Maslow's time, to some unsolvable problems. The central one concerned *why and how* need-gratified people can *fail to self-actualize* when they have everything they need for their basic needs.

• As a guarantee for self-actualization, need-gratification alone is inadequate. It is essential, but not sufficient. Something else is needed to explain and facilitate self-actualization. So while self-actualization is organic and operates naturally, it is not solely organic in that it doesn't need direction. It does. It needs guidance. It needs concepts about growth and meanings that support self-actualization.

• Frick identified what the Human Potential Movement needed —a conceptual orientation. The movement needed *meaning* and all of the mechanisms and structures of meaning-making. And interesting enough, even at that time, this was emerging the Cognitive Revolution through Noam Chomsky, George Miller, Karl Pribram, and others which they launched in the 1950s and 1960s.

• Maslow, along with numerous others, were very close to recognizing the need to include *meaning, symbolic concepts, and conceptual frameworks,* into the Needs Hierarchy. Yet in the end, they did not. That is now up for us to do.

End Notes

1. Journal of Humanistic Psychology, Fall 1982, Vol. 22. No. 4.

Chapter 9

THE GROWTH MODEL

OF SELF-ACTUALIZATION

". . . a baby is only potentially a human being, and must grow into humanness. . ." (1970, p. xviii)

Maslow created a second model or schema for Self-Actualizing or Growth Theory beyond the Hierarchy of Needs. This model is not well known. So if you didn't know that, you are not alone, not by a long shot. I didn't know about it until I began my research and I would estimate that 99% of people don't know about it. Yet he did. Maslow created a schema of a field of forces toward and away from growth. And he even added a bit of a diagram with arrows indicating influences for a person moving toward growth and away from safety and other arrows moving away from growth and back toward safety.

A central idea in this model is that *self-actualization growth is based on safety and moves toward risk.* The premise here is simple: to grow we have to feel safe. We only move away-from safety and toward the risk and the challenges of growth when we have a sufficient foundation of safety. (1968, pp. 46-47).

> "Every human being has both sets of forces within him. One set clings to safety and defensiveness out of fear . . . The other set of forces impels him forward toward wholeness of Self and uniqueness of Self, toward full functioning of all his capacities . . . Safety has both anxieties and delights;

Growth has both anxieties and delights." (1968, p. 46, 47)

A Growth Model
Actually Maslow sometimes even called Self-Actualization Psychology *Growth Psychology*. His ideas about meta-motivation, being-needs, peak experiences, being-values, and the actualizing of potentials were all expressions of "growth" by which he meant toward the full development of human nature. In *Toward a Psychology of Being* it is the fourth chapter that presents self-actualization as a Growth Model.[1]

Figure 9:1

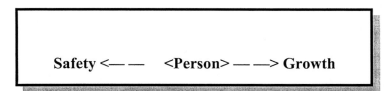

Maslow used a paradigm for this growth model. He used the template of a young toddler learning to walk and venturing away from his mother's knee into strange surroundings. When a young child begins this new development first he clings to his mother and only explores the room with his eyes.

> "Then he dares a little excursion, continually reassuring himself that the mother-security is intact. These excursions get more and more extensive. In this way, the child can explore a dangerous and unknown world." (1968, p. 49)

As the child practices the little whobly steps, the child is growing forward to unleash his or her capabilities. As the child uses his legs, balances, grabs for chairs and other things to stabilize the walk, the innate potential for walking develops.

> "If suddenly the mother were to disappear, he would be thrown into anxiety, would cease to be interested in exploring the world, would wish only the return of safety, and might even lose his abilities, e.g., instead of daring to walk, he might creep." (1968, p. 49)

Principles
What are the principles of this growth model? I have summarized and formatted Maslow's thinking using the following distinctions

about growth as the principles of growth.

1) Growth is self-validating

We grow because growth itself is intrinsic to our nature. We are designed and wired to grow and develop. And as we do, nature or God has made it so that we grow and delight in growing due to the fact that the experience of growth is self-validating. It is more delightful, joyous, and satisfying to grow than to not grow.

It's fun to grow. Because the new growth experience validates itself, we don't need an outside criteria to tell us what's good for us. As a reward itself, growth rewards us as we develop by endowing us with more knowledge and skill. Maslow's formulation of this was "growth-through-delight."

> "Growth takes place when the next step forward is subjectively more delightful, more joyous, more intrinsic satisfying than the previous gratification. . ." (1968, 45)

Principles of Growth
1) It's self-validating.
2) It is exploring.
3) It is existential.
4) It is a choice.
5) It requires courageous vision.
6) It requires safety.
7) It involves small continuous steps.
8) It is coaxed forward.

We see this in small children who are secure in their parent's love as they learn to do new things. With success they experience a sense of inner validation of achievement.

2) Growth is Exploring

We grow by exploring, by trying things out, by seeing what happens if, by experimenting. Being without the instincts to know what a thing *is*, what works, what leads to what—we are, by nature, born as little scientists with an insatiable curiosity to find out things. And this is how we continue to develop over the life-span.

This means that a healthy person is always reaching out in a spontaneous way to discover possibilities and testing capacities to find out what he can do. The states that drive this exploration include curiosity, fascination, wonder, and play.

3) Growth is existential

Growth is *existential* refers to how the basic human experience involves the strain between the inner forces of growth and defense. This existential dilemma is embedded in our deepest nature. And it sets up the force field analysis between the pushing and the restraining forces. And we feel this dilemma as anxiety-and-excitement. We want to grow, delight in it and at the same time we find that it can often be scary. It can produce anxiety, fear, apprehension, worrying, and all of the fretting that goes along with trying out new and different things.

4) Growth is a choice

Paradoxically while growth is wired in, we also have to choose it. There's a reason for this, namely, we can, to our own detriment, choose to not grow. Or we can default on choice and simply not choose to grow. So confronting us at every point of our lives is *the growth choice,* and it is a choice we make dozens, if not hundreds, of times a day. Repeatedly throughout everyday we are encountered by choices for awareness, for responsibility, for understanding, for repression, for avoidance, for denial, for truth, for lies, and for a hundred other choices.

In choosing the steps and experiences of growth, the challenge is to become a good chooser— wise, informed, deliberate, thoughtful. No one can choose for you. These choices count unless you default on choosing, but of course, that's also a choice. And where we make a choice for others, in doing so we actually enfeeble them and undermine their powers.

5) Growth requires courage and vision

Because growth is a choice, because it involves the risk of change, of the unknown, of effort to cope, etc., and because it involves existential anxiety, it first takes vision to choose to grow. After that it then takes lots of courage to grow, to discover ourselves, and to unleash our highest potentials. How daring are you in your growth? Do you have sufficient vision and courage to keep growing?

6) Growth requires safety

We grow forward when we feel safe enough to venture forth. Without safety, we feel endangered and that elicits the defense and escape mechanisms to protect our fragile ego. Without safety we regress into less adult, less mature, and less effective coping strategies. Our sense of safety then is the pace of our growth. Maslow put it in these words, "Safety needs are prepotent over growth needs." (1968, p. 49).

If we make approval too important, or conformity too important, we endanger our self-actualization. If we make disapproval a terror, that is, a terrifying danger for another person, we undermine the growth process toward our own autonomy and self-direction.

All of this underscores the importance of *driving out fear* as a base state of mind-and-emotion. As Edwards Deming warned managers in business, fear shuts people down and with it shuts down creativity, joy, growth, and self-actualization. Yet most of our fears do not relate to actual dangers to our person. There's no real threat. Most relate to psychological dangers, that is, dangers that we have mentally mapped to our ideas, values, identity, future, etc. We feel threatened because we scare ourselves by the fearful meanings we give to things.

7) Growth involves small continuous steps
Most growth forward customarily takes place in little steps, one step after the other, with no obvious big positive results. It requires learning— that is, know-how experimentation as we try things out and develop insights and skill. These are the steps on the pathway of competency.

Growth forward occurs as we trust. We experience it as we trust ourselves, others, the world, and the experiences of learning and growth. So the more we develop these trusts, the safer we will feel and the more easily we can be coaxed into ever higher levels of growth.

8) Growth is coaxed forward
We cannot force growth. We cannot command or order our psychological growth nor another's. Instead, because growth is grounded in safety, at best we can only call it forth gently and persistently. In this, it can be coaxed out of us. We can enable others to grow by making it more possible. In this we can beckon, invite, and seduce others toward the pathway of growth and competency.

Away-From Self-Actualization
The first set of forces in the Growth Model are those that *endanger* our sense of self and well-being—these are the away-from forces. Anything and everything that maximizes the dangers of growing toward self-actualizing elicits move-away-from energies and emotions. It increases our fears, insecurities, and apprehensions. It evokes our defenses so that we begin to regress. This is the regressive nature and power of our lower needs when they are not

gratified sufficiently. The deficiency that we experience through inadequate gratification then threatens our existential self. Similarly the more meaning and importance we give to safety and security, the less energy for moving forward we have of self-actualizing.

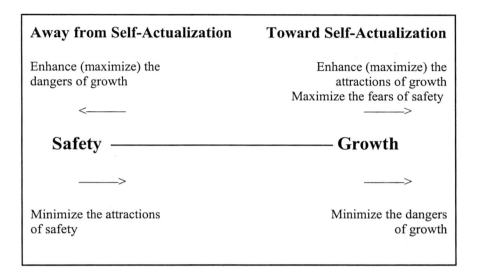

If we ask, "Why is it so hard and painful for some people to grow forward and to self-actualize?" the answer is now clear. *They are too insecure to grow forward.* They are too deficient of the necessary inner and outer security to move forward. For these also anything that enlarges the sense of the danger or challenge or risk of self-actualization, increases the forces away-from growth.

Moving Toward Self-Actualization
The second set of forces in the Growth Model are those that maximize the attractions of actualizing our potentials and growing to become the best versions of ourselves. These are the moving-toward forces. The forces for growth first are those that enable us to gratify the lowers needs so that step by step we learn to effectively cope with our needs, get along well with others, and give accurate meanings to our needs.

The next forces of growth are those that call us forward toward healthy, wholeness, and our own unique authenticity. A rich and exciting vision of growth does this as do good examples or models of growing self-actualizing people.

The Growth / Fear Dialectic

The bottom line is that there are two forces pulling at us, not just one set. We have within both pressures for health and pressures for regression. So while we may at moments be pulled and tempted toward the rewards of virtue, the beauties of goodness, the inherent health of self-actualization, we also often perversely refuse to step forward into such growth? Why? Mostly due to weakness and ignorance. We are reluctant, afraid, or unable.

> "Growth forward is *in spite* of these losses and therefore requires courage, will, choice, and strength in the individual as well as protection, permission, and encouragement from the environment." (1968, p. 204)

Key Points in this Chapter

- At the heart of *Self-Actualization Psychology* is human growth or development. This psychology of the bright side of human nature concerns how we can keep developing over the span of our lives and grow forward as we see the advantages of growth and overcome the fears of against growth.

- Within *the Growth Model* are field forces—the forces for growth and forces against growth. We have moving-away-from forces that move us to regress to safety in fear of growth and we have moving-forward forces that creates an excitement of the vision of becoming more of who we can become.

- Self-actualization results from enhancing the growth forward forces while simultaneously reducing the intensity of the fear forces. Then the actualizing of the innate potentials within us occur as delight and self-validation.

End Notes:

1. That chapter in *Toward a Psychology of Being* actually originated from a lecture prepared for a conference in 1956 and published that year.

Chapter 10

MODELING

SELF-ACTUALIZATION

PSYCHOLOGY

Your theory of mind
determines and governs your mind's operations.

"It is the theory that determines
what we can observe."
Albert Einstein

elf-Actualization Psychology begins from a belief in unleashing
human potential and a belief in the importance of unleashing
those potentials. The next step is to *model* it through detecting
and unpacking the structure of self-actualization as a process and to
create a workable model for replicating the abilities and states of self-
actualizing people. Modeling self-actualization in this way is much
more challenging than just setting the vision.

The *Human Potential Movement* successfully created an inspiring
vision of the possibilities, shifting the perspective in psychology from
what's wrong and sick in human nature to *what's right* and *what's
possible*. Yet in the end that same Third Force movement which
initiated this new perspective did not deliver on its promises. It did

not operationalize the self-actualizing process nor did it create a useable model to guide the self-actualizing process. Maslow certainly started the process, but he did not bring it to completion.

The foundation of *Self-Actualization Psychology* began when two incredible human beings impressed Maslow to an astonishing level. As he stood back and marveled at these incredible human specimens, he said his studies in traditional psychology were completely inadequate for understanding them. That was the mystery which initiated his first interest and curiosity so that he began his exploration into self-actualizers.

What Maslow subsequently achieved was a qualitative study of the traits, qualities, and experience of these individuals. He called them "peak experiencers," those who were "fully human," and he identified many of their critical traits. This began his "Good Humans" research and from that study emerged the first model in the field of self-actualization, his *Hierarchy of Needs*.

The Needs Hierarchy postulates that human nature is developmental, driven by felt needs as impulses that move or motivate us, and that it is structured hierarchically so that as one level of need is gratified, the next higher level emerges into consciousness. As such, the Needs Hierarchy was, and continues to be today, revolutionary in its impact.

Yet what Maslow did not create, nor did Carl Rogers, nor anyone in the first Human Potential Movement, was an actual model of the process of self-actualization. Maslow set forth the premises. He created a new paradigm of human nature and he explored the how question, How does the process work? While Maslow modeled self-actualizers to understand the syndrome by means of indepth interviews (1971, pages 72-73). He did not generate a model that facilitated the development of self-actualization using the mechanisms that he and others discovered to reliably enable others to actualize their potentials. And it is precisely this that is needed today.

So while we have so many of the pieces of the puzzle, we still do not have them organized into a consistent model. We do not have them sequenced into one or more processes that we can use to guide ourselves or others who want to unleash a particular potential. This is what a *Self-Actualization Model* for today must provide.

Modeling Self-Actualization

If we want to detect, unpack, articulate, and replicate the experience of self-actualization, the process whereby a person enters into a self-actualizing life, the first step is to understand the process of modeling itself and what a full model looks like. I offer the following questions about models to move in this direction:

- As a process, *how* does self-actualization work?
- What are *the mechanisms* that facilitate the unleashing of human potential to actualize new possibilities?
- What *modeling* has already occurred about the self-actualizing process?
- What *models* do we currently have that detail how a person can achieve the unleashing of his or her potentials?

In response to the question about the modeling of self-actualization, very little modeling has been done apart from Maslow's original work. Maslow was decades ahead of his time. Even today most people find his articles and books so incredibly rich that they are overwhelmed in terms of offering so many possibilities. It was, and is, demanding enough just to understand his genius.

Another complication regarding the modeling of self-actualization is that it is much easier to model a specific area of self-development, than the life-long project of self-actualization. Actualizing to become "the very best version of you" speaks about an entirely different thing than seeking to develop in a specific area of life like being a better husband, leader, entrepreneur, writer, etc. This is what we find when we look at the literature of the Human Potential Movement, of Esalen, and of every field that emerged from the Human Potential Movement.

So rather than modeling self-actualization in the lineage of Maslow, those within the Human Potential Movement focused on specific facets of self-development—relaxation, meditation, healing past hurts, succeeding in reaching goals, making more money, being successful in a particular area, etc.

The Need for Modeling

If modeling the life-long process of self-actualization itself seems too much, another factor also discouraged such modeling. It was the assumption that governed Maslow and Rogers, as the leaders of the Human Potential Movement. I'm speaking about their assumption that self-actualization is "an innate process that just naturally unfolds." This led to one of the primary rules which they then proposed, namely, to not interfere with the natural organic growth of a human being. Assuming that the innate drive toward self-actualization was sufficient for self-actualization, they did not probe in depth how to intervene and facilitate the self-actualizing processes. As a result, they did not create a model of self-actualization—its processes and development and so did not identify specific patterns or processes for it.

The metaphor that informed their thinking was that of nature, of organic processes, and natural growth. They used the metaphor of the incredible potentials inside a small oak seed. How does it develop? How do we unleash the potentials within such a seed? Simple. We provide the right environment for soil, water, sun, etc., and we then leave it alone. Mostly we *avoid interfering* with the seed. There's a sense in which we don't "grow" the oak tree, so neither do we "grow" ourselves. As an organic process, we provide the necessary components, then we step back to *let it happen.*

While this insight is true, it is only part of the truth. *Getting out of the way to let self-actualization emerge and transpire is indeed one key to facilitating the unleashing process.* This is certainly *one* key, but it is not the only key, and it is certainly not *the* key.

> To self-actualize, first stop the interferences and get out of your own way!

It is true that when we "try" too hard to grow, or "force" ourselves, our children, or others to develop in a certain way or direction, we interfere with our natural learning and change. This can seriously interfere, and even damage, our growth. The metaphor of "trying hard to grow" shows up whenever we attempt to impose our values, beliefs, and outcomes on ourselves or others, or when we suppose that growth has to fit some rigid pattern. More often than not, this interferes with the human development of potentials.

Yet merely getting out of the way and eliminating interferences isn't enough. Nor is the nurturing of the environment, as important as that is. This organic growth metaphor works beautifully with plants, and with animals as well, but not with humans. And why not? Simple, because *human development is not fully determined.* It arises through an interaction of our creation of meaning—*as we human beings need guided assistance.* Without instincts of content knowledge, while we have a general tendency to grow and develop, we don't know how or into what. In our case, we need the guidance of correct information and we especially need the guidance of healthy and supportive beliefs. In our case, having no instincts we intimately participate in the process as does our social group.

The Art of Capturing Expertise
In positing how self-actualization works, Maslow, Rogers, May, Perls, Frankl, Assagioli, Allport, Jourard, Moustakas, Polanyi, Bugental, and others in the human potential movement talked mostly about *activating, releasing,* or *unleashing* potential. They spoke about the *uncovering* techniques of encounter groups, gestalt explorations, non-verbal and body techniques, dance, etc. Our intelligence potentials, as well as our emotional and spiritual potentials, emerge when we find and tap into our innate talents and resources, using our understandings and emotions, and following our passions.

Of all the developers, Maslow offered the most ideas and research about *the processes* of self-actualization. These showed up in his mapping of human needs into lower and higher needs and the Hierarchy of Needs which he wrote about extensively.

My first interest in self-actualization arose first when I was working on modeling the genius state of being in the zone or "flow" using the Meta-States model. Out of that research the foundational trainings in Neuro-Semantics arose, *Accessing Personal Genius, Living Personal Genius* and *the Stroke of Genius* trainings.[1]

But it was later when I began modeling executive and personal coaching that I revisited the literature of self-actualization and sought to find a model for Self-Actualization Psychology. Assuming that there was such a model, my aim was to simply use it as the core model in the Meta-Coach Training System that I was developing with Michelle Duval. At that point in researching the field of Coaching I realized that *if* we were going to design a training system, we would need an explicit model of *Self-Actualization Psychology.* We would need to specify what it is, how it works, its mechanisms and processes, and how we could mindfully use it in facilitating the unleashing of potentials in people.

As I interviewed numerous experts coaches around the world and read widely the literature of the field to discover the relationship of coaching to self-actualization, I discovered that *the facilitative process of coaching* itself, by theory and practice, *enables self-actualization.*

This means that the coaching conversation process itself offers a methodology for actualizing potentials. What we have in the methodology of coaching, along with specific technologies, is to a great extent a missing piece for unleashing human potential and facilitating self-actualizing. Rather then merely getting out of the way, the coach works to *facilitate* the natural processes and offers guidance about self-actualization—about the process of how we make actual what is potential within.

What's Required for a Model

Modeling begins with finding a best practice or an expertise that demonstrates what's possible. Then we step back to identify the experience's structure. Modeling is about unpacking an experience to detect patterns in an attempt to understand its dynamic structure. From there we can design and re-design an experience, streamline it, enrich it, make it more elegant, or add new and empowering qualities to it. The final step in modeling is training and coaching the model to replicate the experience so that many people can make it real in their lives.[2]

Realizing all of this I decided to revisit Maslow, May, Rogers, and other pioneers of the idea of human potential to take a fresh look at their ideas about how to make self-actualization possible. I also wanted to see if I could translate them into a specific *model* with specific patterns, processes, and techniques.

In this, I didn't want to simply create a model in the sense of a step-by-step pattern, I wanted something more. I did not just want a small "m" model, that is, merely a pattern or process. I wanted a full-fledged model (model with a capital M). And I knew that a systematic approach would include four things which could then be tested for validation or falsified: a theory, guidelines, variables, and patterns.

1) *Theory*

To create a model of self-actualization that can fully guide us in unleashing potential we first have to identify *the theoretical understandings* of Self-Actualization Psychology—the principles, premises, and concepts that describe what this model is and how it works.

That's what a theory does. A theory sets forth the conceptual frameworks that define, describe, and explain *what* it is, *how* it works, and *why* it works. We use a model to make sense of some phenomenon and we do so by being able to identify several hypothetical assumptions and beliefs about the phenomenon. With our hypothesis about some facet or variable of it, we can then test our theories and assumptions to see if we can validate them as true or false. When nothing can falsify a theory, we don't have a theory, only a belief. Maslow certainly contributed a lot in this regard, constantly suggesting various hypotheses of self-actualization for testing.[3]

2) *Variables.*

Within the theory and guidelines are the numerous variables and elements as the component pieces of the model. These pieces or facets of the model enable us to work with the model with regard to some phenomenon. These are the facets of experience, or of human experience, that we work with in the model. In Self-Actualization Psychology Maslow contributed such variables as lower and higher needs, prepotency, the meta-levels, deficiency, the being-level, peak experiences, etc.

3) *Guidelines.*

From the development of a theory, we need to specify the guidelines for using and working with the conceptual understandings. What are the rules, processes, and meta-understandings for working with the model? What heuristics, or rules of thumb, guide and govern our use of the model? For understanding how to work with an experience or phenomenon, the guidelines provide a general understanding of what works, how, in what way, and what does not work. Guidelines can offer a formula for use, similar to a recipe.

4) *Patterns.*

The final task of generating a workable model is to organize some of the variables into patterns and processes—techniques by which we can actually use the model to replicate the phenomenon, in this case, the peak experiences of self-actualizers. While we sometimes call these patterns and processes a "model" (small "m"), they are but the final result of a well-formed model.

Three Self-Actualization Models

As this book goes to print we now have three Neuro-Semantic models for describing, detailing, and facilitating the process of self-actualization. These are built upon the premises of Self-Actualization Psychology and incorporate the role of meaning from Cognitive Psychology, General Semantics, and Neuro-Semantics.

1) Self-Actualization Psychology Model

Starting with the four factors of a model (theory, variables, guidelines, and patterns) enables us to make the content of a Self-Actualization Psychology explicit. With that, we can use the model to mobilize our resources to experience peak experiences more often and use them to move persistently to create peak performances in a given area. The Self-Actualization Model was presented in Chapter 6 which included a summary of the theory and concepts, the components and variables, the guidelines, and the resultant patterns.

2) The Self-Actualization Quadrants

This model is based upon the twin-roles of *meaning* and *performance* in the process of actualizing our best (chapter 14, also see *Unleashed*, 2007, chapter 7). It is in the special synthesis of *meaningful* performance and *performance* of our highest and best meanings that enables us to give birth to self-actualization as a flow experience. We can also use the Quadrants model to identify where we are in that synthesis, and if we need to play more to the inner or the outer game in order to further our own self-actualization. The Quadrants was the first model developed in Neuro-Semantics for describing the self-actualization process and is now the foundation for the workshops, coaching, and trainings in self-actualization.

3) Self-Actualization Matrix[4]

The third Neuro-Semantics model for conceptualizing and working with self-actualization is *the Matrix of Self-Actualization* (Chapter 11). Using the distinctions of the Matrix Model, this model details the meaning, intention, and states of self-actualization. Then it details the dimensions of self as the self grows and develops—which lies at the heart of self-actualization.

This model highlights the inescapable role of meaning since meaning creates all of the frames of the Matrix. This gives us a systemic look at the holographic nature of our needs and drives and what we can do to tap into their energy to unleash more potentials of talents, creativity, skills, and possibilities. The Self-Actualization Matrix enables us to identify specific patterns that facilitate self-actualization for actualizing potentials.[5]

Patterns for Unleashing

The bottom line of a complete Model is the presence of actual techniques or patterns that we can use for facilitating self-actualization. And if the lack of specific patterns created a vacuum of "human technology" and so contributed originally to the demise of the human potential movement (Chapter 21), then to launch a new Human Potential Movement requires that we create specific patterns for actualizing potentials. Only then will we be able to translate the vision of self-actualization into everyday life.

Now regarding patterns for self-actualization, there are several questions to explore:
- How can we determine if a pattern truly encapsulates a technique that we can use to facilitate self-actualization?
- What *criteria* should we consider as validating a given pattern?
- What new and exciting patterns can be developed for actualizing one's highest potentials?

Patterns for Self-Actualization

A *pattern* is a step-by-step process for guiding yourself into a particular state of mind-body-and-emotion and which elicits, evokes, and even provokes you into beginning to *experience* a given desired outcome. In the previous book, *Unleashed*, you can find a dozen Neuro-Semantic patterns for self-actualization.[6]

In setting forth a pattern, prior to the specific *steps* of the pattern, we first declare the purpose of the pattern. What will the pattern do? What thoughts and feelings, what experiences will the pattern generate? Once we know its design, we state when and where and with whom to use the pattern, the conditions, contexts, and perhaps set forth some boundary statements as to when it will not be appropriate or useful.

When we write a description of a pattern, we write something like an executive summary. Patterns generally read like a recipe so that each step describes a separate thing to do such as eliciting a state. If each step can be elicited and facilitated by specific questions, the better. This format enables anybody to use the pattern in facilitating a particular experience. Patterns for actualizing potentials typically involve a synthesis of the things we do in our head as we frame meaning and then the things we do externally with our body which activates that meaning.

Typically at the end of a pattern, and sometimes within one or more of the steps, we *run a test*. We can run a virtual test by asking the person to imagine being in a situation and noticing what happens mentally-and-emotionally within him or her. Or we may run an actual test as we put the person in a situation to see if sufficient resources have been mobilized for a new response to emerge. Self-actualization patterns can be thought of as techniques for *coaching the inner and outer games* to empower and to actualize untapped potentials.[7]

There is a final analysis and question for any pattern: Can we use it to actualize ourselves and our talents in a specific way? Can we use it to actualize our thinking skills, our emotional intelligence, our relational connections, etc.? The design of a pattern is that we can use it to "become all we can become" and becoming "fully functioning" human beings.

Key Points in this Chapter
- *Modeling* maps an experience so that we can work with that experience, replicate it, and/or streamline it to make it better. In this way, modeling can accelerate our learning and enable us to work with the very structure and form of an experience.

- Our objective in modeling self-actualization is eminently practical—so that we can *unleash* untapped potentials and experience the fullest range of who and what we can be.

- There are currently three models for mapping self-actualization in Neuro-Semantics: Self-Actualization Quadrants, Self-Actualization Matrix, and the Self-Actualization Psychology model.

End Notes:

1. See *Secrets of Personal Mastery* and the Training Manual, *Accessing Personal Genius.* Even in NLP, as a cognitive-behavioral communication model for developing personal resources for bringing out one's best, there are only a few general patterns. There are some patterns for creating more resourceful states, the Circle of Excellence, for reframing negative meanings, i.e. the Reframing and Mind-Line patterns, and creating new behaviors, i.e., New Behavior Generator. Yet there is not a single pattern for "self-actualizing" as such. In fact, the term self-actualization has been almost non-existent in the field of NLP.

2. For more about modeling, see Robert Dilts' *NLP The Structure of Subjective Experience* (1980), *NLP Going Meta* (2004), the training manual for *Neuro-Semantic Modeling*, and the manual for *Cultural Modeling.*

3. This is in spite of the fact that both Maslow and Rogers wrote extensively about research and about operationalizing the language of self-actualization. Maslow even wrote a book on *The Psychology of Science* and posited that psychological research needs to include qualitative factors.

4. I have included the Matrix Model briefly in the next chapter. It is more fully developed in the training manual and the book *The Matrix Model* (2002).

5. Key patterns in Neuro-Semantics for unleashing potentials for self-actualization are the following. These can be found in the *Accessing Personal Genius* training manual and in *Meta-State Magic.*

Meaning Enrichment Patterns
1) Systemic State Accessing pattern
2) Meta-Stating pattern
3) Meta-Yes-ing pattern
4) Meta-No-ing pattern
5) Intentionality pattern
6) Self-Esteem-ing pattern
7) Meta-Stating Emotional Permission pattern
8) Matrix Detection pattern (with meta-questions)
9) Matrix Transformation pattern
10) Meta-Pleasuring

11) Meta-Stating Possibilities (miracle assuming)
12) Genius pattern
13) Matrix Framing pattern
14) Dragon Slaying and Transforming
15) Gestalting
16) Super-charging your Attitude pattern
17) Decision Destroyer
18) Swishing to a New Self-Image
19) Movie Rewind pattern

Performance Enhancement Patterns
1) Mind-to-Muscle pattern
2) Owning Response-Powers
3) Distinguishing response-ability *for* and *to*

4) Meta-Alignment pattern
5) New Behavior Generator
6) Anchoring new responses
7) A SWOT analysis
8) Strategy Analysis, Unpacking, and Installation

6. For *self-actualization patterns*, see *Source Book of Magic, Volumes I and II.* Volume I has 77 of the basic NLP patterns and Volume II has 143 Meta-State patterns. In *Unleash,* there are several key patterns for facilitating self-actualization.

Updating Cognitive Distortions (chapter 3)
Creating a Crucible (chapter 7)
Accessing Personal Genius (chapter 12)
Well-Formed Outcomes (chapter 13)
Intentionality (chapter 13)
Giving and Receiving Feedback (chapter 14)
Building Ego-Strength (chapter 15)
Unleashing Possibilities (chapter 17)

7. See *Winning the Inner Game* (2006).

Chapter 11

THE SELF-ACTUALIZATION

MATRIX

"Any person in any of the peak experiences takes on temporarily many of the characteristics which I found in self-actualizing individuals. That is, for the time they become self-actualizers. . . . We may define [self-actualization] as an episode, or a spurt in which the powers of the person come together in a particularly efficient and intensely enjoyable way..." (1968, p. 97)

Given the *Self-Actualization Model* in Chapter 6 we can now take these descriptions and use them to detail the meaning frames within a *Matrix of Self-Actualization.* I briefly introduced the Matrix Model in chapter eight on *Recovering Meaning* as a general overview. In this chapter I will now describe that model in more depth as I apply it to the experience of self-actualization. The result will be a *Self-Actualization Matrix* that we can use to integrate the distinctions in Self-Actualization Psychology.

The Matrix Model
The Matrix Model is comprised of three *process* matrices and five *content* matrices. This makes the model a combination of both processes and content. Via the psychological process mechanisms (meaning, intention, state) we create our content about our *self* which then enters into us so deeply that it feels like part and parcel of us, or our nature, of what is *given* in human experience, rather than what we have created. Yet we have created it and we have embodied it with our neurology.

Within the three process matrices are the most essential processes, the mechanisms by which we construct all of the meanings that govern our lives. While meaning and intention are part of the same fabric, they are distinguished in this model to distinguish two facets of awareness, namely, the things that are *on* our mind and the things *in the back* of our mind. The things *on* our mind are our constructed meanings — representations, associations, words, evaluations, etc. The things *in the back* of our mind are our intentions— our motives, agendas, purposes, outcomes, intentions, etc.

In the Matrix Model we portray and illustrate the Meaning and Intention matrices as a spiraling double-helix. A spiral of two lines of thought, thoughts in the front and in the back of our mind, create a double-helix of meanings. That is, behind every meaning that we represent and encode, we have motives in the back of the mind. Then with State, we ground the matrix in reality. The entire Matrix of meanings is grounded in our mind-body state because it is from that place that we encounter the world beyond our skin.

The *content* matrices indicate those ideas and concepts which comprise the meaning frames that we create and which we take everywhere we go. The categories of this content are those of that arise developmentally as we grow and develop as persons. In the Matrix Model they are classified as the following categories: Self, Power, Others, Time, and World.

With the Matrix Model we are able to map systemically how we engage in the framing of meaning. As a result, it gives us a systemic look at the holographic nature of our needs and drives and what we can do to tap into their energy to unleash more potentials of talents, creativity, skills, and possibilities.

Matrix Questions
To facilitate your awareness of your own Matrix, use the following Matrix Questions to explore your current meanings and your embedded belief frames about self-actualization.

States: What does self-actualization feel like to you?
                     What states do you want to experience as you self-actualize?
                     What are your best states when you are self-actualizing?
                     What states of self-actualization will bring out your best and unleash more of your capacities?

Meaning: What does self-actualization mean to you?
What else? And what else after that?
What are the most empowering meanings that support unleashing your potentials?
What limiting and toxic meanings or beliefs do you have that undermine self-actualization?
What could you believe that would empower your self-actualization even more?

Intentions: Why self-actualize? What will you get from that?
What are your highest intentions that facilitate realizing your full potential?
What intentions would you like to commission to self-organize your Matrix?
Are there any intentions that sabotage the creating of the best version of you?

Self: Who do you need to be in your self-definitions to actualize your best self?
What do you need to map about your self-worth (dignity, respect, value)?
What do you need to map about self-confidence in your talents and skills?
Who will you become as a self-actualizing person?

Power: Do you fully distinguish yourself as a human *being* (your worth and value) from who you are as a human *doing* (what you can do and accomplish)?
What mental and emotional resources unleash your self-actualization potentials?
What talents, aptitudes, and gifts do you have that you want to unleash?
How do you need to frame your fallibility so that mistakes and failings will not stop your self-actualization?

Others: What do you need to map about others and relationships that will help unleash your potentials as you actualize your interpersonal and social self?
What relational or social skills would move you to greater self-actualization?
What belief or frame which gets in the way do you need to release?

Time: What do you need to map about time so that it supports the unleashing of your potentials?
What beliefs or meanings about time free you to be more present in this moment?
Does your meanings about time, scheduling, the past, the future, etc. enrich you and facilitate your development?

World: What mental maps will you develop to support your self-actualization in your area of passion?
What worlds or universes of concern would you like to explore?
In what area will you self-actualize?
In what domains will you actualize your highest and best?
What other worlds will you need to explore and develop familiarity with in order to fully actualize your best?

The Self-Actualization Matrix

From all of these starter-questions, it is obvious that a great many beliefs and meanings come together to create a full and well-integrated Self-Actualization Matrix. How full and well-integrated is your personal Self-Actualization Matrix? *The content matrices* describe your sense of self in five dimensions whereas *the process matrices* describe your style of thinking and your explanatory style as you construct meaning in multiple ways and at multiple levels.

Self

The *self* of self-actualization is your best self which has the integrity and authenticity to be true to your values and beliefs. Self-actualization requires that you be true to yourself as you find and develop your best gifts, intelligences, and opportunities given the events and circumstances of life. The identity you construct and develop as a self-actualizer arises as you give rich and robust meanings to yourself as a meaning-maker and someone seeking to fully actualize your highest potentials.

As a self-actualizer your sense of self develops to give you your own sovereign center. This develops as you increasingly assume responsibility for yourself. This gives you an internal locus of control. Then you will have within a personal "supreme court" for your own referencing and for knowing what you want, feel, belief, etc. This is the first category that Shostrum used in his instrument (the POI, *Personal Orientation Inventory*) for measuring self-actualization.[1] As a way of moving through the world the self-actualizer lives from within and has internal references with an external check. He or she checks on the outside (externally) with others and with expert sources, but ultimately makes the choice.

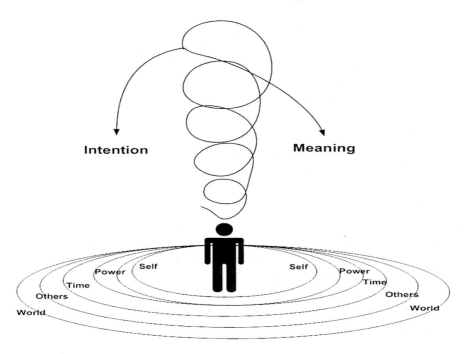

In self-actualizing, we experience ourselves well grounded with a solid sense of self-esteem, self-confidence, then self-efficacy. We first value ourselves unconditionally as a fully valuable and lovable human being (self-esteem). This is the foundation for being real and authentic with nothing to hide, nothing to defend against. And when we have that, then we cultivate confidence in what we can *do* (self-confidence as a human doing).

In the end, the self that's self-actualized becomes increasingly more integrated and less split. The self becomes more open for experience. And as our self becomes more idiosyncratic, we become more truly ourselves.

Powers
In self-actualizing, we develop our skills, competencies, and abilities

so that we become increasingly independent and autonomous. This brings about a self-efficacy in handling the challenges of life. To develop your capabilities, look inside, identify your strengths and your weaknesses and learn to cultivate your best. In the realm of your powers and resources, translate your dreams and hopes into action, take courage to make real what you sense as a potential.

Self-actualization involves owning your responses as you become a fully response-able person. This leads to the proactivity of taking initiative to follow your inner dispositions and actualize your innate talents. And this also supports the authenticity of choosing your way as you experience the freedom of choice to chart your own way.

The aim in self-actualization is that you become a "fully functioning human being." And that means becoming more expressive and spontaneous. It means becoming more creative. And most importantly, it means being able to get yourself to do what you dream about and believe in.

When you are in a peak experience you usually feel yourself at the peak of your powers, and using all of your capacities in the fullest way. You feel more intelligent, more perceptive, stronger, and in top form. At such moments there is no waste of energy as things feel effortless. Not only is there a higher quality to the behavior, but you also perform with grace and ease.

Others
Maslow noted that a trait of self-actualizing people is that they have deep and intense relationships. Accordingly, self-actualizing involves giving to and receiving from others. It involves connecting, bonding, supporting, and developing your best potentials socially and relationally. As social beings, our consciousness is formed within the contexts of relationships. And because self-actualizers think of others as equal human beings with lower and higher needs, they are able to reach out to them to create friends, colleagues, family, loved ones, and community. This inter-dependence arises from independence and enables you to create intimate contact, another scale in the POI that measures self-actualization.

In self-actualization, you are no longer dependent on others for love and so do not need it as a deficiency. Your need for love at this level is more of *a need to give love,* to care for others, to value, to respect others, and to intimately connect in a non-needy way. Without any need to cling to others, the self-actualizing person actually has a strong need for privacy and solitude. Then the *Being*-love that results from this solitude is not a need to receive from others, but to give to them.

In self-actualizing, we become more accepting of life as it is, people as they are, and ourselves with all of our strengths and weaknesses. This, in turn, gives birth to a gracious humor—the ability to laugh at ourselves. It also endows us with an amused, non-hostile, and philosophical sense of the irony of life.

Time

In self-actualizing, you become highly competent in your experience and use of time. In the POI, after *internal* referencing Shostrum described "time competency" as the second of the two key categories for measuring self-actualization. *Time competency* of self-actualization means living in the present, able to be fully present in the moment, using the learnings of the past and heading toward the future.

This means that in the self-actualizing life, you are more present in the here-and-now which enables you to "be all there" in your engagements. Consequently, you listen better. You listen without all of the contamination from past and future expectations.

World

The environmental context of self-actualization involves first and foremost the specific world of activities that describe where you live, your home, environment, culture, your career, hobby, and all of the other worlds of meaning that you navigate. It involves the experience of your best skills and competencies. In what context are you most keen on actualizing some potential? Is it in the business world, social world, world of mathematics, art, marketing, etc.?

There are so many human universes of meaning and in the self-actualizing life we are able to be creative and flexible as we move in and out of them. We can adopt roles easily and drop them just as easily, recognizing as we do that they are but roles that we play and not our inner authentic self.

Maslow noted that self-actualization requires both B- and D-cognition, both *contemplation* (B-cognition) and *action* (D-cognition) as we navigate various worlds. In solving problems or resolving paradoxes, we sometimes need the D-cognition that recognizes limitations, constraints, and reality factors. Yet we also need the B-cognition of possibilities for new creations and innovations.

States

What are the states of self-actualization? What does a self-actualizer feel? What emotions specifically characterize a self-actualizer? At one level, they include almost every emotion possible for a human being since self-actualizing means being real and authentic to the rich multiplicity of our experiences. After all, self-actualization involves having the flexibility and choice of the full range of emotional states, to feel and emote appropriately to the contexts and events of life as it changes.

In self-actualization we can be fully present to our emotions knowing that they are just emotions rather than tools of cognition. They do not tell us what is right and wrong, what is real or what is false. Instead, they tell us more about the difference between our mental mapping and our experiencing.

Yet mostly in self-actualization we are captivated by life and its possibilities. We are curious, playful, explorative, always learning, enjoying ourselves, engaged, fascinated, in awe, respectful, in love with life and others, etc. In this, as a self-actualizer you experience more of *the being-values states* since these are the values and value-states that we ultimately seek as human beings.

Intention

The intentions of self-actualization begin with the intention to discover and become your best self, to become a fully functioning person, and to actualize specific talents, possibilities, and talents. Your intention above these intentions is to live fully and not to waste your time, energy, or life. The self-actualizing intention is to actualize possibilities and to avoid things that diminish you as a human being.

Meaning

The meaning of self-actualization is that of living fully, being fully alive / fully human. The meaning is to experience one's best in actualizing the highest of one's potentials. The meaning is to be true to yourself, authentic, and congruent. It is to release the music within and to find and fully develop your unique contributions.

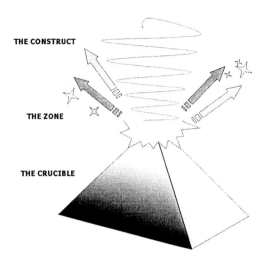

THE CONSTRUCT

THE ZONE

THE CRUCIBLE

Key Points in this Chapter

- We create a *Matrix of Self-Actualization* by putting all of the multiple meanings about self-actualization into the Matrix Model. This gives us lots of specific content descriptions for what self-actualization looks like in terms of belief frames about each of the content matrices.

- As a result, the Self-Actualization Matrix gives us a way to think about the processes of self-actualization in a systemic and systematic way. It enables you to see and understand how your self grows and develops.

End Notes:

1. POI stands for the *Personal Orientation Inventory* which is an instrument created by Maslow and Shostrum in 1964 for measuring self-actualization. This is the subject pursued in Chapter 13.

Chapter 12

PROCESSES FOR

UNLEASHING POTENTIALS

"What does one *do* when he self-actualizes?
Does he grit his teeth and squeeze?
What does self-actualization mean
in terms of actual behavior, actual procedure?"
Maslow (1971, p. 43)

Suppose your phone rang today and a CEO of a very important corporation was on the line. And suppose she said, "If you can answer two critical questions, you will receive the corporate contract with my company that we've been talking about." And suppose this is a contract you have been dreaming about for years. So you listen carefully to the questions:

"I need to know two things. First, *how* does a person specifically find, identify, and unleash his or her potentials? And second, *what* are the specific processes and mechanisms in Self-Actualization Psychology that explain how this unleashing of potentials works?"

If that call were to come in right now, how many mechanisms could you list and what processes would you use to actually facilitate a person's unleashing? This was the driving question as I started researching Self-Actualizing Psychology. This also was what I sought to answer in my first book on self-actualization, *Unleashed: A Guide to Your Ultimate Self-Actualization* (2007).

So, what are some of the steps involved in the process of mobilizing your resources that will enable you to unleash your potentials? This chapter provides a summary of the processes listed in *Unleashed.* Becoming familiar with these mechanisms and how they work will enable you to use them to empower yourself and others for unleashing human capacities, powers, talents, and potentials.

What unleashes potentials? First there has to be a vision of possibilities. Without a vision, there's nothing to pull you forward. Without a vision that there is more, that there are abundant potentials to be unlocked, you will not extend yourself. And yet even with vision, there has to be the ability to face reality for what it *is* and deal with your situation as you find it.

We call this ego-strength. It takes a strong sense of self and of your skills and abilities to solve problems to take advantage of your strengths and opportunities. Following this you need to know yourself, you need the kind and quality of self-awareness that allows you to enter into the uniquely human adventure of discovering yourself—your passions, predispositions, talents, opportunities, strengths, weaknesses, etc. And as you do, the mechanisms of just witnessing, just seeing what *is*, non-judgmentally exploring and releasing all judgment enables you to discover what you can achieve.

Activating and actualizing potentials begins with these first four powerful responses as unleashing mechanisms: envisioning your life dreams, developing the ego-strength to face life, opening yourself up to reality as it is, and accessing a state of non-judgment for pure witnessing. From there you are ready for the drama of self-actualization which occurs in three scenes.

The first scene: Entering into *the construct of meaning* where you use your creative powers of meaning-making to create a robust sense of meaning and meaningfulness. You unleash nothing without rich and compelling meanings that invite you into the challenge of life. If self-actualization is a function of the meanings you discover and create, there's no escape from the necessity and the responsibility of creating rich meaning.

The second act: Enter into the fire, into *the crucible of change and transformation,* into the place where you are able to get to your own core. And there you experience a self-encounter. You encounter your emotional core, your core of needs, impulses, drives, and motivations and all of the learnings that you have about these experiences. This is a place of construction and de-construction. Here you bring old forms and structures of your life that need to be de-constructed. And here, with your transformative crucible you form and reform, de-construct and re-construct empowering realities in the image of your meanings.

The third act: Enter into *the zone of self-actualization*— the zone of performance. This is the place where you can authentically express yourself and your gifts, where you can actualize your best meanings and visions in actual performance. Here you experience the synergy of meaning and performance. Doing this enables you to experience peak experiences and become a *peaker* as you take your actual skills to new levels of competence so that you experience peak performances in the real world.

What other unleashing mechanisms are there? Within each act of the self-actualization drama there are many.

Scene I: Creating a Robust Construct

1) *Meaning-making:* It all begins with your recognition that your meaning-making creates your reality, your interpretative schemes, and the activation your fundamental powers. Step up to your creative powers of meaning-making by learning how to both suspend and construct meaning at will.

2) *Quality controlling:* The purpose of quality controlling is to check out the quality of your meanings and to make sure that they are not toxic or ineffective. Then you can detect or create rich meanings to activate your highest passions. This will also enable you to reframe meanings so you can set quality meanings that are robust and enlivening. Installing a quality control mechanism in your mind enables you to detect and be alerted to low quality meanings.

3) *Synethesizing meaning and performance:* Discover how to synthesize the dual roles of meaning and performance to get on the self-actualization path that will take you into the zone of self-actualization. Refuse the delusion of any "learning" which is detached from acting upon that learning. Decide always to translate your knowing into doing. Make a commitment to never leave the scene of an insight without doing something about it. This will enable you to close the knowing-doing gap, a powerful factor in actualizing human potentials.

4) *Need Gratification:* Gratify your *deficiency* needs with true and adequate satisfiers. This will create for you a personal foundation for moving beyond your lower needs to your higher needs. Create a solid foundation by developing the coping skills for your basic animal needs of survival, safety, love and affection, and self-respect. Begin this by welcoming your needs as legitimate needs that require adequate gratification. As you do this, learn to be (as Maslow put it) a good healthy animal.

5) *Transcend your lower needs:* Activate your highest needs, the needs of *being* and *meaning* where your true passions emerge. These are the needs that cannot be gratified to extinction. Gratification of these do the opposite, they create greater capacity for these higher needs. So welcome the never-ending restlessness of your higher needs so they propel you forward.

Scene II: Entering the Transformative Crucible
6) *Stepping back for expansive awareness:* Experience the magic of stepping back from yourself, your needs and emotions, and observe yourself with a non-judgmental awareness. Witnessing yourself at higher levels (which use your self-reflexive consciousness) puts you at choice point. And in doing this you access the executive levels of your mind for higher quality decisions.

7) *Activating Powers:* Find and take complete ownership of your innate powers so that you can play to your strengths while simultaneously managing around your weaknesses. As you activate your innate powers of the responses that no one can take from you, you create the gestalt state of "responsibility." As you do this, you develop your personal sense of being in control of your life, your responses, and your destiny.

8) *Choosing:* Step up to your executive power of choice to take control of your focus, meanings, emotions, identity, attitude, and direction. Accessing your power of choice transports you into the truly human dimension of consciousness where you "run your own brain" and use your consciousness with intentionality.

9) *Esteeming Self:* Validate your unconditional value and your individual uniqueness by distinguishing your person from your behavior. Such unconditional positive regard will empower you to get your ego out of the way which, in turn, will free you for the transcendence of self-forgetfulness. This will give you the ability to

stop striving to become "a somebody," recognize that you already are a somebody, and then begin to live in a way that expresses your "somebody-ness."

10) *Centering Self:* Create personal and social safety nets for being able to take smart risks as you stretch beyond your comfort zones. With the safety nets, you'll feel centered enough in yourself to take risks, set ambitious stretch goals, and live far more boldly than you ever thought possible.

11) *Synergizing opposites:* Overcome the limitations of dichotomizing polarities by creating synergy between conflicting forces. As you refuse to be cornered and leashed by either-or thinking, you free yourself to experience higher level solutions that resolves the artificial polarities that dominate so many facets of life.

Scene III: Entering the Zone of total Engagement

12) *Engagement:* Use your flow state to be totally present in your engagements as you take your performances to ever higher levels of excellence. Enjoy losing yourself in the moment as you experience peak experiences where you feel fully alive with all of your resources available. Practice stepping in and out of "the zone" of self-actualization until you can do it at will.

13) *Stretching:* Set compelling goals that stretch you to the next level to actualize your highest self and best performances. Step up to use "big, hairy, audacious goals" as a way to put more energy and vitality into your life. Refuse to sell yourself, human nature, or your potential short by putting up with small wimpy goals.

14) *Receiving Feedback:* Welcome specific feedback in real time as a mirror of reality to more quickly and flexibly adjust to changes. Transform your attitude about feedback so that it seems and feels like an exciting opportunity to enhance your skills and accelerate your learning.

15) *Capitalizing problems:* If "problems" are a human construct and are entirely within your power to frame and reframe, then welcome them. Adopt a "bring it on" attitude toward problems. As this stops the internal flight and fight, it will enable you to develop quality problem-solving skills so you can capitalize on your problems and use them to energize yourself for unleashing new possibilities.

16) *Loving:* Within the zone is the *being*-love of self-actualization and this is the love that enables you to fall in love with the adventure of life and meaning. Step up to the B-love of caring and investing yourself in others. Doing this will enable you to actualize more of yourself and in the end you'll fall in love with life itself.

17) *Playing:* When you live in the zone you become joyfully playful as you give yourself to the adventure of self-actualization. Playfully create, experiment, and innovate your self, your life, and the gifts that you can bring to others.

18) *Valuing:* Because the *being*-values are in the zone of self-actualization, be sure to step up to embrace the *being*-values as "the meaning of life." You can make *valuing* as a way to look at life and others with fresh eyes of continuous appreciation.

19) *Culture:* "Cultivate" your mind, heart, and interactions along with others to create the good conditions required for self-actualization. Invite other self-actualizers to join you in creating self-actualization companies, businesses, and communities. Self-actualization is not an individualistic thing. It involves others and it requires the support of a self-actualization culture.

So what are the Mechanisms?
Let's now stop and step back from this list of two-dozen processes that contribute to the unleashing of potentials. As we step back and ask, "What are the actual mechanisms?" the answers fall into two categories: meaning and performance. If there's no meaning, no meaningfulness, no significance, no value, no challenge, no vision, no desire, no hope—nothing will be evoked and released. Why would anything be unleashed? And if there is all of that, but no action, no response, no neurological activity, no performance—then there will be hoping, wishing, desiring, wanting, envisioning, but no actuality.

The mechanisms that enable you to unleash your potentials is *the performance of your highest meanings and the enrichment of meaning in your current performances.* This means that it is the synergy of meaning-and-performance (challenge and competency) that makes our potentialities real.

Unleashing Your Potentials

Potentials can be unleashed, and they are unleashed via numerous processes. In the three scenes of the Construct of meaning, the Crucible of change, and the Zone of engagement the drama of self-actualization occurs. In this drama we continually recycle through meaning-making, de-construction of old meanings about emotions, needs, and motivations, so we can experience the synergy of being in the zone when challenge and competence optimally combine.

Each of these distinctions are described in *Unleashed* as well as their relationship to self-actualizing. And yet these mechanisms are only the beginning of the self-actualizing life. There are more of these and there is much more to be said about how to actualize your highest visions and values.

Key Points in this Chapter

*   *Life is all about becoming*—becoming all you can become, becoming the best version of you. We call this self-actualizing.

*   There is rhyme and reason to how the process of unleashing of potentials works which enables us to actualize our highest possibilities. Identifying those mechanisms gives us an insider's view on what's required for living the self-actualizing life.

*   By learning and using these mechanisms of self-actualization and the specific processes and we move to a higher level where we become self-actualizing persons living a self-actualizing life.

Chapter 13

SELF-ACTUALIZE

OR BE DIMINISHED

"The adult fixated at the safety or love level is a diminished man and must
be treated accordingly and *spoken* to accordingly; he can understand
experientially only the language for that level."
Abraham Maslow

A vision drives *Self-Actualization Psychology*—a vision that
informs and guides its direction. That vision is that within
each of us are immense potentials for greatness. It is the idea
that we can find, cultivate, and release our highest possibilities. We
can actualize the incredible possibilities within ourselves. This urge
within all of us is an urge that reflects our highest (and deepest)
instinctoid nature. That is, we are made to develop and create our
best version of ourselves. It is part and parcel of human nature. We
do not stop when we turn 18, 25, 50, or 65, but we continue to
develop throughout our entire life-span. We do unless we interfere
with the process and diminish our potentials.

If that sounds radical, here's what Maslow wrote about this:
"Capacities clamor to be used, and cease their clamor only
when they *are* well used. That is, capacities are also needs.
Not only is it *fun* to use our capacities, but it is also *necessary
for growth*. The unused skills or capacity or organ can
become a disease center or else atrophy or disappear, *thus
diminishing the person.*" ((*The Maslow Business Reader*,
2000, p. 41, italics added)

In Self-Actualization Psychology, our capacities not only reflect our *needs*, and so "clamor to be used," but when they are not, something terrible happens. Dis-use of our capacities initiates pathological processes. To not *use* what we have, what we *are,* what we are called to— *diminishes us.*

The pathology of needs not gratified, capacities not used, and potentials not developed highlights the dimension of meta-pathologies in human nature and experience. *Meta-pathologies*? These are the diseases unique to us humans, diseases that affect our need for meaning—hopelessness, helplessness, victimhood, boredom, futility, meaninglessness, etc. In fact, Maslow took the time to create extensive charts and lists showing the relationship between needs, their gratification or deficiency, and the various psychological illnesses that result.[1]

In fact, Maslow framed things in this way quite intentionally:
> "Human diminution (the loss of human potentialities and capacities) is a more useful concept than 'illness' for our theoretical purposes." Growth forward *is in spite* of these losses and therefore requires courage, will, choice, and strength in the individual, as well as protection, permission, and encouragement from the environment." (*Toward a Psychology of Being* 1968, 204)

What this means is that self-actualization is not a luxury for us, *self-actualization is a need.* It is a necessity and a requirement for full humanness, for being fully alive/ fully human. Unless we self-actualize our highest and best, we diminish ourselves, we diminish our capacities, our quality of life, and our sense of joy in life.
> "Each neuroticized need, or emotion or action is a *loss of capacity* to the person, something that he cannot do or *dare* not do except in a sneaky and unsatisfying way. In addition, he has usually lost his subjective well-being, his will, and his feeling of self-control, his capacity for pleasure, his self-esteem, and so forth. He is diminished as a human being." (p. 46)

If self-actualization is a *need,* then to fail at it does something worse than simply cause us to miss out on some good things in life. We have so much freedom available to us that we can even ignore, repress, or deny our highest needs, yet when we do so we diminish our *humanness.* We condemn ourselves to living a diminished life.

Maslow (1968):

> "People with intelligence must use their intelligence, people with eyes must use their eyes, people with the capacity to love have the *impulse* to love, and the *need* to love in order to feel healthy. Capacities clamor to be used, and cease their clamor only when they *are* used sufficiently. That is to say, capacities are needs and therefore are intrinsic values as well. To the extent that capacities differ, so will values also differ."
> (*Toward a Psychology of Being*, p. 152)

Destiny or Diminished

As Maslow thought through the consequences of the diminishing our potentials, he described it and equated it to the terrible things that can happen to personality. In *The Journals of Abraham Maslow* (1972) Maslow wrote the following in Feb., 1965. Because it was a journal, he wrote in shorthand using the equation sign (=) to mean "equals."

> "What you are fitted for— that is your destiny, which you must accept and give yourself to wholly, and train yourself for in the best way possible. All this then reads at the highest level: which of the B-values are you going to specialize in? Because you detect in yourself specialized capacities or possibilities or become some B-value tasks 'call for' you more strongly; i.e., they need you, so you respond. . . . Becoming less than you were capable of becoming = voluntary self-diminution = voluntary 'castration' = voluntary suicide and renunciation or wasting of life = you are not a good member of the species = misery = the intrinsic guilt of evading growth and self-actualization and therefore misery, self-punishment, and sense of having failed." (p. 124)

This brings up the question of *non*-self-actualizing. *How* do we account for people *not* self-actualizing especially when they have all the conditions required for actualizing their best? What explains that? If we are designed for actualizing our highest potential, *why do so many people not self-actualize?* Why are they not psychologically healthy? Why do they fight the B-values? How do we account for this *diminution of the person*? Or, to quote Maslow, "Why is he this kind of less-than-whole person?"

Maslow used the concept of intrinsic guilt to describe as what occurs when we betray our potentials, when we betray our best self and do not live up to our potentials, when we waste our potentials, or try to be someone other than ourselves (*Journals*, 1982, p. 166).

> "I think one consequence of the hierarchical theory of basic needs is a hierarchical or 'levels' way of thinking about much else: politics, economics, religion. etc. It also implies a theory of personality levels. The adult fixated at the safety or love level is a diminished man and must be treated accordingly and *spoken* to accordingly; he can understand experientially only the language for that level." (*Journals,* p. 177)

What does it mean to be diminished? Maslow described it as a person having lost important human capacities, pleasures, and rewards. Of course, this occurs along a continuum—a continuum of losing more and more capabilities. In the extreme,

> ". . . a diminished person can't really 'enjoy' anything in the high sense, can't love, never experiences real friendship, real trust, identification with others. Certainly gets no peaks, only 'kicks.' Shallow emotions, impoverished consciousness. Easily bored, can only achieve lower pleasures. No meta-motivational pleasure." (*Journals,* p. 185).

If by accepting, loving, and respecting our inner nature enables us to facilitate our psychological health and self-actualization —

> "Then it is by self-denial, asceticism, and rejection of the demands of our organism that we produce a diminished, stunted, and crippled self. (199).

When we are diminished, we almost inevitably neuroticize one of our needs, emotions, or actions. We land upon a comprised way that's ultimately self-defeating in terms of meeting our actual needs (205-206).

What does it mean to be diminished? It means—
    — Operating at a fraction of your capacity
    — Defaulting on self-actualization
    — Shrinking from being the real me
    — Undermining and dampening my real aspirations
    — Draining off one's energy in unrewarding areas
    — Disintegrating into fatigue and depression
    — Achieving only a small fraction of one's potential intelligence, potential love

Key Points in this Chapter

- Self-Actualization is not just a nice cap on things for those with sufficient affluence. It is a requirement for living in a fully human way at all stages of development.

- One excellent way to understand self-actualization is by examining its opposite which is *diminition,* that is, being diminished as a human being in capabilities, resources, powers, and experiences.

- From the theory of Self-Actualization, *diminition* offers us a new frame of reference for understanding what has historically been labeled as neurosis, sickness, psychosis, etc. When a person suffers from neurosis, that person suffers from being diminished as a human being.

- Diminition, rather than the sickness metaphor, enables us to more objectively and neutrally ask, "Does this build up and enrich? Or, does it undermine and make one less than one can be?"

End Notes:

1. Here is the list of B-values that Maslow developed from his study of self-actualizing people along with his list of meta-pathologies.

B-Values	Meta-Pathologies
Truth	Mistrust, cynicism, skepticism
Goodness	Hatred, repulsion, disgust, reliance only on self and for self
Beauty	Vulgarity, restlessness, loss of taste, bleakness
Unity; wholeness	Disintegration
Dichotomy-transcendence	Black / white thinking; either/or, simplistic view of life
Aliveness; process	Deadness, robotizing, feeling oneself to be totally determined, loss of emotion and zest in life, experiential emptiness
Uniqueness	Loss of feeling of self and individuality, feeling oneself interchangeable with anyone

Perfection	Hopelessness, nothing to work for
Necessity	Chaos, unpredictability
Order	Insecurity, cynicism, mistrust, lawlessness, total selfishness
Simplicity	Over-complexity, confusion, bewilderment, loss of orientation
Richness, totality,	Depression, uneasiness, loss of interest in world comprehensiveness
Effortlessness	Fatigue, strain, clumsiness, awkwardness, stiffness
Playfulness	Grimness, depression, paranoid, humorlessness, loss of zest, cheerlessness
Self-sufficiency	Responsibility given to others
Meaningfulness	Meaninglessness, despair, senseless of life

Chapter 14

THE POWER TO

SELF-ACTUALIZE

"It looks as if one way to breed grown-up people
is to give them responsibility, to assume that they can take it,
and to let them struggle and sweat with it.
Let them work it out themselves,
rather than over-protecting them, indulging them,
or doing things for them."
Abraham Maslow (1971, p. 220)

If self-actualization doesn't occur without our awareness, choice, and response, and if self-actualization doesn't occur without effort on our part, then core powers enable us to self-actualize?

From the previous chapters I'm sure it is now obvious that responsibility plays an exceptionally important role in *Self-Actualization Psychology*. In fact, responsibility plays so central a role that it is only through accessing and assuming responsibility that we are able to actualize our highest and best potentials. Conversely, without acceptance of personal responsibility for self-actualizing, we diminish ourselves as persons and limit our possibilities for being all we can be.

- What is the relationship between self-actualization and responsibility?
- Can we self-actualize without accepting full responsibility for ourselves?
- To what degree is self-responsibility a precondition and requirement of self-actualization?
- Can a person unleash potentials without self-responsibility ?

Obviously, these questions are rhetorical. Of course we can't self-actualize without accepting responsibility for ourselves. Of course, self-responsibility is a precondition for actualizing our best potentials. What would you say if someone questions this? "Why is that so? Why can we not self-actualize without self-responsibility?"

Would you not explain that *responsibility lies in the nature of self-actualization*? Would you not say that because self-actualization is not an inevitability, but a personal choice, then it is only through making responsible choices that we self-actualize. Would you not explain that the ability-to-respond to our talents, dreams, and passions and fully developing them involves ongoing effort, focus, and vision?

This highlights an important fact: self-actualization is not something that happens *to* us apart from our awareness, choice, and effort. Self-actualization does not happens like winning a lottery. That's why self-actualizing is not for the passive, the lazy, the unimaginative, those following the path of least resistance, or blamers. Nor is it for complainers or whiners. It is for *response-able* people who develop their personal vision of finding and following their talents and passions and unleashing their potentials to become their best and making a contribution in the world that makes a difference.

The key thinkers of the Human Potential Movement who introduced the idea of responsibility into *Self-Actualization Psychology* were William Glasser, Viktor Frankl, and Rollo May. This had been a missing element in the older psychologies.

No wonder self-responsibility is as one of the prerequisites of self-actualization and without it, there can be no actualizing of your best. Self-actualizing doesn't happen apart from mindful responses. In fact, it is a function of your responses, your best responses— the performances that you create day-in and day-out as you seek to turn your dreams, visions, and values into reality.

Core Powers of Human Beings
Self-responsibility begins with the four basic human powers of thinking-and-emoting and speaking and behaving. These responses create a zone of power which each of us have as our basic heritage as human beings. That's why owning and fully claiming these powers facilitates the unleashing of potentials and develops the powerful state of self-responsibility.

How self-responsible are you? Test yourself. Take the following sentence stem and generate a dozen endings. Keep repeating the stem until you generate a dozen or more endings.[1]

> "If I took complete responsibility for what I think, what I feel, what I say, and what I do ..."

Don't worry whether the endings you generate are positive or negative, that's not the point. The point is first to increase awareness and second to download what's in "the back of your mind." That's because it is what's in the back of your mind that makes up your frames and meta-frames[2] about responsibility and these may be leashes holding you back. Third, doing this will also put you *at choice point* where you can use your executive level of mind to forge your highest path.

> "If I were to take full responsibility for all of my words . . ."
> "If I were to take full responsibility for all of my states ..."
> ... for my attitudes, happiness, resilience, playfulness, seriousness, relationships, values, goals. etc.

Self-responsibility describes the ability to own and express your innate powers. When you are self-responsible, you take a proactive stance to do the things that you need to do to fulfill your dreams. Here's another sentence stem you to use for developing self-responsibility:

> "If I were to take full responsibility for making my dreams and visions come true ..."
> "If I were to take full responsibility for actualizing my best potentials. . ."

The Challenge of Self-Responsibility
Self-responsibility is not for the faint of heart or for those with low ego-strength. Nor is it for those who make their self-esteem, value, and worth *conditional*. To do that puts your self-esteem on the line. Self-responsibility takes you a long way along the path of self-actualization because you stop wasting energy blaming, accusing, complaining, and whining. You get on with things. You look for what needs to be done, and you *do* it.

So what is *self-responsibility*, how do we describe it and what are the ways that we facilitate its development? Because those who are self-responsible are also proactive, they initiate action, they think through decisions, they continuously question and learn, they identify their values, their visions, and stand up for them, they pursue their goals, they bounce back from set-backs, they keep awakening their resources, they keep accessing new strengths, they boldly make decisions and follow through, they turn new learnings into habits, they make themselves accountable to others, they operate as great team players, and they work with and through others. They allow others to hold them accountable and, in fact, search for and build structures of accountability.

Nathaniel Branden in *Taking Responsibility* (1996) describes self-responsibility in the following way:

> "The essence of self-responsibility is the practice of making oneself the cause of the effects one wants, as contrasted with a policy of hoping or demanding that someone else 'do something' while one's own contribution is to wait and suffer. It is through independence and self-responsibility that we attain personal power." (p. 13)

If the heart of self-responsibility is *making oneself the cause of the effects one wants,* how do we do that? How do you make yourself *the cause* of your desired effects? How do you develop the sense or feeling that you are *the source* of your actions, your thoughts, your choices?

The Power of Self-Efficacy
The answer goes back to the state of *self-efficacy* (actually it is a meta-state).[2] This refers to the sense, the understanding, the belief, and the realization that you are able to make a difference, that *you can always do something,* and that you can trust your basic powers of mind, emotion, speech, and behavior for navigating your way through life. Unlike self-confidence which demands proof, historical evidence, and successful references, self-efficacy describes how you relate to the future about those areas in which you have not yet successfully navigated. It is a state of trust in yourself. It is the sense, "I can figure it out, develop the skills, hone the required competencies, and make it happen." When you develop that frame as your meta-state, then you are able to truly "make yourself the source and the cause" of the results you want.

What is your current level of self-responsibility from 0 (none) to 10 (absolute)? If you were to become even five percent more self-responsible, what difference would that make toward actualizing your best self?

Achieving Self-Actualization via Self-Responsibility

In the Self-Actualization Quadrants, the flow zone is in the fourth quadrant. It is here that you begin moving toward full optimization of your *highest meanings* and *robust performances*.

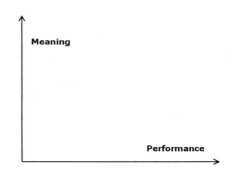

Quadrant 1 is where we all begin. It reflects how we begin undeveloped in terms of development in meaning and performance. Quadrant 2 gauges the development of your skills your as competencies grow. This quadrant refers to your performances and actions leading to your achievements. Quadrant 3 gauges the development of meaning, including such things as vision, passion, inspiration, great ideas, etc. This quadrant measures the kind and quality of your meanings, your meaning-making powers, and the flexibility of your mind to generate supportive meanings and your ability to suspend meaning.

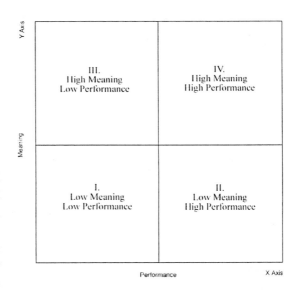

Now inspiring meaning without performance is just dreaming. And performance without rich meanings is just empty and compulsive behavior. So it is in *the synthesis* of meaning-and-performance that enables us to actualize our best meanings and embody our best performances with the most robust meanings. All of this describes our sense of challenge and inspiration from our meanings as we synergize the development of our competencies to create a new level of synthesis. And in this way we are propelled into both peak experiences and peak performances.

This overall process of how we self-actualize unites the two axes. And with this, we enter into "the zone" of being at our best and fully engaged with whatever activity we're involved with. The same axes that create "the flow zone" in Csikszentmihayli's model also creates the self-actualization quadrants. And whereas I have identified them as the axes of *Meaning* and *Performance*. Csikszentmihayli labels them *Challenge* and *Competency*.

Here we have a confluence of Positive Psychology and Neuro-Semantics and that typically raises several questions: How do these models relate? How do they describe provide different perspectives on the same experience? How do these relate to self-responsibility?

Activities or experiences that you endow with *meaning*, and that become highly *meaningful* to you, are those that *challenge* you to grow. They push you past your current competency level and stretch you to your higher levels. You need that kind of challenge. Without challenge, your life becomes stale and boring. You feel disinterested, reduce your level of awareness, and stop extending yourself. For an activity to be meaningful, it has to challenge you at an appropriate level of signficance.

Your *performances* depend upon the ongoing development of your skills and competencies. As you keep using your skills, you refine, hone, and develop them more fully. Doing this enables you to then take on more challenge since it is in actual *performance* that actualizes the meanings in your body via your competencies.

On the *Meaning* axis, if you go for too big of a meaning, too much of a challenge, you overwhelm yourself. And with overwhelm, you go into the panic or overwhelm zone. And that causes people to shut down and inwardly give up. If they continue to dream, *they dream without doing*. They may create dreams in the mind, but they do not make them real in their lives.

On the *Performance* axis, if you have too much skill for something, you experience it as too easy, too simple, "kid's play," and you will feel it as boring and unchallenging. And with under-whelm, you enter the drone or bored zone. In both instances, too much or too little challenge, you will fail to optimize your best. You will not enter into the flow state of the Self-Actualizing Zone.

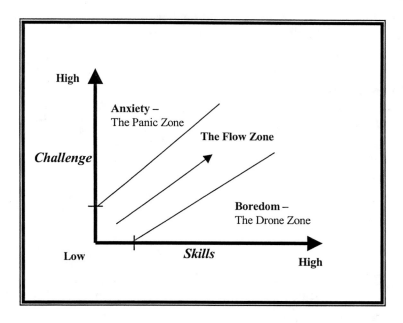

It takes the proper combination of both. Only then will you be able to *synthesize* meaning and performance, challenge and competency and *optimize* both into the self-actualizing experience. So given all of that, How does this relate to self-responsibility?

To think about these two axes, the Self-Actualization axes of meaning and performance and the flow axes, think of them in terms of self-responsibility. As you do, let's rename these axes *Responsibility* and *Capability*. When you do this, you can see that the higher the level of *responsibility* which you assume and own moves you upward into more *meaning* and *challenge*. That's the vertical axis. Similarly, the more capability you demonstrate over time as you grow and develop, the more you move along on that axis in terms of *competency* and *performance*. That's the horizontal axis.

In other words, *the level of responsibility that you assume* describes the meaningful vision, goals, hopes, dreams, etc. that you accept and hold yourself to. Taking on too much, all at once, creates the overwhelm. Taking on too little corresponds to little, or no, development. As you give yourself time (which necessitates the states of patience, persistence, commitment, resilience, etc.) to keep developing your performance / competency as the capacity is developed, you keep fulfilling one level of responsibility. That prepares you for the next. If you go too slow, boredom will overtake you so you'll quit. If you push too fast with too much impatience and not enough persistence, you'll be overwhelmed and defeated.

In all of this, *self-responsibility* is the meta-state[1] that enables you to use the right amount of pull and push for setting stretch goals, holding yourself accountable and inviting others to hold you accountable. In all of this you will be synthesizing your dreams, meanings, and responsibilities with the development of your performances.

Does self-actualization depend on self-responsibility? You bet it does! It depends on lots and lots and lots of self-responsibility. That explains why *only the self-responsible self-actualize.* Those who depend on others, or luck, or circumstance and those who wait for the right time, the right circumstances, the right motivation, etc. typically never get around to it. Self-actualizing requires that you keep finding your current capability level and assuming responsibility to stretch beyond that level just a little bit as you keep exerting focused effort day in, day out.

Putting this altogether, the axis of meaningful challenges includes *responsibility.* And the axis of performance competency includes *capability*—two components of self-responsibility. And because you are responsible *for* your capabilities, accepting and owning that facilitates the process of actualizing your highest and best.

Self-Responsible Growth

When it comes to self-actualization, you have to do it yourself. No one can do it for you. You've got to walk the path of self-actualization all by yourself. Due to our social needs and constitution, and that we are social creatures, we can and do walk the pathway of self-actualization with others—in relationships, collaborations, being a good team player, etc.

The bottom line about self-actualization is that it occurs through *the individualizing process* as you become more fully yourself mature, grown up, able to stand on your own two feet, autonomous, differentiated, and able to find the strengths, talents, and gifts that you have to develop and offer to others. In this, self-actualization arises from relationships and ends in relationships.

This explains why it takes a lot of self-responsibility to enter into and maintain self-actualizing. Why is this? Because it takes a lot of independence to be inter-dependent. Only then can you enter into relationships with others while maintaining a strong sense of self and contributing your voice, your opinion, your gifts, your creativity. It's only through complete differentiation in discovering how to be true and authentic to yourself that you are enabled to become a truly good and effective team player and colleague to others.

In all of this, it's through fully accepting *the challenges of self-responsibility* that we are able to actualize our gifts and become a full participant in healthy relationships. Responsible self-actualization is all about having enough of self, and a strong enough sense of self, so that when we are in a relationship, we can be fully present and available. In this, self-responsible actualization goes beyond self-esteem, self-confidence, ego-strength, and glories in the higher quality of self-efficacy.

Self-Efficacy
All of this reminds me about the ongoing debate that's been raging in educational circles in the United States for perhaps the past thirty years. It's the debate about whether teachers should focus on the 3-Rs (reading, writing, and arthmetic) or whether they should put more focus on addressing a child's level of "self-esteem." Of course, an *either/or debate* like that doesn't have to be dichotomized in that way. Why not address both? Why not create a healthy synergy to work toward and achieve both a strong sense of self and academic skills?

Yet even doing both doesn't resolve the problem. That's because when we take the time to ask educators what they mean by "self-esteem," their answers are typically vague to the point of being useless. Most use the term "self-esteem" as a synonym for self-confidence and so confuse two very different states. The next largest group uses it an equivalent for "feeling good about oneself" (a sense of emotional pleasantness), others use it for a sense of personhood and worth, yet others use it as a synonym to one's social self, and so it goes. With such confusion and ambiguity about "self-esteem," no wonder there are scores and scores of processes trying to raise the level of "self-esteem," while simultaneously undermining one's learning competencies.

What's really needed is *self-efficacy*. This meta-state operates at a higher level to the other states of *confidence* in your ability to do some particular task (self-confidence), *positive feelings* about yourself (self-appreciation), *esteeming and valuing* yourself as a human being of unconditional worth and dignity (self-esteem), and acceptance by your peers and social group (other-esteem).

While self-confidence speaks about past skill and competency, the faith-in-yourself (con-fideo) that you can *do* something, and while self-esteem speaks about an abstract evaluation of unconditional value in oneself, you develop self-efficacy as you conceptually move above specific confidences as you realize that you count and don't have to prove anything to be a somebody. At that higher level, you can then abstract that as you have used your mind-body, your senses, coping skills, etc. to figure things out, so you can with things that you will yet learn and master. Self-efficacy is the feeling, and evaluation, that you can *trust* your talents, gifts, consciousness, etc., to cope and master challenges yet to come as you move out into your future.

Self-efficacy grows along side of "ego-strength." This state of mind empowers you to look reality in the face without blinking. It enables you to face what *is* without falling apart, caving in, or activating the fight/flight syndrome. In self-efficacy, you experience the presence of mind to face what you have to face without falling back to rely upon ego-defenses.

What children need in school, and what we all need for ongoing learning, development, and transformation is *the self-efficacy to trust ourselves*. To trust your mind, to develop trust in your intuitions, to trust your problem-solving skills, to trust your questioning, to trust your ability to build supportive relationships, and so on. This is what develops a solid and vital sense of self-efficacy. And with that, then a person is more ready to actualize potentials, explore latent talents, experiment with weird possibilities, think out of the box, take calculated risks, etc.

Measuring Self-Efficacy
Self-efficacy, then, is one of those magical qualities that facilitates the unleashing of potential. It's one of the ways that we can enable the self-actualizing process so that we can increasingly move to actualizing more and more of our potentials. If we were to test for self-responsibility, if we were to benchmark it, what would we measure and test for?
•   Do you think ahead, and take initiative, in your own growth

and development?

- Do you assume full responsibility and accountability for your actions?
- Do you accept full responsibility for your happiness, mood, emotions, and states?
- Do you stand up for your values and principles?
- Do you continuously question, explore, and expand your possibility thinking?
- Do you plan for new changes and transformations?
- Do you apply truths, principles, insights to yourself?
- Do you proactively approach your relationships?
- Do you discern what you're responsible *for* and whom you are responsible *to*?
- Do you access and awaken new resources?
- Do you keep expanding your problem solving skills?
- Do you regularly step back, evaluate where you are, get accurate feedback, and then make adjustments?

Self-Management and Self-Actualization

We self-actualize as we develop self-responsibility. By owning our innate responses we are able to make things real in our lives. Through the self-efficacy of trusting and committing to our own growth, we discover that self-actualization corresponds to *self-management*—the ability to manage oneself .

Self-development techniques need a strong focus on self-application and self-management. Otherwise they often end up being used for doing things *to* others. When that happens, they typically degenerate into covert forms of manipulation. That's why self-management techniques are best when we use them for co-creating with others their best states and effective performances. Then we can use them for self-actualization as we work collaboratively *with* others.

The promise of a map and navigational tools for "running my own brain" first attracted me to NLP. When I read the line, "If you don't take charge and run your own brain, someone else will!" I intuitively recognized the wisdom in that and so began my adventure into the field of self-management. Managing ourselves means managing our thoughts—our hopes and dreams, our imaginations and memories, our construct of meaning, and the quality of our representations and framing. Managing ourselves means managing our emotions—our states, meta-states, moods, and attitudes. It means managing our activities, choices, time, relational skills, growth, mistakes, learnings, health, and much more.

Actualizing your best requires that you take charge of yourself; it means the practice of both self-leadership and self-management. In this, the *leadership* of self is easier than the *management* part. Catching a vision, setting the course, establishing the operational frames for the inner game, etc. is actually much more exciting than the everyday management tasks by which you translate the self-leadership into practical lifestyle. Yet it is in self-management that we turn our highest dreams into reality.

It is also in self-management that you discover the reality and quality of your self-responsibility. Are you fully able to be a responsible adult in owning and exercising your responses to bring your vision to life? Are you truly able, as a responsible, grown-up adult, to figure out what you have to do to actualize your potentials and then discipline yourself to follow through on your action plan? Those childishly dependent are forever in need for someone else to do it for them.

The question, "What vision or meaning do you want to actualize?" elicits your self-leadership. After you answer that question, it then takes self-management to create an action plan for managing your mind, emotions, time, energy, and responses and making it happen. Can you do that? Even more important, Will you do that?

Now apply this to each and every area of life. What vision or meaning in your career do you want to actualize? What dream or significance in your relationships? In your health and fitness? In your finances? When you exercise the meta-state of self-responsibility so that it becomes habitual, it becomes part of your Matrix, part of the mental-emotional atmosphere that you live in. Then you operate from the joyous pleasure of being a self-directed person—self-directed in your career, money, fitness, skill development, continuous learning, etc. And that puts you on the path for becoming a self-actualizer.

Key Points in this Chapter

- It takes awareness, effort, choice, and personal responsibility to self-actualize. It takes a healthy and vigorous sense of responsibility to develop and unleash your potentials.

- In *Self-Actualization Psychology* being willing and able to take control of one's responses is a prerequisite for self-actualization. As you take charge of your core powers you eliminate defeatism, victimization, and resignation.

- Self-efficacy, as a very special state, is a meta-state that enables you to trust your wits that you will figure things out as you go. This exceptionally powerful state enables you to move out into your future with trust, hope, and optimism.

End Notes:

1. I learned the use of *sentence stem exercises* from Nathaniel Brandon.

2. A meta-state is a state about one of our states. As part of our self-reflexive consciousness, it is the thinking-and-feeling we engage in as our second thoughts and feelings about previous thoughts and feelings. See *Meta-States, Secrets of Personal Mastery.*

Chapter 15

THE SELF-ACTUALIZING

LIFE

"Self-actualizing people, those who have come to a high level of maturation, health, and self-fulfillment, have so much to teach us that sometimes they seem almost like a different breed of human beings." (1968, p. 71)

". . . the most fully-human people, a good deal of the time, live what we could call an ordinary life—shopping, eating, being polite, going to the dentist, thinking of money . . . Peak-experiences . . . whatever their relative frequency may be seen . . . to be exceptional experiences even for self-actualizing people." (1968, p. 124)

Self-Actualization Psychology is the model of psychology that describes the self-actualizing process of unleashing potentials, experiencing peak experiences, and living a self-actualizing life. If the self-actualizing life is the ultimate goal of this psychology, it is natural to ask:

- What is the self-actualizing life like?
- How does that kind of life differ from how we typically live?
- Is the difference primarily in the quality and kind of living or are there certain conditions and quantities also involved.
- When we describe the life of a self-actualizer, are we describing something extra-ordinary, super-natural, other-worldly or something very ordinary?

The problem in describing the self-actualizing life is that it entails lots of paradoxes and things that at first seem counter-intuitive. This results in making self-actualization something that is not easy to describe. Our words often fail us in our endeavor to describe the self-actualizing life.

Self-actualization refers to a dynamic life. We see this in the way the self-actualizing person grows toward health. It is a life devoted to fulfilling highest values, actualizing best dreams, and being creative about the way one lives life. As a life of continually actualizing potentials and capacities the self-actualizer seeks to hear his or her inner voice and develop a personal authenticity in living one's mission.

It is a life that's both intentional in a direction while spontaneous and open in style. It is a life of acceptance of self, others, nature, and reality that enables a higher level of autonomy and transcendence of culture. It is a life characterized by a freshness of appreciation, a richness of emotion, and a higher frequency of peak experiences. It is a life that while less dependent upon others is more democratic in character. It is a life free of biological needs and more focused on solving problems and contributing to the well-being of the whole human race.

I have written the following description from the thirteen characteristics that Maslow gathered from his study of self-actualizers in 1955 (*Toward a Psychology of Being*, p. 26).[1] For him, self-actualization meant growth as "the various processes that bring the person toward ultimate self-actualizing." This means that it is "going on *all* the time" and that it is not a process that has an end-point so that it will culminate somewhere. No one is self-actualized in any final sense. The dynamic nature of self-actualization means that we, at best, can learn to live a self-actualizing life.

This separates the self-actualizing life from the mythical state of perfection wherein all human problems are transcended and people "live happily forever after." Self-Actualization is not like that at all. It is more on the order of what Maslow noted when he said that self-actualizers transcend the *pseudo*-problems of life and the *neurotic* problems of hurt and poor parenting so that they can graduate to *the real existential problems* of human existence (Maslow, 1968, p. 115).

In the following eight categories, I have summarized Maslow's vision of the self-actualizing life and what it means.

1) Self-Actualizing Motivation
For Maslow, the self-actualizing person is meta-motivated or growth motivated. At the lower levels we experience motivation as getting away from the tension of our drives and needs. Need-reduction is the

quality of that kind of motivation. But everything changes at the higher levels. Now we have impulses and needs that we actually enjoy. We have impulses and needs that are pleasurable, even enjoyable tensions.

At this level also our motivation grows with gratification. By fulfilling our meta-needs, the gratification "breeds increased rather than decreased motivation."

> "The appetite for growth is whetted rather than allayed by gratification. Growth is, *in itself,* a rewarding and exciting process." (1968, 30)

So what is the motivation? It is to be more, experience more, have more, do more, think more, feel more, give more, contribute more, and make more of a difference. It is to life fully and completely as oneself without a compulsion to try to live up to somebody else's criteria or even cultural standards. It is always to explore new possibilities and to never settle or be satisfied. It is to enjoy a higher level restlessness.

2) Self-Actualizing Enjoyment (*Being* and *Becoming*)

Something else happens to us as we learn to live a more self-actualizing life. The character of our goal-seeking activities changes from being *instrumental* in motivation to being *intrinsic*. At the lower levels, we think and act instrumentally. That is, we're out to do things, to achieve things. We look at things in terms of how they help or hinder the attainment of our goals. What we do is always a means to some end, and never an end in itself.

Yet this changes when we move to the meta-motivation level. We begin transforming even our instrumental activities so that we enjoy them as if they were end-activities— *enjoyable in themselves and for themselves.*

This is the kind of change that many people experience when they move beyond "having to make the bed and clean up one's room" to first wanting and enjoying a clean room and made-up bed, and then to actually enjoying the beautifying process itself. Eventually, we enjoy making things neat, orderly, well-formed, in order, beautiful. Then the "cleaning" itself becomes an act of creativity, of beautifying, of structuring, of investing a bit of ourselves into the world. And this "intrinsic validity of living" arises from learning how to experience it as a pleasurableness that's inherently valuable and enjoyable in itself.

Maslow described this as the cultivated ability of healthy people to transform means-activity into end-experience (1968, p. 31). This higher kind of pleasure is not the relief from tension, but an ecstasy and serenity in its own right. Here we come to enjoy the tension as an eustress (good stress). In self-actualization—
> "Joy has been attained which means a temporary end to the *striving* for joy." (1968, p. 110)

3) Self-Actualizing Valuing
(Continued Freshness of Appreciation)
When we *value* something, whether it be a person, event, activity, thought, or emotion, we look at it as something that adds to the quality and richness of life, as *a good* in and of itself. The end result is this activity of valuing is what we then call a "value." And what creates the value is *the process of valuing*—the mental, emotional, and behavioral activity of valuing.

So it is in *the valuing process itself* that we are able to transform activities that are typically instrumental in nature into those that are intrinsically valued and enjoyed. And when we do that, we experience more joy, more happiness, more of a sense of the value and preciousness of life. We are able to *sacrilize,* that is, we are able to see the sacred in the secular, to see life from the perspective of eternity. This is part and parcel of the self-actualizing life.

Sacrilizing enables us to live the self-actualizing life in the realm of the *Being*-values. It is here that we develop more of an aesthetic appreciation of life, of the arts, and of the creative ways that we can express our life-force. This leads to the gratitude of self-actualization, the ability to perceive the world as good and beautiful.

The magic here is that when valuing becomes our mind-set, we move through the world with eyes of appreciation and have "a continual freshness of appreciation." This enables us to experience *being*-love and to become a *being*-lover. Maslow described this kind of love as non-possessive and admiring in nature. It is a love that enables us to see potentials in others and to nurture others so that it calls forth these potentials. In this way *being*-lovers are penetratingly perceptive (1968, p 73).

In his study of Grumbles, Maslow noted the widespread tendency to under-value the need-gratifications which we have already achieved. He also noted that failing to appreciate, to be grateful, to count our blessings is a form of pathology (1970, p. 61). By way of contrast self-actualizing people are capable of such gratitude that they experience all of life as precious. This appreciation is closely associated with a hunger for beauty. He also noted that just as we get sick from ugliness, we are also often cured by beauty.

4) Self-Actualizing as Experiencing One's Uniqueness
Here's another challenge in the inquiry about how to describe the self-actualizing life. When we ask about the specifics of the self-actualizing life, we are hindered by the fact that it is, and always will be, different and unique for each person. And it is uniqueness which prevents sameness. Maslow described this uniqueness:

> "Self-actualization is idiosyncratic since every person is different." (1968, p. 33)

Once we have gratified our basic needs, we become less dependent and increasingly more autonomous and self-directed. This means a freedom from the need to conform to any given culture and the freedom to *be* and *become* our own unique self. In the lifestyle of self-actualizing we are forever discovering more and more about ourselves, our inner nature, our inner gifts and potentials, and finding the courage to move forward to a higher quality of authenticity.

All of this requires a lot of ego-strength. This is the paradox that we experience in the self-actualizing life. It is the person in whom ego-strength is at its height who more easily forgets and transcends the ego. And we can only transcend our ego when we have a strong and robust sense of self and so have no fear of losing ourselves. Then we can center ourselves on the world, on problems, and on finding solutions, on making a difference.

Maslow's way of explaining this was to say that the tasks of self-actualization are largely intra-personal rather than inter-personal. In self-actualizing we shift our focus to discovering our self, to selecting the potentialities to developing our gifts and talents, to inventing our meanings, to constructing our life outlook, to actualizing our competencies, etc.

5) Self-Actualizing Passionate Life-Long Learning

School is never out for the self-actualizer. Life is one long adventure and discovery where we are always learning, changing, and being surprised. For those self-actualizing, one is forever embracing change, the changes of life in the developmental process of growing, and the changes of the world as the world's pace of change continues to accelerate.

And what is it that takes a life-time to learn? Mostly how to create synergy, how to create new synthesis between what seems like polarities, opposites, and contradictions. Mostly we keep researching and learning how to bring all of the pieces and parts together to see and experience the wholeness of life, of ourselves, of others, of the world. In self-actualizing we are able to see all of the variables as parts of a larger interpenetrating system. And so we see and think and respond more holistically. This results in self-actualizers resolving such dichotomies as selfish or unselfish, work or play, inward or outward, mind or body, etc.

Maslow speaks about being led to a particular differentiation by his studies of self-actualizing people. In my words, they are able to "meta-detail."[2] *They can hold higher level awarenesses while at the same time detailing out the specifics.* And this kind of perception enables the self-actualizers to perceive holistically. In his words, he described two abilities:

> ". . . simultaneously the ability to abstract without giving up concreteness and the ability to be concrete without giving up abstractness." (1968, p. 89)

Living the self-actualizing life as a life-long learner makes us *becomers*. We are forever becoming more and more of who we can be. We become *explorers* of the farther reaches of our nature. "What more can we become?" This is the adventure of life that our self-actualizing meta-needs conspires to move us into.

Now we can get down to the business of facing, enduring, and grappling with the *real* existential problems of life instead of the pseudo-problems. The self-actualizing life is not about an absence of problems, it is rather about becoming competently able to focus on the problems that require higher level solutions. When we are fully human we still have problems and pains. Yet there is good news:

> "Yet it remains true that these problems and pains are quantitatively less and that the pleasures are quantitatively

and qualitatively greater." (1968, p. 116)

6) Transcending and Peaking

The self-actualizing life also involves having more and more peak experiences. These are the experiences of awe that we stand in wonder about, the god-like possibilities that we catch glimpses of in those special moments when we transcend ourselves.

"Peakers" is the term Maslow used for those who experience peak moments when we fully and exclusively attend to one thing, when the figure of our awareness becomes *all figure* and the ground disappears completely. At that moment we are totally absorbed, fascinated, and engaged in something in which we invest ourselves. And emotionally we feel that we have become one with the object of our engagement.

In such moments we are "in the zone." This is the zone of self-actualization wherein the world goes away, self goes away, and time goes away. We become self-forgetful, we transcend our ego, we become whole as we become completely engaged. Here we experience the sense of transcending—transcending self and time and the world. As regular language fails us here, we inevitably turn to religious and mythic language and to metaphors to describe this flow state.

The experience of the peak experience typically feels as if we are "surprised by joy," to use C.S. Lewis' captivating phrase. It feels as if it happens to us and that it is *a grace*—an undeserved gift from above. It feels as if we are outside of time, and sometimes even outside of space, as we become oblivious to our surroundings.

In all of the peak experiences from the hundreds upon hundreds of people that Maslow interviewed,

> ". . . the peak-experience is only good and desirable, and is never experienced as evil or undesirable. The experience is intrinsically valid . . . perfect . . . complete and needs nothing else." (1968, p. 81)

Out of the god-likeness of this experience we become more tolerant of human nature, *being*-amused, and *being*-accepting.

7) Self-Actualizing as Creating Meaning and Meaningfulness

The self-actualizing life is informed and governed by meaning. Due to our abilities to abstract, we can make of things whatever we wish. Maslow recognized this power when he wrote, "We create it." (1968, p. 90).

This also makes for some special changes. On the one hand, we need to be able to de-construct our abstractions and sense of reality so that we can, on the other hand, construct new maps of reality that enable us to see a rich and wondrous world.

In the de-constructing, we have to be able to see the world with "innocent eyes" again, to see things with a new freshness as if for the first time, to see the uniqueness of things. This requires the ability to suspend meaning, to suspend categorizing things, "to fight our tendency to classify, to compare, to evaluate, to need, to use." (1968, p. 90). Only then can we see afresh the many-sidedness of things, people, and events. This is where *being*-perception comes in. To see as in merely witnessing, accepting, without evaluations and judgments.

8) Self-Actualizing as Easy Self-Discipline

As self-actualizing people synergize more and more of life, they come to experience duty and pleasure as a singular thing. They work at their play and they play at their work. Their work is their play. And what others would call discipline, the self-actualizing person sees first as just a requirement, and then as part of the exciting challenge for the next step in development.

On the subject of fitness, Robert Carkhuff (1981) says that

> ". . . actualizers maintain rigorous fitness programs without making a fetish out of it. They draw upon their physical resources to serve other more important purposes; they value their fitness highly because they recognize it as a necessary but not sufficient condition of their life purposes. They treat health crises as opportunities to learn more about themselves and others." (55)

For self-actualizers, discipline of self is easy because they are clear about what's important. It's easy also because they distinguish means from ends and so they can get themselves to follow through on their goals. They plan and then they follow their plan. In this, they implement in action what they conceive in mind. In his book, *Toward Actualizing Human Potential* (1981), Robert Carkhuff writes,

> "Actualizers can operationalize any goal in their speciality

area and develop the necessary systems and technologies to achieve it." (p. 56)

They can translate the great meanings that they generate in their minds into practical action in their everyday behaviors and life style. For them, these are not separate functions, but operate systemically.

Seeing Self-Actualizing People in Action

Maslow said that one of the first problems that presented itself to him in his studies of self-actualizing people was the vague perception that their motivational life was in some important ways different from all that he had learned. In *Toward a Psychology of Being* he wrote:

> "Self-actualizing people, those who have come to a high level of maturation, health, and self-fulfillment, have so much to teach us that sometimes *they seem almost like a different breed of human beings."* (p. 71, *italics* added)

They are different due to the motivational level *where* they live on the Hierarchy of Needs and the kind and quality of motivation that life at that level generates. They are different due to the *being*-space where they live, due to their B-values, B-love, B-relationships, etc.

What is it like when you self-actualize? Maslow (1971) wrote this:

> "Self-actualization is a matter of degree, or little accessions accumulated one by one. Too often our clients are inclined to wait for some kind of inspiration to strike so that they can say, 'At 3:23 on this Thursday I became self-actualized.' People selected as self-actualizing subjects, people who fit the criteria go about it in these little ways: They listen to their own voices; they take responsibility; they are honest; they work hard. They find out who they are and what they are, not only in terms of their mission in life, but also in terms of the way their feet hurt when they wear such and such a pair of shoes and whether they do or do not like eggplant or stay up all night if they drink too much beer. All this is what the real self means. They find their own biological natures, their congenital natures . . ." (p. 49)

So with that comment, I now pose the question again, "What is a self-actualizing person like?" Or to make this more personal, "What will I be like as I become more self-actualizing? What will that mean in terms of my thinking, feeling, speaking, and behaving?"

Describing self-actualizers as *peakers,* they are those who regularly experience peak experiences of the "flow" states.　　What are the attitudes and states of these self-actualizers? What do we actually *see* in what they do and think and feel?　Here is Maslow's list of the characteristic of self-actualizing people.

- They tolerate uncertainty
- They heartily accept self and others
- They are spontaneous and creative
- They enjoy privacy and solitude
- They have deep and intense relationships
- They genuinely care and love others
- They are altruistic in their actions
- They are self-transcending
- They have a sense of humor and lightness
- They are inner directed
- They have an absence of artificial dichotomies (love/hate; weak/strong; work/play, etc.)
- They have a more efficient perception of reality
- They have a simplicity and naturalness about them
- They have an autonomy that makes them independent of culture
- They have no need for conformity
- They experience mystic or peak experiences frequently
- They are more democratic in their attitudes and dealings with others
- They discriminate between means and ends
- They are philosophical in their attitude about things
- They have a greater sense of the sacredness of life
- They have a continued freshness of appreciation

Does this vision of life excite you? Are you ready for the adventure of actualizing your highest self and your best potentials?　Then this is the call for the self-actualizing life and these are its qualities.

Key Points in this Chapter
- Because we all have moments of peak experiences in life, all of us take on at times some of the characteristics of the self-actualizing life. Yet we only do so temporarily which means we don't live the qualities as our way of life.

- Yet all of us could live more of a self-actualizing lifestyle. This is a very real possibility.　In this self-actualizing is not an either-or nor all-or-none proposition.　It is a matter of degree and extent.

End Notes:

1. We can take these characteristics of self-actualizers and arrange them in various ways. The following classification reorders them into what we can call the dimensions of self-actualization.

> *Cultural dimensions*
>> Autonomy
>> Resistance to enculturation
>> Identification with humanity

> *Philosophical dimensions*
>> Accurate reality perceptions
>> Detachment
>> Sense of humor

> *Emotional dimensions*
>> Spontaneity
>> Freshness of appreciation
>> Mystical experiencing

> *Interpersonal dimensions*
>> Acceptance
>> Interpersonal relations
>> Democratic character structure

> *Intellectual dimensions*
>> Problem-centered
>> Discriminating means and ends
>> Creativity

2. Meta-detailing refers to the synthesis between thinking globally (generally) and specifically in details. See *Sub-Modalities Going Meta* (2006) for an entire work on meta-detailing as a prerequisite for mastery and genius.

Chapter 16

MEASURING

SELF-ACTUALIZATION

"A philosophy is not constructed in the same way as a bridge. A family and a crystal must be studied in different ways. . . . we *must* psychologize *human* nature."
(1970, p. 7)

A s we think about the life-long process of self-actualization, *how* can we tell if we or someone else is self-actualizing, if we are in the process of self-actualizing, or if we are living a self-actualizing life? How can we tell when a person has become a self-actualizer? In asking this, we are asking about metrics and measurements. Can self-actualization be measured? If it is possible, then how do we go about it? What are the signs, signals, indicators, and clues of self-actualization?

The First Self-Actualization Instrument
During summer of 1962, Everett Shostrom consulted with Abraham Maslow about this very question of how to measure self-actualization. As they put their heads together to create an instrument to provide measurement of self-actualization, they created an instrument—the *Personal Orientation Inventory* or POI.[1]

The POI that was finally developed in 1964 was originally conceptualized by Shostrum. He delineated the initial scale constructs. This instrument is made up of 150 two-choice comparative value and behavior questions. The items reflect significant value judgments as seen by therapists in practice and are based on the theoretical formulations of several writers in humanistic psychology including Maslow, Riesman, Rogers, and Perls. (POI, 1987, p. 33)

There are two primary measurements in the POI, *Other versus Inner Directedness* and *Time Competency.* As Shostrum and Maslow conceptualized the key factors indicating that a person is actualizing her or her best, they decided on these two central ideas. First, the operating from out of his or her own sense of self fulfilling his or her best skills and potentials based on self-awareness, skills, aptitudes, and predispositions. And second the person is living in the present with full awareness and contact with reality.

1) Other versus Inner-Directedness
The Inner-Directed person appears to have incorporated a psychic gyroscope so that the person is able to maintain his or her sense of balance and direction regardless of the ups-and-downs and even traumatic challenges in life. Typically this is initiated early in life by healthy influences as good parenting and education. Although for others, that inner gyroscope is developed and created later in life by new understandings or by an empowering decision.

Other-Directed persons are often very good at getting along with people and impressing people yet this is, more often than not, only at a facade level. Looking outside of themselves for direction, their social skills are often "manipulations." They manipulate others to take care of them and give them directions via pleasing others and insuring constant acceptance.

This first characteristic determines how real and authentic the person is in living his or her own life, instead of trying to live someone else's life or living the idealized life that a given culture promotes. In being inner-directed, you find and develop your own unique skills and consciousness as you discover and express your own uniqueness. This creates self-integrity and congruency—key indicators of self-actualization.

Example questions from the POI that explore this include the following:

     5. I am afraid to be myself.
         I am not afraid to be myself.
    15. I put others' interests before my own.
         I do not put others' interests before my own.
    21. I do what others expect of me.

I feel free to not do what others expect of me.
41. I justify my actions in the pursuit of my own interests.
    I need not justify my actions in the pursuit of my own interests.
44. I live by the rules and standards of society.
    I do not always need to live by the rules and standards of society.
46. Reasons are needed to justify my feelings.
    Reasons are not needed to justify my feelings.

If your locus of control is within you, then you become the author of your life. We describe this experience as the meta-program of being *internally referenced.*[2] This means that in terms of authority, your reference point is within, not without. You are your own authority using your beliefs, values, judgments, opinions, etc. for guidance. Studies indicate that we are most healthy when we are *internally referenced with an external check.* The "external check" means that we check outside to see how others are responding to us, to see how our ideas correspond with authorities, and to check with others perhaps have more experience than we do. Yet we live from within ("internally referenced") assuming responsibility for our own choices and responses.

2) Time Competency

Actualizing one's best also involves being fully present in the here-and-now. Without full presence, we would not be all there and so not fully present, so we would be less likely to actualize our fullest potential. The time incompetence / time competence ratio measures the degree to which a person is time competent or present oriented. This is in contrast with time incompetence or living primarily in the past (with guilts, regrets, and resentments) and/or in the future (with idealized goals, plans, expectations, predictions, and fears).

Example questions from the POI that explore this include the following:
59. I strive always to predict what will happen in the future.
    I do not feel it necessary always to predict what will happen in the future.
88. I worry about the future.
    I do not worry about the future.
90. I prefer to save good things for future use.
    I prefer to use good things now.
105. I spend more time preparing to live.
    I spend more time actually living.

This measurement of time competency relates to the *time zone* we mostly live in—the past, present, or future. It also relates to how much of our mental-and-emotional energies are spent in the three zones. It now seems that the ability to live in the present is the human challenge—and yet the more we can do that, the more our actions can relate to actualizing today's possibilities.

The 10 Other Scales

In addition to inner-directed and time-competent, there are ten subsidiary scales for self-actualization. These are designed to tap values important in the development of the self-actualizing individual. This is how the POI describes them:

1) *Self-actualizing value:* measures the primary values of self-actualizing persons, and in particular the B-values.

2) *Existentiality:* measures the ability to situationally or existentially react without rigid adherence to principles. This reflects one's flexibility in applying values or principles to one's life.

3) *Feeling reactivity*: measures sensitivity of responsiveness to one's own needs and feelings. A high score reflects sensitivity to personal needs and feelings, whereas a low score shows insensitivity to one's self.

4) *Spontaneity*: measures freedom to respond spontaneously or to "be oneself." A high score indicates the ability to express feelings in spontaneous action. A low score indicates being fearful of expressing feelings behaviorally.

5) *Self-Regard*: measures affirmation of self because of worth or strength. A high score indicates the ability to like oneself because of one's strength as person. A low score indicates low self-worth.

6) *Self-Acceptance*: measures affirmation or acceptance of oneself in spite of one's weaknesses or deficiencies. A low score indicates an inability to accept one's weaknesses.

7) *Nature of Man— Constructive*: measures the degree of one's constructive view of the nature of man. A high score indicates the belief that human nature is essentially good, reflects the self-actualizing ability to be synergistic in one's understanding of human nature. A low score sees human nature as essentially evil or bad.

8) *Synergy*: measures ability to be synergistic, to transcend dichotomies. A high score indicates the ability to see opposites of life as meaningfully related. A low score indicates that the person sees opposites as antagonistic. The synergistic person sees that work and play are not different, that lust and love, selfishness and unselfishness are similar dichotomies that are not really opposites.

9) *Acceptance of Aggression*: measures ability to accept one's natural aggressiveness as opposed to defensiveness, denial, and repression of aggression. A high score indicates the ability to accept anger within self as natural. A low score indicates that the person denies such feelings and avoids expression of them.

10) *Capacity for Intimate Contact*: measures ability to develop intimate contact relationships with others, unencumbered by expectations and obligations. A high score indicates the ability to develop meaningful, contact-relationships with others. A low score indicates that the person has difficulty with warm interpersonal relationships.

The POI and the Matrix

In chapter 11 I introduced *the Matrix Model* as part of the description of the Self-Actualization Matrix. It will again serve us here as we think about how to measure self-actualization. Here the Matrix model will enable us to pull together a lot of mental-and-emotional *frames* about the variables indicating that a person is self-actualizing.

We will use the Matrix Model here to pull together into one model *the key processes* by which we create our experience of self-actualizing. This will pull together our sense of the experience itself in terms of meaning, intention, and state. And it will pull together the key dimensions of our sense and concept of self as it develops over the lifespan. This is the contribution of Developmental Psychology within the Matrix Model for the self, power, others, time, and world matrices. The result is that the Matrix model enables us to think systemically about both the processes and content of our consciousness and experiences.

In this way, we can now relate the Self-Actualization Matrix to the POI as a measuring instrument. Doing so allows us to begin to measure the various aspects of self-actualization and see how it relates to our matrix of frames.

Self and Power

The POI begins with the content matrices of Self and Power. It does this by first addressing and measuring *the support scale* with 127 questions. According to the POI (1987),

> "The support scale is designed to measure whether an individual's mode of response is characteristically 'self' oriented or 'other' oriented. Inner or self directed people are guided primarily by internalized principles and motivations while other directed persons are to a great extent influenced by their peer group or other external forces." (p. 4)

> "The inner-directed person goes through life apparently independent, but still obeying this internal piloting. The source of inner-direction seems to be implanted early in life and the direction is guided by a small number of principles. The source of direction is inner in the sense that internal motivations are the guiding force rather than eternal influences. This source of direction becomes generalized as an inner core of principles and character traits." (p. 15)

Being inner-directed in one's own internalized sense of support describes the *authority meta-program* of referencing internally with an external check.[2] The person develops his or her own principles, values, beliefs, understandings and then lives, decides, and acts according to them. This is the person who *authors* the script of his or her own life. Self-actualization requires that we develop a strong and robust sense of self—a self that we can trust, depend on, and look to for our sense of direction.

> "Self-actualizing people appear to have liberated themselves from rigid adherence to the social pressures and social expectations to which normal and non-self-actualizing people conform." (p. 15)

So in the Self and in the Power matrices, to become more self-actualizing in our person we build meanings about *self* and *power to respond* that allows us to develop, find, cultivate, and operate from a set of principles. These are our life principles that we adhere to and use as a map as we navigate through life.

The Time and Power Matrices

The time scale of the POI measures the degree to which we live in the present as contrasted with living in the past or future.

> "The time competent person lives primarily in the present

with full awareness, contact, and full feeling reactivity while the time incompetent person lives primarily in the past with guilts, regrets, and resentments, and/or in the future with idealized goals, plans, expectations, predictions, and fears." (p. 4)

If self-actualization is a process of development over time and through time, then our concept of "time" plays a significant role in determining the degree and extent of our self-actualizing. So the competency for handling "time" as a concept comes down to the ability to live fully in the here-and-now with an openness for contact with others and engagement in significant activities.

"Such a person is able to tie the past and the future to the present in meaningful continuity; appears to be less burdened by guilts, regrets, and resentments from the past than is the non-self-actualizing person, and aspirations are tied meaningfully to present working goals. There is an apparent faith in the future without rigid or over-idealistic goals." (p. 13)

The psychologically healthy person in self-actualizing uses the past for reflective learning regarding what works and what doesn't and then reflects upon future anticipations and consequences as a way to chart his or her future. In processing each time dimension, we do not use the past or future for feeling bad, but for coping and mastering life's challenges. By way of contrast, the non-self-actualizing person fails to discriminate well between past and future. Such persons have "undigested memories and hurts of the past" that they have not interpreted in an effective or a meaningful way which allows them to learn from previous events, make the necessary personal adjustments, and move on.

Time competency implies that the self-actualizing person is constantly able to synergize between the past and future for the sake of the present. In this we do not live in the future "always a step ahead of actuality." Nor are we always dragging our feet in the past by constantly engaging in archeological expeditions or letting the past determine the future.

The end result is the ability to be present in the moment and to respond appropriately and relevantly to the events that are currently happening. This creates a realness, an openness, and an authenticity. As being in the moment describes a freedom from the past and future and because there's no need to be defensive or to escape, time competency facilitates in us an openness to being in full contact with reality in this moment.

The Pairing of the Sub-Scales
Regarding the ten sub-scales, the POI Manual (1987) puts the sub-scales together into pairs and sees them operating in a synergistic way to create a life balance critical to self-actualization. The POI even offers several synergistic terms for the gestalts that result from these pairs. I have indicated these words used in the instrument by putting them in quotes to identify these terms. Then in the sections that follow I have expanded upon them.

Self-Actualizing Values (1) and Existentiality (2)
> combine to create "valuing" which occurs in the *Intention, Meaning and Power matrices.*

Feeling Reactivity (3) and Sponaneity (4)
> combine to create "feeling" in the *State matrix.*

Self-Regard (5) and Self-Acceptance (6)
> combine to create "self-perception" in the *Self matrix.*

Constructive Human Nature (7) and Synergy (8)
> combine to create "awareness" which we would locate in the *Meaning and Intention matrices.*

Acceptance of Aggression (9) and Capacity for Intimate Contact (10)
> combine to create "interpersonal sensitivity" in the *Others matrix.*

Intention and Meaning Matrices —> Valuing
The sub-scales of Self-Actualizing Values (1) and Existentiality (2) unite to give what the POI designates as "valuing." This occurs in the *Intention, Meaning and Power matrices.* This points out how as self-actualizing people we are able to create clear values which we flexibly apply in our everyday lives. This prevents us from suffering valuelessness or becoming compulsive or rigid regarding our values. *Valuing* enables us to live for the rich meanings which Maslow identified as the *being*-values.

Values and living existentially with sufficient flexibility enables our self-actualizing in terms of living meaningful lives. By valuing we live for something important and significant. Life counts for us. We ourselves count. We also use flexibility as we live (existentiality) so that we don't obsess about the meanings that we value or become compulsive in living those meanings. We value, we value highly, and we value with the grace of flexibility so that our choices are relevant and life-affirming. *This is sacrilizing.*

This was a central focus in Maslow's work. He often spoke about how his model could lead to a scientific definition and understanding of values as he argued against the non-sense of a value-free society, science, school, etc.

State Matrix —> *Feeling*
The sub-scales of Feeling Reactivity (3) and Spontaneity (4) united to give us the quality labeled "feeling." This occurs in the *State matrix.* In self-actualizing, we develop an openness to ourselves, to our needs, desires, emotions, and from this intra-personal awareness we are able to effectively express ourselves. This facilitates our communication and expressiveness skills, enables us to "know ourselves" and assert ourselves appropriately.

What these two scales measure we today call *emotional intelligence* or *emotional quotient* (EQ). As self-actualizing people, we are open to ourselves and all of the human impulses of needs and emotions. We are not distant, standoffish, stiff, but spontaneous, joyful, and even playful. This is the "second childhood" in self-actualizers as they recover that which is childlike in learning, curiosity, and wonder. Self-actualizers enjoy life, feel it, and are in touch with their feelings. They are neither afraid of their emotions nor do they blindly trust them. Instead they test them, acknowledge them, and then use their energy to empower them in taking effective action in life.

Do feelings play a role in the process of self-actualization and, if so, what role do they play? The answer is that our feelings enable us to be sensitive and responsive to contexts and people and they inform us about how to use our emotions intelligently. So, *yes,* they are important and play a significant and contributing role.

Self Matrix —> *Self-Perception*
The sub-scales of Self-Regard (5) and Self-Acceptance (6) unite to create what the POI calls "self-perception," which obviously refers to the *Self matrix.* Self-actualizing people value themselves and hold

themselves in high regard as human beings. They can simultaneously acknowledge, honor, and appreciate themselves for their strengths while simultaneously humbly accepting themselves in spite of their weaknesses. This saves them from crippling perfectionism on the one hand and arrogance and superiority on the other. It enables them to be democratic in relations with others, treating people with equality and respect.

How do you think of yourself when you are self-actualizing? When you are living a self-actualizing life, is your self-perception richly layered with *acceptance* of your weaknesses and fallibilities, yet *positive regard* as a human being? This, in turn, gives you a solid sense of self so that you can become self-forgetful as you can lose yourself in present-moment engagements.

The synergy here between high regard and acceptance of weakness enables you to take off the blinders to yourself and to realistically "know yourself." Your self-perception is therefore well balanced in self-assertion and a modest humility as you accept and appreciate both your strengths and weaknesses.

Meaning and Intention Matrices —> *Awareness*
The sub-scales of Constructive Human Nature (7) and Synergy (8) unite to create "awareness," according to the POI. This refers to the *Meaning and Intention matrices* that govern our explanatory styles as well as our thinking patterns. Cognitively, self-actualizing people view human nature as basically good. Hurt and evil is then interpreted as a distortion of human nature and as arising from the lack of a sense of safety or from the desperate deficiency of some basic need. Simultaneously we are able to take opposites in life and transcend them to create a new synergy from those forces. And as this allows us to avoid either-or thinking, we also avoid creating of false dichotomies between work and play, lust and love, selfishness and unselfishness, etc.

Philosophically, self-actualization is a function of believing in the goodness of human nature and the goodness of life itself. This is the same belief that Einstein lived by, "We live in a friendly universe." Believing in goodness allows self-actualizing people to search for goodness, find it, create it, cultivate it, support it, and live in an awareness or mindfulness of goodness. To not believe in goodness leads to discounting goodness when we do find it. It prevents us from see, discovering, and creating goodness in the presence of pain and problems.

With all of this in mind, the word "awareness" is such an insipid term to describe the richness that's implied in the idea of synergy—seeing the whole embedded in an awareness of goodness in the world. This rich and complex "awareness" of these two qualities generates an accepting, valuing, optimistic, and resilient awareness. And with it, we are enabled to live in an enriched world not torn apart by Aristotelian either-or thinking which reflects a childish stage of thinking that if perpetuated into adulthood creates false dichotomies, pseudo–choices and problems, and prevents the fuller perspectives as both-and thinking and systemic thinking.

With this rich mindfulness, a self-actualizing person moves through life "aware" of the positive possibilities for creating new experiences and for creating synergy out of things that otherwise seem polarized and torn into conflicting opposites.

Others Matrix —> *Interpersonal Sensitivity*
The sub-scales of Acceptance of Aggression (9) and Capacity for Intimate Contact (10) unite to create "interpersonal sensitivity." This unified trait refers to the *Others matrix.* Self-actualizing people value, accept, and interpret anger as "just an emotion." They see it as an emotion which indicates a sense of threat or danger. So in them there's no fear of anger or rejection of anger in self or others. So as they simultaneously accept their own life force for self-protection ("anger"), they accept it in others.

This then facilitates the ability to make intimate contact with others in an I-thou relationship in the here-and-now and so anger does not ruin the relationship. In other words, in spite of the presence of "anger," we can make and hold real authentic contact with others. By not being put off by anger or aggression, we can maintain meaningful contact as we empathetically seek to understand the sense of danger and explore the source of the perceived threat. All of this allows us to continue to love and accept self and others and use the intimacy which these emotions create.

By way of contrast, when a person rejects anger, it leads one to denying anger in self and others and then to repressing anger. Then as anger is feared, disowned, not countenanced, but interpreted as dangerous, it distorts personality, fogs the mind, and reduces one's ability to fully develop. Rejecting anger leads to being less authentic with oneself and others, less real about one's true thoughts, values, judgments, and emotions, and less able to compassionately connect to self and others. By accepting anger (and by way of extension, all other "negative" emotions) as a legitimate facet of the self-actualizing life, we are able to get to the heart of things, deal with interpersonal reality, and live more authentically and intimately in our relationships.

So as we are self-actualizing in relationship to others, we welcome emotions as emotions and do not semantically overload them and attribute to them an importance they do not have. They are just emotions; just the difference between our mental mapping of the world and our experiencing of the world.[3] As a result this enables us to be real and authentic and to care and respect others.

How do we Measure Self-Actualization?

The POI, as a psychological instrument, is designed to evoke and measure all of these attitudes, feelings, states, and behaviors and to use them as cues for measuring self-actualization. In this, the POI measures self-actualization in terms of these qualities and interactions:

__ Inner directed
__ Time competent
__ Valuing the *being*-values
__ Flexibly living by your principles in the here-and-now
__ Emotionally aware and attuned to your needs
__ Spontaneously free to respond
__ High self regard for one's value
__ Self-acceptance for one's weaknesses and limitations
__ Valuing human nature as basically good
__ Sees opposites as meaningfully related, synergizing dichotomies
__ Acceptance of negative emotions as just emotions, especially anger
__ Meaningful contact with others in I-Thou relationships

Key Points in this Chapter

- To measure self-actualization we must first operationalize the attitudes, states, and actions so that we can create a behavioral description of the responses from low to high. This is what Shostrum and Maslow attempted to do in creating the POI.
- Self-Actualization is primarily taking ownership of oneself (inner directed), of one's mental and emotional powers and

using those powers to be authentically yourself. To use them to follow your values and to create a meaningful life in what you do and who you relate to. It is making full and authentic contact with yourself, your environment, your skills and abilities, and your relationships, and to do so in the here-and-now. This essentially facilitates our full development and growth and unleashes our potentials. As such, it is natural, simple, and organic—and it is perhaps the biggest and most profound challenge of life.

End Notes:

1. The POI instrument is produced by EDITS (Educational and Industrial Testing Service), San Diego, Ca. To see a more recent measurement tool that we have created in Neuro-Semantics, see the Synergy Measurement of Meaning and performance on the websites.

2. *Meta-Programs* are the perceptual filters that we use as we see, perceive, and interpret things. Perhaps the best known meta-program is the optimistic / pessimistic filters around whether the amount of water in a class is half-full or half-empty. "Locus of control" is generally measured from internal to external (Rotter, 1966). A person with a strong internal locus of control tends to attribute outcomes to self-directed efforts rather than to external factors. See also the article, "Owning My Own Authority," www.neurosemantics.com.

3. "Emotions" result from *the difference* that we sense between what we "map" within our mind-body system to what we experience as we encounter "the territory." Emotions are therefore relative to our mental mapping and relative to the skills we have in actually coping with the demands and challenges of life. For more about the Neuro-Semantic perspective on emotions, see *Secrets of Personal Mastery*, article on www.neurosemantics.com "When the Emotional Scale Turns Downward."

Chapter 17

SELF-ACTUALIZATION

AND PEAK EXPERIENCES

"The climax of self-actualization is the peak experience."
Abraham Maslow

"Self-actualizing people . . . count their blessings . . . grateful for them and avoid the traps of mainly either-or choices."
(1970, p. xvii)

"Peak experiences do not last, and *cannot* last. Intense happiness is episodic, not continuous."
(1970, p. xv)

What comes to mind when you think about the pinnacle of *Self-Actualization Psychology*? Do you not immediately think about those experiences that Maslow called *peak experiences*? If not, then let me have the privilege of describing a peak experience and how these experiences play a critical and an influential role in Self-Actualization Psychology.

The term *peak experience* is a generalization for a person's best moments, for his or her happiest moments of life, for experiences of ecstasy, rapture, bliss, profound aesthetic experiences, creativity, moments of mature love, ecstatic sexual experiences, etc. Maslow explored such experiences by asking hundreds of people, "What was the most ecstatic moment of your life?"

In the process of interviewing hundreds of self-actualizing people, he also asked them to describe how the world looked to them during their peak experience moments. From the hundreds of words of description he then boiled things down and came up with the following list:

> Truth, beauty, wholeness, uniqueness, order, dichotomy-transcendence, aliveness-process, perfection, necessity, completion, justice, simplicity, richness, effortlessness, playfulness, self-sufficiency (1971, p. 102).

From this Maslow concluded that apparently almost all people have peak experiences even though many people don't seem to notice them or give them any conscious attention.

Defining Peak Experiences

What is a peak experience? Maslow described them as what you feel when you "gain authentic elevation as a human being." It is "an experience of heaven" that you step into for a period of time that you simply and fully enjoy. Afterwards, you can use the experience to feed upon with your memory as a source of inspiration. This means that peak experiences can be used to create very important consequences in your life.

Peak experiences are self-validating by nature. Peak experiences underscore that life is precious, joyful, and full of possibilities. There is a sense of total life-affirmation in peak experiences—times when we *feel* the meaningfulness of life. Maslow commented about peak experiences in the following way:

> "... life has to have meaning, has to be filled with moments of high intensity that validate life and make it worthwhile." (1971, p. 180)

The way we all experience the ordinary life most of the time involves striving to meet needs and reach goals. Ordinary life is a life of *becoming* and approaching possibilities. By contrast, the peak experience describes what we are ultimately designed to experience —*being*-ness, they are experiences of *being*.

> "We are forever becoming, driven to strive for a state of ultimate humanness. We are again and again rewarded for good *becoming* by transient states of absolute *being* by peak experiences." (1968, p. 154)

As I mentioned earlier in chapter 15 on *The Self-Actualizing Life,*

Maslow used the term "peakers" for those who regularly experience peak experiences. At such moments we are fully and exclusively attending to one thing and the figure becomes *all figure* as the ground disappears completely. In our peak experiences that we are totally absorbed, fascinated, and engaged with something, something that we use to derive a sense of life's meaningfulness.

If peak experiences are so powerful, so special, so much at the heart of self-actualization, then why are peak experiences also so short and so temporary? Maslow argued that the reason that these wonderful experiences are ordinarily transient and brief is because we are not strong enough to endure them more often or for longer periods (1971, p. 36-37).

> "Peak experiences do not, and *cannot last.* Intense happiness is episodic, not continuous." (1954, p. xv)

Components of Peak Experiences

Maslow discovered that peak experiences contain two components. One is an emotional component—the sense and feeling of ecstasy, of standing out from ourselves, of transcending ourselves, of merging with an object of engagement. The other is an intellectual component—that of illumination, an insight, new awareness, new understanding.

Maslow also held the view that peak experiences are entirely good. As quoted earlier, his precise words were:

> ". . . the peak-experience is only good and desirable, and is never experienced as evil or undesirable. The experience is intrinsically valid . . . perfect ... complete and needs nothing else." (1968, p. 81)

Yet he may have stacked the deck to have reached that conclusion. That is, it may have been his particular research and the way it was framed that led to that conclusion and created his results. Here is how he asked the research question:

> "I would like you to think of the most wonderful . . . experiences of your life; happiest moments, ecstatic moments, moments of rapture, perhaps from being in love, or from listening to music or suddenly 'being hit' by a book or a painting, or from some great creative moment . . ."

Did he tilt the scale by adding the words "wonderful, happiest, ecstatic," etc.? It certainly seems that way to me. What if he had just asked about the most intense experiences of life that led to insights, transformation, or a change of direction or value in life? Would that not also identify some peak experiences that might have arisen in crisis or even trauma? Without question, people do at times experience life changing insights and transformations from negative experiences as well as positive. History provides plenty of examples of such.

Loaded with Benefits

Peak experiences have a great many positive benefits for us. In Maslow's studies it led to the sense that life is good and worth living, the sense of joy of being alive, the sense of mystery and of the sacred, the specialness of the now, the connection with others, even all of humanity, love for others, and deeper democracy.

Peak experiences typically are moments of tremendous joy and vitality and they occur in the lives of all people and during all ages of development. As such, they are little tastes and appetizers of self-actualization.

Controlling Peak Experience

So far the description of a peak experience implies that it happens to us, and, that it comes upon us at unawares. Quoting C.S. Lewis, Maslow even said that when they occur, we are mostly "surprised by joy."

Yet could we take charge of the experience and learn to control it, that is, to step in and out of it at will? Is it possible to so identify the components, elements, and processes that we could manage the experience itself? Could we come to know ourselves and the structure of the experience that well?

It was Maslow's opinion that we could not and so he said that a peak experience is not a mood or state of mind, but "a genuine revelation of reality." This also explains, at least in part, why Maslow thought of the peak experience as not merely human projection, but a true revelation of the best values. And although an avowed atheist, it is in the peak experience, as described by Maslow, that he reveals a robust spirituality. For him the peak experience was a mystic experience.

> "Peakers also seem to live in the realm of Being: of poetry, esthetics; symbols; transcendence; "religion" of the mystical, personal, non-institution sort; and of end-experiences."

"There were the same feelings of limitless horizons opening up to the vision, the feeling of being simultaneously more powerful and also more helpless than one ever was before, the feeling of great ecstasy and wonder and awe, the loss of placing in time and space with, finally, the conviction that something extremely important and valuable had happened." (1954, p. 164)

I'm not along in questioning Maslow's belief about peak experiences being something that we wait for and that we experience passively. One of his biographers, Colin Wilson, also questioned him. If peak experiences are the same or even only similar to the experiencing of being "in the zone" of the flow state, then the axes of challenge and competence, or of meaning and performance, govern how they operate. And precisely because these axes describe the variables that determine peak experiences, we can now consciously and intentionally create these moments.

Key Points in this Chapter
*   All of this means that peak experiences, as highly desired subjective experiences, are human experiences with a structure. And if structured, then as we learn the workings of the inner mechanisms, we will be increasingly able to turn the experiences on and off at will.

*   Peak experiences are those special moments when we get so lost in an experience that for a few brief moments, we live in an eternal now fully present in our engagement with a rich sense of life's meaningfulness.

*   Peak experiences exercise a powerful influence on our mind, emotions, and relationships. Entering into the world of *being*, even just momentarily, enables us to see ourselves, others, life, and everything "under the aspect of eternity."

*   Peak experiences in the end are subjective experiences that have structure and structures that we can identify, learn, and then replicate to take charge and recreate them as we so desire. And when you can do that, your ability to move beyond the lower needs, move into the self-actualization needs, and unleash your potentials will move to a whole new level.

Chapter 18

REWORKING

THE NEEDS HIERARCHY

"If I have seen further
it is by standing on the shoulder of giants."
Isaac Newton

- If self-actualization is a process, how can we picture it as a dynamic and fluid experience?
- If meaning lies at the heart of unleashing, how can we best conceptualize and "see" *meaning* itself as a living process?
- What can enable us to move beyond the static and rigid images of *Hierarchy of Needs* so that we can think about the unleashing of our potentials in a systemic way?

As a new approach in psychology Maslow, Rogers, May, Frankl, *et al.* launched the revolutionary idea of *modeling psychologically healthy people*—self-actualizing people. Their idea was to explore healthy personalities to identify what enables people to fully develop, become all that they can become, enjoy peak experience moments, and continually take their performances to ever-new and higher levels.

The subject of their modeling—*human nature at its best*. By way of contrast, Maslow called human nature at its worst "the psycho-pathology of the average." The developers of the Human Potential Movement set out to describe human nature *at its optimal best* when not interfered or sidetracked through trauma or drama.

Because they assumed that we naturally and positively develop as we move through the stages of mental, emotional, social, personal, sexual, interpersonal, and spiritual growth, theirs was also a developmental psychology. What we primarily need, they said, is a supporting environment that has available the necessary requirements and resources. When human nature or development goes wrong, it goes wrong due to the things that *interfere* with the innate forces of development.

Maslow and others also argued that we cannot infer a healthy psychology model by studying human trauma, pathology, and failures and then inverting our discoveries. *Inverting* something that's distorted, false, misinformed, or that's gone off in a wrong direction, will not necessarily give us the right direction, the optimal, let alone the ideal for self-actualization. That would be like studying the rejected plans of the engineers in an automobile company, invert where they went wrong, and then postulate an ideal car.

It only takes a glance at Maslow's *Hierarchy of Needs* pyramid to appreciate its simplicity and how it contributes to understanding that our needs operate at different levels. The hierarchy enables us to appreciate the sequence from lower to higher needs and the different motivations that occur at each level. Obviously we need air, food, and water in a more fundamental way than we need love, affection, approval, and self-regard. The hierarchy also provides a picture of how we move up the levels. By gratifying the needs at one level, we move to the next. Without gratifying the lower motivations to some degree, we are not able to move up to the higher or meta-motivational levels.

This is the contribution of the pioneering efforts of Maslow as well as the other pioneers of the Human Potential Movement. As I have engaged, and continue to explore this area, in updating and remodeling their work, any ability I have to see further rests entirely on the fact that they first explored this territory. It is because I stand on their pioneering work in mapping self-actualization that you and I can now move more quickly through this terrain. In this, we owe much to those pioneers of human potential for their initial mapping of psychologically healthy people. It is also their work that now allows us to see things they missed in their initial modeling.

I'll offer this re-modeling in two chapters, this one and the next. In this chapter the focus will be on looking at the Needs Hierarchy and expanding it with developmental psychology. In the next chapter we will continue the metamorphosis by adding meaning to transform the pyramid allowing it to become dynamic and exploding into a volcano.

Taking Things to the Next Level

As we now step back from the *Hierarchy of Needs,* we can see several things lacking and inadequate with it as a Model. The biggest problem is its rigid and static nature. The pyramid and hierarchy metaphors implies something staid and unmoving. And because every metaphor has entailments—there are unmentioned and unconscious features which every metaphor drags with it.[1]

What are the entailments of the pyramid and hierarchy metaphors? Due to the *diagram* of a pyramid and the *metaphor* of a hierarchy, Maslow unwittingly wedded the idea, and so the feeling, of our needs, and the level of our needs, to a static and rigid image. This happened in spite of his own emphasis on process and the ever-changing nature of reality.

The truth is that Maslow was a big crusader for process, growth, systems, and the process world of continuous change. So this is a tremendous irony. After all, no one crusaded against "dichotomizing," rubricizing, and "reductionism" more than Maslow. He continuously spoke about self-actualization as not static, but a never-ending process of growth.

> "The aim of this chapter is to correct the widespread mis-understanding of self-actualization as a static, unreal, 'perfect' state in which all human problems are transcended, and in which people 'live happily forever after' in a superhuman state of serenity or ecstasy. This is empirically not so . . ." (1968, p. 115)

Yet it was, and is, the metaphorical images of a hierarchy and a pyramid that carries the entailment of something*static* and rigid. Both metaphors imply that self-actualization is *linear* (we experience the "needs" in one direction only, from lower to higher) and *non-dynamic.* After all, what is more unmoving and non-dynamic than a pyramid? So when we look at the Hierarchy of Needs, what do we see? Do you see any movement in it? Any action? Anything alive? Sadly, we have to admit that the image does not convey the process or dynamic nature of self-actualizing.

As a result, *Maslow failed to map the fluid nature* of *how our consciousness with its meaning-making powers actually influences and transforms our needs.* He failed to map human needs as fluid and moving energies. Because our instinctoid needs lack content programming they leave us open to learn what things mean as we create meanings that we live by. In this way we come to understand what things are, what works, what doesn't, and what it all means. So our lower needs do not tell the whole story. To get the full story, we have to explore our unique meanings.

Figure 18:1
*The Spiraling Energy within
and the Hidden Pyramid above*

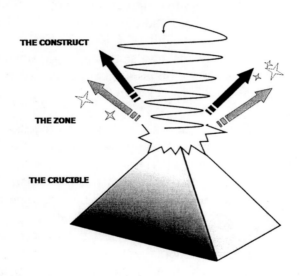

Give that after our experience of the lower needs, we invent and create meanings about these needs and how to satisfy them, how can we picture this in a dynamic way? And given that as we reflect on our meanings, we create layers of meanings as beliefs and belief systems that infiltrate our needs with our meanings, how can we picture all of this mental and emotional energy as it occurs inside the pyramid? How can we draw a picture of this movement? How can we incorporate fluidity and movement and process within the hierarchy?

To answer these questions, I have created new images of the pyramid to depict our evolving development within our hierarchy of needs.

These new images now enable us to picture the spiraling energy of our essential human instinct of meaning-making as the spiraling and swirling of our thoughts and feelings layering level upon level of meaning. Now we can see it as a visual image of fluid energies moving up and out of the top of the pyramid where it becomes an inverted and invisible pyramid above the hierarchy levels.

As noted earlier, in addition to the rigid and static nature of Maslow's model, the most important problem is that *he left meaning entirely out of the pyramid as the dynamic that informs our drives.* Yes, Maslow explicitly detailed the nature and workings of our needs showing them as our initial values, and how they work developmentally to create our hierarchy of needs. Yet he did not connect or explore the influence of the meanings that we attribute to our needs and values in his model. In this, he essentially left out the cognitive / conative/ affective dimension of our meaning-making in relation to our needs.

Yet without meaning, needs are just impulses. They are just energies without a set content or value. *Meaning gives content and value to our impulses.* And because we can give them one meaning at this moment and another meaning at another moment, our meaning-ascribing is fluid and dynamic. This changing and fluid nature of our meanings is seen in how our needs take on and express different meanings at different times. So if we ask, "What does this need mean to you?" we also have to ask, "Does it change so that at different times you experience it as meaning something else?"

The Metamorphosis of the Hierarchy of Needs
Given all of this, it is my opinion that we need to do four things for us to refine and extend Maslow's original modeling of self-actualization.

- First, we need to inject *fluidity of representation* into the model so it comes alive and dances with energy to give us a sense of what's going on. This will transform the pyramid from being static and rigid to dynamic.

- Second, we need to give *meaning, cognition, and explanatory style a central role in the self-actualization process.* This will marry need and thought, impulse and mind, and affect and consciousness to create a more holistic approach.

- Third, we need to include *the developmental process* within the Hierarchy to indicate that our meanings grow and mature over time. This will encode the fact that developing involves experiencing our needs in different ways over the lifespan as we develop from incompetence to competence, and then to mastery.

- Finally, we need to include a *dynamic, non-linear systems model* so that we can imagine how all these processes operate at the same time over the years of our lives. This will make the model systemic.

If the basic human needs are *dynamically influenced by our meanings* so that as we grow and develop in understanding, the meanings we give to our needs evolve to change the way we experience those inner drives, then the hierarchy diagram needs to transform into something more dynamic.

Figure 18:2

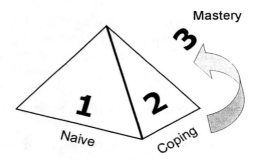

Our Needs Developmentally

To begin the metamorphosis, let's add the developmental distinction. Developmentally, we can think of experiencing our needs in at least three life stages as we actualize our thinking, emoting, and skills.

- *The naive stage*
  In our first experiences of feeling our needs, we simply feel urges that drive us. We experience these biological urges in a naive, direct, and simple way. Our needs are needs. Hunger is hunger. Feeling of cold and exposed to the elements calls for warmth and shelter. Here we experience our *driving needs* as inner urges without any cognition or

awareness about them.

- *The coping stage*
  At this stage we learn to cope with our needs as we learn how to gratify our inner impulses. As our needs are colored and filtered by our meanings and understandings so they govern our coping skills. Here our how-to knowledge as well as our lack of effective coping skills influence the quality of our coping, whether we are coping well or ineffectively whether we are making a good or poor adjustment to life.

- *The mastery stage*
  When we get a solid handle on our drives and are able to effectively satisfy them in service of our self-actualization, we master our needs so that *we have them* rather than they have us.

The Naive Stage

In growing up we first experience the deficiency needs in the innocence of a child's mind and body. At first we hardly know what we are feeling, let alone know anything about how best to gratify our drives or what they mean about us or about life. Naively we experience and express our biological urges as they are in nature untouched by mind and meanings. We simply experience our need for food, water, sleep, comfort, safety, and later friends, stimulation, etc. as mere sensory stimuli, as impulses of the mind-and-body. There's simply a tension of deficiency toward which our mind-body system is activated to reduce. We don't know what it means. We don't know what to do. We just feel needy and dependent.

In the naive stage, the drives have us. When we lack something that we need, *we feel it as an intensely demanding drive.* And so we cry and throw tantrums and demand that we get what we want! Lucky for us, as babies we are not only needy, but cute, adorable, and loveable. Otherwise, they'd kill us for being so demanding! In the basic deficiency needs, we *need* food, water, air, etc. The need screams and so we respond from that deficit. When we fulfill the need, the drive and impulse of that need vanishes. It goes away and simply disappears. Poof! It vanishes, and then we even forget how driving it was. As deficiency makes us desperate, we turn into desperate creatures. Gratification returns things to normalcy so that life feels good again. This stage begins at birth and perhaps extends to around two-years of age.

The Coping Stage

With repeated experiences of need and gratification during infancy, something new begins to happen. We develop our first ideas and understandings about our basic needs. Of course, at first our understandings are childish ideas, full of a child's way of making sense of things. Over time we are told what the impulses are and what to do about them. We think. We reflect. We learn. We develop beliefs about our urges, what they are, what they mean, how to satisfy them, what they say about us, etc. We learn to understand them in various ways.

With this infiltration of meaning into our needs, everything changes. Now we experience our needs through the filter of our meanings. As a result, our needs become increasingly governed, colored, and dominated by our meanings. They become semantically determined, and even semantically loaded. In this, we discover the power to reduce the drive of some needs and the ability to turn up the drive of other needs. *Human* motivational dynamics now begin to enter into the picture. They are driven by our cognitions as structured in our understandings, beliefs, decisions intentions, and definitions.

As we learn to cope with things, *we cope in terms of the meanings that we have created, learned, and attributed to our basic needs.* The problem at this point is that if we don't develop accurate and productive meanings, we will not develop effective coping skills. Instead we will misunderstand the urges, fear them, develop erroneous ideas and beliefs about them, what they say about us, and how to cope with them. In this, every limiting belief and toxic thought undermines our ability to cope so we become increasingly anxious and our anxiety then leads to our poor adjustment to reality. Every limiting belief operates as a frame that leashes and imprisons us.

Our first coping skills are infantile by their very nature and during their development, we mostly adopt the coping skills of those around us, of our parents and our culture. We take on ways of dealing with the world from what others around us have adopted.

All of this creates one incredible phenomenon. Namely, *our needs and impulses metamorphosize* as we embed them within meanings —our understandings of what the need is, our how-to knowledge for coping with it, our beliefs about what it is and what it means about us, our beliefs about what needs and drives are permitted and which are taboo, etc.   As our meanings frame and reframe these needs, they alter how we experience them. In this way our meanings and intentions significantly influence our

> Our *meanings may so transform the deficiency urges so they become a positive expression of our vision and mission.*

experiences with these raw and primitive urges.

So in the beginning we experience the needs as driving, powerful, and even all consuming. Then over time *our ways of thinking and our explanatory styles* about them, about ourselves, our world, and our coping skills *change how our basic needs affect us.* They change how we experience our needs.

I'll illustrate with food. If we have learned effective meanings and developed effective coping skills, we can now recognize our hunger feelings without feeling desperate. We might even *enjoy* the feeling of hunger believing perhaps that it *means* we are exercising self-control on a diet, or using it to signify protest against an injustice, fasting for a spiritual reason, or numerous other things. *Meaning now runs the show.* Now we can experience criticism or rejection and take it in stride without having a tantrum.

In this way we frame and reframe even our basic "needs" as we meta-state our experiences and give new and different meanings. What is food? How do we experience eating? For energy, for vitality, for love, to de-stress, for sociality, for reward, for love? What about sexuality— what is it for? Procreation of the race, love, fun, play, nurturing? This explains how we can meta-state our needs and frame them in a way that powerfully distorts the needs and creates a semantic overloading. Doing this leads us to experience psycho-eating, psycho-sexing, psycho-working, psycho-relaxing, etc. Our psycho-logics create our psycho-responses.

In the coping stage, our meanings transform how we experience our needs.   Sometimes this is for our benefit, sometimes it is to our detriment. Inadequate meanings lead to poor coping skills which then undermine our effectiveness. Toxic and morbid meanings create neurotic needs which then diminishes us as human beings.

The Mastery Stage

If meaning shifts our relationship with our basic needs from naive experiencing to infantile coping, then childish coping, then young adult coping, the change becomes even more dramatic as we move to the level of mastery. In fact, everything shifts dramatically at this level. As we master our meanings, intentions, understandings, etc. our meaning attributions completely transform our experiences. It can even do so to such an extent that the *lower* needs can completely lose all of its power to drive us.

We enter the stage of mastery over our basic needs as we construct ideas and understandings about the needs that are accurate, useful, and empowering. This enables us to experience them from the perspective of highly effective meanings. As young adults, we move into the coping stage so that our meanings influence how we cope with things. In the coping phase, we may experience dozens of different meanings and beliefs and so experience the "needs" from a multitude of coping perspectives.

In the mastery stage we move to a higher dimension. Here, like Mother Teresa or Nelson Mandela, *we may even choose to experience the deficiency needs of the lowest levels.* In mastery, we can experience deficiency without responding to the urges with desperation as we did when children.

> *Meanings can so transform our deficiency urges of the lower needs that they become a positive expression of our vision and mission.*

This explains how some people can deny sex, and actually experience the deficiency of that need as a sign of spirituality, or how others can deny sex in the moments of temptation and passion so they can have a fuller experience in a loving relationship of marriage. As a result, they don't feel lack or dissatisfaction, but joy and integrity in living up to a higher value. Some accept disapproval of friends and family to follow a vision, others seek disapproval of one group to validate approval in a new group.

When we learn to master our drives in terms of understanding and effective skills, we no longer live at the level of the lower needs. Now by resourcefully handling our deficiency needs, we are able to move to the higher needs— to the self-actualization needs.

Key Points in this Chapter

- The Hierarchy of Needs, while insightful on several accounts, is inadequate for portraying the dynamic nature of our human needs. That model does not convey at all the governing influence of our meanings about our needs.

- The first development of the *Hierarchy of Needs* is the addition of the developmental phases of coping and experiencing our needs. This gives us the three-faces of the pyramid and puts meaning in the center.

- As we put meaning in the center, *meaning now becomes the core of energy within us*—an energy that can blast us out the top into spiraling layers of yet more meanings, and these meanings then set the frames that, in turn, govern our needs for mastering them.

Chapter 19

THE PYRAMID'S

METAMORPHOSIS

"The ultimate of abstract, analytical thinking
is the greatest simplification possible,
i.e., the formula, the diagram, the map, the blueprint,
the schema, the cartoon . . ."
Abraham Maslow (1968, p. 209)

I began reworking the image of the hierarchy in the last chapter so that we view it as a pyramid with three faces. That occurred by adding the developmental awareness regarding how we experience our needs as they change and grow. As we learn to cope and understand our basic impulses, as we attribute various meanings to the lower needs, our experience of our needs transforms. In this way, as we include the dynamic role that meaning plays in our experience of our D-needs, we add movement and fluidity to our mapping of the basic needs.

In this chapter, I now want to do the same with the rigid and static idea of *a hierarchy*. The design here is to complete the metamorphosis so that Maslow's triangle (or pyramid) becomes a volcano.

The Challenge of Drawing
Representationally, we know that it is easy to draw or imagine *static objects* like chairs, cars, houses, trees, dogs, etc. If the object stands still almost everyone can draw or sketch it without too much difficulty. When it won't stay put, but moves about, jumps and dances, it becomes more difficult to draw it in a way to indicates movement. How do you draw movement? One way is to shift your

representation from a snapshot to a movie or animation. This allows a person to picture external dynamic experiences. How difficult is it to imagine or sketch a person running, selling, coaching, negotiating, etc.?

Yet all of this becomes even more difficult when we attempt to picture *internal dynamic experiences* like imagining, thinking, self-actualizing, creating meaning, etc.   Try it.   Or even more challenging, try to picture something entirely abstract. Picture your "instinctoids." Make a mental movie of "giving meaning to your needs and drives."   This is the challenge—representing concepts, abstractions, paradigms, and models. How can we see meaning in a drawing?

Now given all that's gone before, *what we need to model in self-actualization is meaning.* It is precisely meaning that we want to include in the model. We want to do this because the content information regarding how to fulfill our needs and how we experience our needs is supplied by our meanings, not our DNA. *It is our meanings and construction of meaning that most essentially govern our lives.* This is what I referred to in *Unleashed* as "the Construct." Yet, how do we picture that? How do we portray the meanings we give to our needs which govern our experience of motivation, feelings, and actions?

To add to the difficulty, and to make this even more challenging, as we picture meaning and meaning-making we need to do so in a fluid and dynamic way. This "knowledge" about what to eat, how much to eat, when to stop eating, how to feel regarding the feeling of hunger, and many other facets of food does not come from within. It is not "instinctive." We lack the instincts that provide that kind of detail programming. Devoid of such, we have to learn and choose. So, what does that look like? How do we see *learning* and *choosing* as active inner processes?

What most uniquely describes the human experience is this neuro-semantic freedom for *choosing* and *assuming responsibility*. We are infinitely free to think and evaluate as we desire, yet as we do so, *the meanings that we create govern, determine, and control the way our mind-body-emotion system works.*

What this means is that ultimately *we are only as free as our meanings, we are only as free as our frames.* The matrix of meaning that we create is self-reflexive to such a degree that as each of us create our own unique personal theory of mind (what we think about our mind, emotions, self, nature, etc.). Then that theory of mind governs, to a great extent, how our mind works. This is the ultimate catch-22,[1] is it not? We have to use our mind to change our mind! The "mind" we create by our thinking then influences *what* we think and *how* we think.

> We are only as free as our meanings. We are only as free as our frame.

In all of this, our needs are not absolute, but relative to the meanings we give them. Even the most biological of the needs, the survival needs, are not absolute and all-determining. We can resist them, ignore them, and even act against them. If this was not so, suicide would not be possible. Nor would eating disorders be possible. So even our biological needs are conditioned by our semantics.

Seeing Meaning as Frames
* So what does meaning look like?
* What images can we use to portray meaning and meaning-making?
* How can we picture the relationship of our meaning-making and how it influences our hierarchy of needs?

One way that we do so using the Meta-States Model is to picture our meanings as *frames*—as frames of meaning. And what is the connection between frames and meaning? I can best answer by illustrating with a conversation.

Conversational Frames and Framing
Suppose you meet a good friend on the street and when you ask how he is, he says, "I am fed up to here with arrogance." What do you say to that? Do you not intuitively ask,

> "Jim, what are you talking about? Who or what are you *referring* to?"

Before you can understand what he means you have to know his *frame of reference*. Without knowing the *point of reference* that he's using as he makes that statement it is impossible for you to know what he means or how to respond to him. So Jim says,

> "It's Larry. He is so arrogant. It really puts me off. I just don't want to be around him."

Ah, now we are getting a little more of *the reference situation* that has triggered Jim's response. So we say, "Yeah, Larry can be kind of stand-offish at times."

"No! That's not what I'm talking about!" Jim explodes. "Larry has just blown the biggest job we could have ever had as business partners, all because he had to do it his way. Damn him! He is so arrogant, never even asked me my opinion about it!"

It is the external reference situation of the context that gives meaning to *the words, tones, and behaviors.* In this, meaning is a function of context. But, of course, in your meeting now with Jim, Larry is not present and that event is no longer happening. That event is done and over. It's gone. Well, at least externally. If it still exists at all, it is happening entirely inside of Jim's mind. It is now entirely *a movie* playing on the theater of his mind—a *represented reference.* Jim has brought the outside world inside his mind-body system. That's why sometimes you have to say,

"If I could peek into the theater of your mind, what are you seeing and hearing? What's playing in there? What old DVDs and movies are you watching?"

Figure 19:1
Reference System

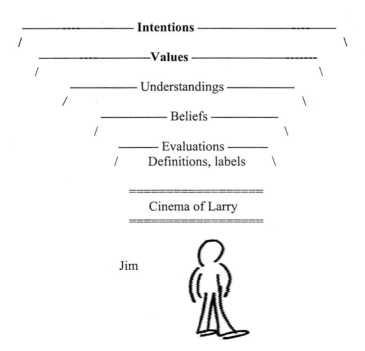

-202-

If we don't know that, we won't know the person's *mental context* out of which his or her words and actions make sense. *Contexts* are not only external and "out there"—the events that happen to which we respond. *Contexts* are also inside our thinking processes as the frames that we use inside to make sense or meaning of things. That's why, if you want to spend some time with Jim and help him through his distraught state, we would ask,

> "Jim, that sounds absolutely dreadful. It sounds like you're really upset and frustrated and maybe even angry with Larry. What does it mean that you've lost this big account?"

Doing this allows the framework to come alive as a system—as a mind-body-emotion system. It enables the layers of inner contexts to become activated.

Then whatever Jim talks about tells you some of his *higher frames of reference and frames of mind* about it all—he describes the frames that make up more of his internal contexts. And it could mean all kinds of things; loss of income, difficulty meeting payroll at work, loss of status, "failure" in losing that account, disappointment because now he cannot take his family on a long anticipated holiday, and so on.

From the first external reference to the layers and levels of internal references, "meaning" arises as the embedded frames within embedded frames, as a holistic framework of references that make up the mental contexts of a person's mind. These are *the frames* by which we make sense of things.

The Matrix as a Model of Frames

We can now use this as a way to *picture* our meanings as frames, layers of embedded frames. At least this begins to give us a way to *see* a symbolization which enables us to begin to conceptualize "meaning" as an image (Figure 19:2). Yet this still is not very fluid. So our next step will be to put in some arrows and lines indicating *the flow of energy* (mental, emotional, personal, and interpersonal energy) *as it moves through the system*. Doing this will allow the framework to come alive as a system—as a mind-body-emotion system.

In Neuro-Semantics, we do this with *The Matrix Model*.[2] Conceptually, the Matrix model is comprised of three process matrices and five *content* matrices. *The process matrices* are those processes by which we create and construct meanings. In the Matrix Model, we label these as the Meaning, Intention, and State matrices. *The content matrices* are those that indicate those ideas and concepts (as meaning frames) that we never leave home without and whcih refer to our development of "self." We call these the Self, Power, Others, Time, and World matrices.

Figure 19:2

The System Loops of the Matrix

The "System Loops" of the Matrix

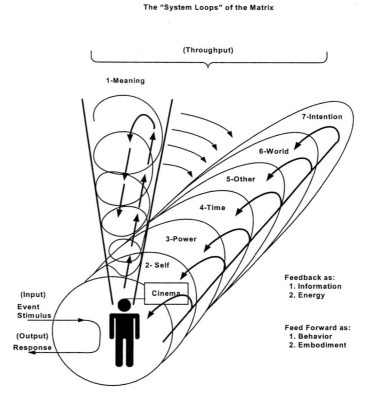

The Matrix Model enables us to *picture* concretely the feedback loops and the feed forward loops of our meaning-making and meaning-performance. In *feeding back* to ourselves, we draw conclusions, create beliefs, make decisions and do other meta-cognitive things in our mind-body system. This takes us *up* as we set frames about frames, beliefs about beliefs, ideas about ideas, feelings about feelings. This *feed back* describes the way we meta-state ourselves, level upon level, as we use our self-reflexive consciousness.

The converse is the feed forward process. In feeding information forward in our mind-body system we create emotions as we get our body to feel and act on the ideas in our heads. This is the way we transfer the contents of the mind into the muscle programs and movements of the body. It is a mind-to-muscle process of transfer and incorporation.[3]

Now we have a much more fluid and dynamic model that allows us to picture the processes of meaning-making and meaning-performing. Obviously because I'm only using flat 2-dimensional diagrams in this book, you will have to use your imagination to see them as 3-dimensional. Once you do that, you can then allow them to flash on and off as *information* comes into the system and *energy* (movement and action) flows out of the mind-body system.

Information in—energy out describes the heart of meaning-making in our mind-body system. As we input data, we process that data as information. Then we continue to process it up all the levels of the mind. We process the data as beliefs, decisions, values, identities, and so on. Then we output that information as we "metabolize" our layers of thoughts and beliefs into energy, as emotional energy, somatic energy, and eventually as the energy of speech and behavior that outwardly expresses our meanings.

Figure 19:3

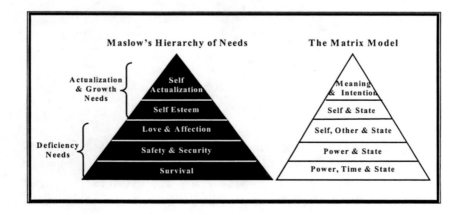

The Holography of the Matrix
The next thing is to imagine the Matrix model as *a hologram*. Imagine it as a living, moving, breathing system (a mind-body-emotion system) that responds as information goes in (data and information which then becomes ideas, beliefs, decisions, expectations, demands, permissions, taboos, etc.) and that then responds with the energy of motion, emotion, and behavior as it comes out.

Mapping a Dynamic Pyramid
Tentatively mapping Maslow's hierarchy of needs onto the matrices of the Matrix Model enables us to recognize where the lower and higher needs fit into the Matrix model (Figure 19:3).

Each need obviously involves some *State*.   As we move up the levels, giving *meaning* to the needs and to the five content matrices (Self, Power, Others, Time, and World), we move from *Time* (when) and *Power* (how) at the lower levels, to the *World* (where), then to *Self* and *Others* (who and with whom). These take us through the deficiency needs. Finally we arrive at the growth or expressive needs of self-actualization, that is, into the *Meaning* and *Intention* matrices where we seek for meaningfulness as we find and express our highest intentions and potentials.

Making the Pictures Jump and Dance
If static metaphors invite us to mentally map our development statically, the solution is to replace them with *dynamic* metaphors.[4] So the next step is to transform the static Needs Hierarchy so that it uses the fluid and dynamic Matrix model and so incorporate non-linear processes in the model. Doing this enables us to map what was rigidly static in a way so that we can imagine it becoming dynamically alive and fluid. It now begins to become a fluid, ever-in-flux and ever-in-change holoarchy, a set of embedded frames within frames making up the Matrix of our meaning frames.

Using this enables us to begin to see symbolically the dynamic mind-body processes. We can now begin to map the multiple dimensions of the needs hierarchy pyramid onto the Matrix model. We can now let the hierarchy morph into a holoarchy.

Holoarchy

A holoarchy? What is a holoarchy? This term refers to a structure of *holons*—wholes that are parts of larger wholes. In a holoarchy, every frame is itself a whole *and* a part of some larger whole which makes the entire structure a set of embedded *frames*.

One of the best descriptions of *holons* and *holoarchy* comes from Ken Wilbur (1996).

> "Arthur Koestler coined the term 'holon' to refer to an entity that is itself a *whole* and simultaneously a *part* of some other whole. And if you start to look closely at the things and processes that actually exist, it soon becomes obvious that they are not merely wholes, they are also parts of something else. They are whole/parts, they are holons.
>
> For instance, a whole atom is part of a whole molecule, and the whole molecule is part of a whole cell, and the whole cell is part of a whole organism, and so on. Each of these entities is neither a whole nor a part, but a whole/part, a holon. . . . Everything is basically a holon of some sort. . . . There are only whole/parts in all directions, all the way up, all the way down. . . . At no point do we have the whole, because there is no whole, there are only whole/parts." (p. 20)

Figure 19:4
Whole/Part Structures — Holons

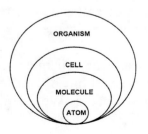
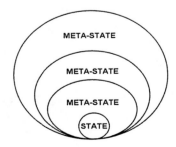

Figure 19:5

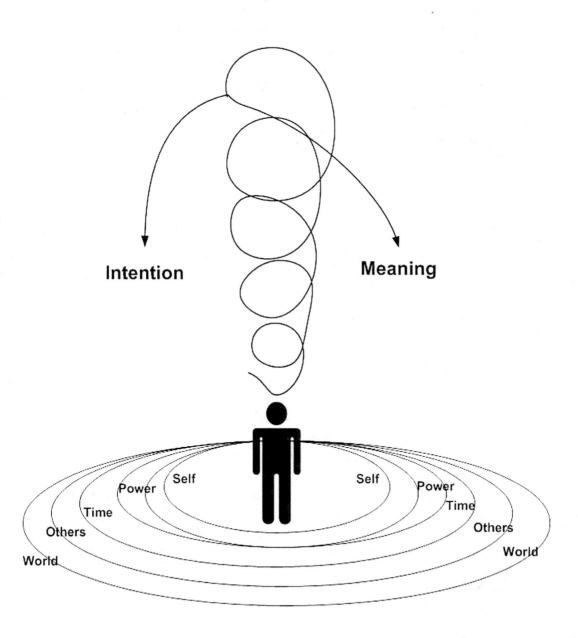

The difficulty with picturing this is that we have to think of *dynamic energy in flux* rather than about static objects. I typically draw the swirling and spiraling thoughts and feelings of it *as a whirlwind,* as spiraling thoughts-and-feelings going round and round. I do that by drawing *spirals* which look like a tornado, or an ebby of water, going round and round. In these images we can actually *see* what looks like a structure even though it is a dynamic structure. We can even take a picture of the spiraling energy of a whirlwind or an ebby of water. Yet while you can see the looping or spiraling forces, if you tried to grab a handful of it, what would you grasp in your hand? A handful of air or water?

Figure 19:6
The Spiraling of Thoughts and Emotions

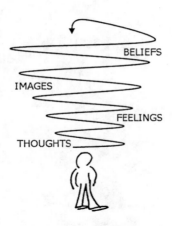

You would get a handful of nothing—nothing other than the content that's already there. The dynamic structure of the spiraling movement is not made up of anything other than the "stuff" that's already there—yet those components are not put together in a static way. The structure itself is *dynamic,* and is structured dynamically, it exists as an emergent property of the system. So we do not have a static structure, we have *structuring* as a process.

So with our mind-body-emotion system that goes round and round an idea, experience, or event. In this sense, we call *meaning* into existence at every moment as we think-and-feel it in our body. In fact, it doesn't exist apart from our thinking-and-feeling processes.

Our human needs share this dynamic nature. If you tried to grab a handful of your meanings, there's nothing there except in the experience of other processes—thinking, feeling, and physiology responses (your mind-body-emotion system). What seems so solid and real on the inside (i.e., your meanings that you hold about some thing) arises as only *an emergent property*. It arises as the winds of your thoughts and emotions spiral round and round. It seems real. It feels real. Yet it is an internal phenomenon—a phenomenon that exists in the world of mind or communication.

All of this becomes real in our body. There it is given substance. If the thought-and-emotion is realizable, then it is in the neurological dimension of our neuro-semantic mind-body-emotion system that we materialize it. If you believe you have innate worth as a human being unconditionally, you will be sending commands to your nervous system which will be making this real in your walk, talk, face, voice, breathing, etc. Of course, everything is not realizable. You can believe in Santa Claus traveling the entire world and visiting every home in one night all you want, but that will not make it so in the external world. At best it will only get you to beg for a Christmas tree and get up very early on December 25 to rush into the living room.

As *meaning* emerges, our body naturally and inevitably seeks to "make it real" (realize or actualize) it in actions, behaviors, skills, and muscle memory. That's why we *feel* our meanings / emotions in our bodies. When something is meaningful to us, *we experience that meaning as an emotion* and we feel an urge to move out [e(x)-motion] from where we are.

The Invisible Pyramid
Since Maslow failed to incorporate *meaning construction and attribution* as well as explanatory style into his Needs Hierarchy model, except as one of the *being*-needs or *being*-values, how and where can we now add that to his model?

What I have done to address this is to open up the top of the pyramid to allow the swirling and spiraling thoughts that we learn or create to spiral and layer upward as the energizing power in the pyramid. It is also above and beyond, where we experience our highest needs—the self-actualization needs. Once we gratify the lower needs, and are ready to jet propel into the higher needs, life as a self-actualizer begins. It occurs as it were, at a whole new level *up and out of* the pyramid altogether.

Representationally this puts the higher needs at the very top of the pyramid—*bursting forth out* of the pyramid. We can now see the top of the pyramid opening up allowing the unique individuality of each person to pursue the cognitive, aesthetic, order, and every other self-actualization needs. As we begin to imagine this, lo and behold—*the pyramid becomes a volcano!*

Then above and beyond that wild area of the *higher growth needs* we can see an invisible Pyramid which is above it and inverted so that it is upsidedown to it. I've put this as *an invisible pyramid* to symbolically represent the meaning/intention matrix that we activate every time we use our cognitive unconscious to construct all kinds of meanings about our lower needs. It is in this ongoing process of attributing meaning that endows our needs with specific content.

All of this portrays dynamic energies inside the previous static pyramid and enables us to represent the fluidity and plasticity of meaning which evolves as we grow and develop. Now we know that what's inside is not merely our needs, but our needs-as-filtered-by-our-meanings.

Seeing the Matrix of Self-Actualization
If we put all of this together, what do we have here that we can see? What can we now picture? How can we now portray the self-actualizing processes with these images?

See a person, a human being with a spark of energy inside —demanding needs like an engine of impulses pulsating at the center and pushing the person to act to fulfill the basic needs for food, water, air, sleep, safety, security, love, affection, etc. See the person's bubble of energy growing and developing as he learns new and effective ways to fulfill his needs. See her, over time, rising up in her mind, spiraling up in thoughts and feelings, giving meaning to these needs and impulses. Picture the person building more and more meaning frames as beliefs and understandings about our innate human needs. And as these habituate, imagine her within a network of embedded frames—a matrix.

Figure 19:7
When the Pyramid becomes a Volcano
The spiraling up of thoughts and feelings
as they move up the levels
of our meaning making matrix

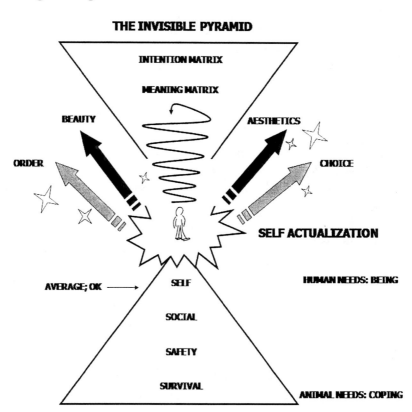

THE INVISIBLE PYRAMID

This matrix is the world of meaning that we live in and operate from. It colors our world. It is also a living, breathing and ever-developing matrix, one forever in flux.

Now watch, as you would a movie, and see this person gratify his lower needs—the survival, safety, social, and self needs and moving above and beyond those deficiency needs to the self-actualization needs. Picture her entering into the higher realm of meaning-making so that she experiences and formulates her understandings of justice, fairness, truth, love, beauty,

> The self-actualizing person is not the ordinary person with something extra added, it is rather *the ordinary person with nothing taken away.*

contribution, time, etc. As she does, it endows her with a rich sense of the meaningfulness of life activating her warp drive for heading for the stars.

See her becoming all that she can become as she identifies and unleashes her potentials. Perhaps her dream is that of balancing home life as a wife and mother with her career as a manager in a marketing company. What will actualize her best meaning in that context? What flow states will be most important to her? What will be the peak experiences that she will step into from time to time?

If a self-actualized person is one who is able to step into the moment and engage fully with another person, thing, or experience, then our mental movie will see the person developing through various stages of life, stretching, getting feedback, learning, curiously exploring, loving, extending self, and experiencing more and more peak experiences.

Figure 19:8

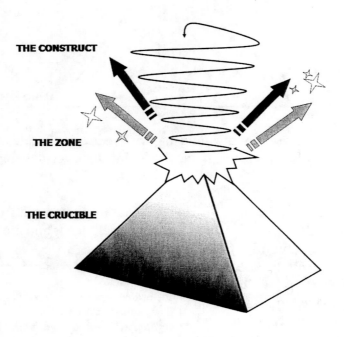

Key Points in this Chapter

• *Self-Actualization Psychology* adds a whole new dimension to psychology enabling us to catch a vision of people at their best. It creates the positive psychology that Maslow envisioned. And that enables us to stand in awe of all human beings and their potentials.

• Standing on the shoulder of the key developer of the Human Potential Movement, Abraham Maslow, we can now see how to shift from the linear, static, and rigid images and shift to more dynamic and fluid images. We can begin to see *meaning as frames*—a holoarchy of frames with information entering and energy exiting the system.

• All of this allows us now to picture meaning as a fluid and moment-to moment creation. It gives us a fluid and living Matrix of frames, a holoarchy of frames, and an expansive pyramid / volcano that opens up for all kinds of new possibilities.

End Notes

1. A *Catch-22* refers to a self-contained structure that imprisons one inside of a conceptual world where there is no solution. It is a negative and toxic double-bind that creates the sense of a no-win situation, often times expressed as the feeling of "damned if I do; damned if I do not."

2. There is a lot to say about *the Matrix model.* For a full presentation of that model, see the book by that title, *The Matrix Model* (2003). Also for an exploration of how the content matrices make explicit the development of "self" over the lifespan, see the article "The Matrix of the Matrix" on www.neurosemantics.com.

3. See *Achieving Peak Performance* (Hall, L. Michael, 2007). This book deals with the mind-to-muscle processes in Neuro-Semantics and how we transfer information so that we actually implement what we know.

4. George Lakoff and Mark Johnson, *Metaphors We Live By* (1990) and *Philosophy in the Flesh.*

PART II:

THE MOVEMENT

Chapter 20

THE FIRST

HUMAN POTENTIAL

MOVEMENT

"Humanistic psychology was a great experiment, but it is basically a failed experiment in that there is no humanistic school of thought in psychology, no theory that would be recognized as a philosophy of science." (Cunningham 1985, in Schulz, 1992, p. 18)

T he *Human Potential Movement* (HPM) exploded on the scene in the 1960s creating a new excitement about psychology, human development, and unlimited potentials. Launched by Maslow as "Third Force Psychology" and picked up by Rogers, May, and others, that movement promised to change the face of psychology. And to a great extent it did and the positive consequences of that change continues with us today. And yet that movement pretty much fizzled out by the late 1980s and seems to have completely disappeared in the 1990s.[1] So what's the story of that dynamic movement? And more specifically —

- How could something as dynamic and powerful as the Human Potential Movement vanish, or disappear, or die?
- What undermined "the Third Force" so that it failed to become a School of Psychology with departments in every major university as is the case with Behaviorism and Psychoanalysis?

Obviously there must have been some weakness or vulnerability, or perhaps several of them, for something so exciting, so vibrant, and so dynamic as the Human Potential Movement to disappear. What made the *Human Potential Movement* vulnerable so that it was unable to sustain its vision and create a form that would endure?

While the movement had a great vision, had created a paradigm shift in psychology, and began with a new model of human nature (the Hierarchy of Prepotency of Human Needs), and while it launched dozens, perhaps even scores of new therapies, the zestful enthusiasm of the movement that arose in the 1960s and exploded in the 1970s, ran out of steam by the turn of the twenty-first century. What explains this or how did this happen? Whatever happened to the Human Potential Movement? Where did it go?

The First Human Potential Movement
Given the premises of self-actualization and the work of Abraham Maslow in the late 1930s and through the 1940s and 1950s, *the Human Potential Movement* (HPM) began to take form. Yet it wasn't until the 1950s and 1960s that a sufficient number of people on the ground level had accumulated so that it blossomed fully in the late 1960s. Many people were involved in this movement as it focused on actualizing human potential and the best in human nature. Maslow designated the movement "the Third Force" in psychology, the first force was Freud's Psychoanalysis and the second was Watson and Skinner's Behaviorism.

Maslow's *Hierarchy of Needs* and *Toward a Psychology of Being* popularized the human potential movement, and even today is studied in psychology, management, leadership, business, human resources, motivation, etc. Maslow also popularized it with his descriptions of "peak experiences" and the idea of actualizing one's self holistically. And by the 1960s the time arrived for these ideas to take hold in the general population.

In 1962, Richard Price and Michael Murphy purchased the property at Big Sur, California and started Esalen as a Growth Center. Their goal was not focused on the psychological, but on the spiritual and religious—namely, bringing Eastern philosophy and religion to the West. Accordingly they welcomed any and every technique that they could find and that anyone offered as a way to actualize human potential. In this way Esalen became the Mecca of the Human Potential Movement in the 1960s, welcoming all kinds of non-verbal and body techniques (psycho-drama, Feldenkrais, Rolfing, Gestalt, etc.) and all kinds of Eastern processes (meditation, etc.) and other things for increased and expanded awareness (Gestalt "contact" and integration, encounter groups or T-groups, etc.).

So in the 1960s and 70s, Esalen became the Mecca of the Human Potential Movement leading the way for the creation of more than 200 "Growth Centers" across the United States and another 200 around the world.[2]

In fact, in 1964 George Leonard caught the imagination of the nation with a lengthy article on the movement in *Look* Magazine. Then Will Schutz wrote the book that captured the wide range of things going on at Esalen as a "Growth Center" of the movement with his best selling book, *Joy* (1967). With this initiation of the Third Force in psychology, a paradigm shift was occurring in the very premises of human nature—premises that had dominated modern psychology for more than half a century.

Those early pioneers in the Human Potential Movement didn't believe that people were just stimulus-response mechanisms who could be helped and fixed through the conditioning offered by Learning Theory (Behaviorism). Nor did they believe that people were driven by powerful anti-social urges and the Freudian instincts of sex, aggression, death, competition, etc. (Psychoanalysis). Instead, they viewed human nature as creative, driven by positive intentions, seeking to evolve and fulfill unique aptitudes, and that people are able and willing to assume responsibility for themselves, and move to a place where they transcended themselves and live for bigger, and higher meanings.

Key Leaders in the Movement
Along with Abraham Maslow was *Carl Rogers* who developed Client-Centered Therapy. It was Rogers who identified the key concepts and "tools" (if there were any) in the Human Potential Movement as he spoke about the power of *accurate empathy, unconditional positive regard,* and *authenticity* for facilitating healing and growth of the human person. These are, he said, the critical dynamics that facilitate healing in effective therapy. He also introduced the non-directive tools as the way to initiate organic growth that would call forth a person's potentials.

Rollo May, Viktor Frankl, and *Erich Fromm* along with many others in the area of Humanistic Existentialism focused on the critical importance of meaning, love, will, and personal responsibility. This introduced the focus on *ego-strength* and *responsibility* which gave further impetuous to the Human Potential Movement. It reflected the spirit of the times also in that numerous other psychoanalysts were creating new forms of therapy that included much of the same focus especially the importance of the present, personal responsibility, and accurate cognitive mapping. *Albert Ellis* created RET (Rational Emotive Therapy), *Aaron Beck* created Cognitive therapy, and *William Glasser* created Reality Therapy and Control Theory.

In Family Systems Therapy, *Virginia Satir* contributed her ideas about "people-making" and then served as the first director of training at the Esalen institute (1966). *Fritz Perls* who created Gestalt Therapy from the Gestalt Psychology Wertheimer, Kohler, and Koffka, emphasized the importance of challenging a client to come into sensory presence to the moment. For Perls and Gestalt Therapy the healing factors are the now of the present, awareness, contact, and fully integrating experiences. *Roberto Assagioli* contributed the trans-personal psychology of Psycho-Synthesis stressing integration and synthesis between polar opposites and dis-identification with expressions of oneself.

In these forms, and many others, the *Human Potential Movement* exploded on the scene creating an entirely new direction for psychology and a new paradigm of human nature and potential. This psychology and movement went under several labels—Growth Psychology, Third Force, Self-Actualization Psychology, and *Humanistic Psychology*. For Maslow the focus was not to eliminate or replace the previous psychologies, but to add correctives to certain errors and misdirections. He wanted to keep what was valuable in both Behaviorism and Psychoanalysis and take psychology in a new positive direction through studying psychologically healthy people.[3]

Many, if not most of the leaders also mostly wanted to move beyond focusing on hurts, dysfunctions, and problems, people at their worst, to focusing on people at their best. They sought to shift focus to the qualities of psychologically *healthy, fully functioning people* and all that would then open up, and the processes for facilitating growth development.

All of those who founded and developed the Human Potential Movement created a truly dynamic legacy. The movement launched a great many dynamic psychotherapies and practices. And most of them directly sought to study the best examples of human experience to use those examples as the basis for theorizing about human nature.

Other Simultaneous Developments
In the same time frame and atmosphere, the Cognitive Psychology movement was emerging. In 1956 Noam Chomsky landed a fatal blow to traditional Behaviorism with his research into linguistics when he created a new model of linguistics called *Transformational Grammar*. Proposing that we are born with a "language acquisition device" that programs us for a language readiness, he argued that this is how we enter into the symbolic dimension. Chomsky's Transformational Grammar revolutionized linguistics, defeated Behaviorism, and launched the Cognitive Psychology Movement.

At the same time George Miller and his associates contributed to the launching of the Cognitive Psychology movement that was revolutionizing many fields—psychology, the neuro-sciences, artificial intelligence, etc. From Miller's research and famous paper, "The Magic Number $7^{+/-2}$", he along with Galanter and Pribram created a new model, the TOTE model as a way to model how we think within "the black box" of our mind, something that Behaviorism not only avoided, but said could not be done.

Ten years later a young professor, John Grinder, and a young university student, Richard Bandler, used the TOTE model and Transformational Grammar to study and model two of the key leaders of the Human Potential Movement—Fritz Perls and Virginia Satir. As they did, they discovered their patterns of communication by which they could replicate their "magic" with people. As they made their communication patterns explicit, they created a new communication model which they called "the Meta-Model of language in therapy" (1976, 1977, *The Structure of Magic, Volumes I and II*). And in doing so, they also used many of the insights of anthropologist and systems thinker Gregory Bateson, another key leader within the Human Potential Movement who was the last scholar in residence at Esalen.

The Models of the Movement
The essential and core model of the Human Potential Movement was Maslow's *Hierarchy of Needs*. With his pyramid of needs, he popularized the idea of self-actualization as a higher and yet biologically-based human need. His hierarchy distinguished lower and higher needs and introduced some of the first uses of the word *meta*—meta-needs, meta-motivation, meta-pathology, etc.[4]

Undoubtedly, the central strength, power, and charm of the *Human Potential Movement* in psychology during the 1960s rested in how it shifted the focus from studying sick people to studying and modeling healthy people. This was *the paradigm shift* of the Human Potential Movement. Maslow, Rogers, Frankl, May, and others shifted the focus on "fully functioning humans" (Rogers) or "full humanness" (Maslow). Maslow studied those who were well-adjusted, had plenty of ego strength, who were not neurotic, or unable to cope with life's demands, but those who greatly contributed, pioneered new creative ideas, and who regularly experienced "peak experiences"—in a word, self-actualizers. At that time, all of this was absolutely revolutionary.

Yet the Needs Hierarchy as a model gives us almost nothing to actually do for ourselves or with others. In this it was left to the creativity of the people of this movement to engage in a wild experimentation to find things that would facilitate self-actualization. With the publication of *Motivation and Personality* (1954) Maslow became recognized internationally and a pioneer thinker in psychology and that put self-actualization on the world's map. This also began the fascination about the farther reaches of human nature.

Key Points in this Chapter
*   The first Human Potential Movement arose from the discoveries of Maslow in the 1940s with his discoveries from modeling self-actualizers that shifted the psychology paradigm from the dark side to the bright side of human nature.

*   When the Human Potential Movement began it was a time of wild and chaotic searchings as people began pushing out the limits and boundaries for this new psychology. Esalen, the first growth center, led the way for the moment as it became the home for psycho-drama, body therapies, eastern religions and meditation, the use of psychodelic drugs, the encounter group, and scores of new ways to actualize human potential.

*   Yet as exciting as the movement was, it didn't last. It also did not create a lasting legacy as a full-fledge model of the bright side of human nature.

End Notes:

1. At least this true for English speaking countries. Juan Lafarga Corona, a colleague of Carl Rogers who translated most of Rogers' work into Spanish began a "Human Development Movement"in Mexico. Lafarga is a psychologist and Jesuit priest, inspired by Rogers and others, has continued to this day to lead conferences and trainings in Mexico. Today much of the Human Development Movement there continues the focus on Gestalt, Client-centered therapy, and yet it includes many, many other therapies, in fact, any that promote the development of the human condition.

2. Third Force Psychology was officially "named" the Human Potential Movement in 1965 by Michael Murphy and George Leonard (Kripal, 2007, p. 207).

3. The term *meta* refers to what is higher, it originated from the Greek word meaning "above, beyond, and about." Maslow and Bateson are apparently the two seminal thinkers who began using the term in the 1930s. And given that they knew each other and spoke with each other and had numerous connections in Ruth Benedict and Margaret Mead, I have not seen any evidence for who first began using the term.

4. Maslow called the Third Force *epi*-Freudian psychology and *epi*-Behaviorism.

Chapter 21

THE COLLAPSE

OF THE HUMAN POTENTIAL

MOVEMENT

If we begin in the 1960s and 1970s with all of the excitement of the Human Potential Movement and then fast forward a couple of decades, we suddenly discover something truly surprising. When we stop and look around to locate that movement, it is not to be found. It has disappeared from sight.

- So, where is it? What happened to it?
- What was left when all the furry and chaos of the initial movement had settled?

The answer is complicated involving many different aspects. Much of the steam of excitement was as much part of the temper of the times, what with the anti-establishment, anti-war, and the drug culture of American in the 1960s and 1970s. There were also some early charismatic leaders—James Pike, Fritz Perls, etc.

Yet when the ephemeral disappeared, much still survived and actually continues to this day. Some of it proved valid and replicable even without the need for charismatic personalities or the need to "believe" in a system. Central to what survived were the ideas of becoming psychologically healthy persons, the farther reaches of excellence in human nature, the positive psychology of being at one's best, and modeling self-actualizers.

- So what happened? What caused its demise?
- How did it collapse as a cultural phenomena?

Problems in the Movement

Why did the Human Potential Movement with its new lease on human psychology, its focus on the bright-side of human nature, and its paradigm shift from studying sick people to studying healthy people *disappear as a movement?* While this movement took a very positive and optimistic position about human possibilities somehow, as a movement, it did not survive. What follows here are some of the reasons, causes, and contributing factors that I believe were involved.

Criticisms of the HPM began to occur very early and did not seem to let up throughout its history. In the 1970s and 1980s the *Human Potential Movement* was criticized for being too idealistic, too individualistic, too narcissistic, too mystical, too abstract, and too "spiritual." This was especially true of Esalen and the Growth Centers. Lacking, and even disdaining, the rigors of the scientific approach of quantifying results, operationalizing terms, and inventing processes and techniques that could be replicated, while the movement did awaken many to the untapped potentials within and spurred many new forms of psychology, primarily it failed to specify the processes of how self-actualization occurs.

Even from within the movement there were criticisms. For example, both Maslow and Rollo May came to strongly criticized Esalen for being superficial, overly-optimistic, and anti-intellectual.

Duane and Sydney Schultz in *A History of Modern Psychology* (1992, fifth edition) described some of the problems with the Human Potential Movement.

> "Despite these symbols and characteristics of a school of thought, humanistic psychology did not actually become a school. That was the judgment of humanistic psychologists themselves at a 1985 meeting, nearly three decades after the movement began."

> "Humanistic psychology was a great experiment, but it is basically a failed experiment in that there is no humanistic school of thought in psychology, no theory that would be recognized as a philosophy of science." (Cunningham 1985, p. 18)

> "Why didn't humanistic psychology become part of the mainstream of psychological thought? One reason is that

most humanistic psychologists were in private clinical practice, rather than at universities."

In the massive 2001 book, *The Handbook of Humanistic Psychology* (Schneider, Bugental, and Pierson, editors), Eugene Taylor and Frederick Martin wrote about the problems with the Humanistic Psychology Movement and spoke of it in terms of it dissipating into a myriad of forms, many so radical that they became absorbed into the psychotherapeutic counterculture and then fragmented into numerous streams. Even back then numerous speakers spoke about humanistic psychologists as dissipating their attention across too many subject areas.

The Vulnerabilities of the Movement

While there were many positive and attractive things about the new emphasis on the bright side of human nature, *the Human Potential Movement,* and even the idea of self-actualization, had its own problems. There were several problems that made it vulnerable— to falling apart—weaknesses that led to its demise.

1) Vagueness

First among these problems was the lofty, vague, abstract, and even mystical and "spiritual" language that the Human Potential Movement developers used. They spoke and wrote

> The Human Potential Movement awakened people with its tremendous visions of new possibilities for people, but could not deliver on its promises.

about focusing on "experiencing," "being with a client," transcending, cosmic consciousness, unconditional positive regard, mystic experiences, oceanic feelings, and shifting the therapist and client relationship to an equal partnership. And while, these inspiring terms contain great ideas that enliven; empirically and scientifically they are problematic. After all, what do these ideas empirically look and sound like? What does "unconditional positive regard" look like in actual behavior?[1]

At the time these concepts powerfully counterbalanced treating clients as objects to be studied or fixed, rather than people to be respected. In this, the Human Potential Movement *re-humanized* therapy, education, business, and even management. It reintroduced the *human person* and the *humane* back into these fields. Yet its concepts were not scientifically well-formed, but stated in language far too mystical and spiritual. Rogers' focus especially was upon *the person*, what it meant to be a person, and the variables that support and develop personhood.

Even "self-actualization," as a great vision was not described in very precise behavioral terms.[1]   If "self-actualizing" speaks about realizing, discovering, and making actual the rich potentials and possibilities of our talents, aptitudes, and inherent passions, how do we do that? If actualizing is probing deep or high enough to discover the things that activate our excitement and push us forward to evoke our best from within, what processes facilitate this?

2) Too Wedded to Therapy
The vagueness problem extended also to the confusion of self-actualization with therapy.   Given their backgrounds in psychotherapy, Rogers, Perls, Satir, etc. used the new self-actualization psychology for *therapy*—for dealing with dysfunctional people and systems, people who need to be healed and fixed. By contrast, with Maslow's experience in the university, he focused more on the psychology of healthy and extraordinary people, and then toward the end of his life, on business. Yet he also primarily wrote and spoke about self-actualization in the context of therapy and, to a certain extent, tied self-actualization and the Human Potential Movement to therapy. This prevented the new psychology from finding its ideal population.[2]

3) Lack of a Single Specific Technique
While there were lots of experiences, the movement as such did not have a focus point technique, one for public consumption and one for branding "self-actualization." In this respect, the movement lacked any specific process or technology to carry out its visions. Yes, it had the vision for human wholeness, but no specific methodology. The movement certainly inspired a whole generation of people about a new exciting hope of a new positive and generative psychology. What it lacked was the necessary technologies to deliver on those hopes.

To complicate this further, because Rogers popularized his client-centered approach as *non-directive,* he did not believe in, nor did he want, "techniques." For him, techniques were de-humanizing and to that extent he viewed them as in conflict with self-actualization. For him, techniques implied *doing something to a person* and so he considered them manipulative. If there were any techniques, they were exhausted in the process of "giving positive regard to the client."

The primary "technique" (if we can even call it that) within the Human Potential Movement was the *encounter group,* that is, the sensitivity training groups (the T-groups) which were popularized at Esalen and other growth centers.[3]   And to that end, the Human Potential Movement used all kinds of things to facilitate the encounter from in-your-face type of confrontations, to drugs, to group therapy, to gestalt therapy, to family systems therapy, to open sexuality, to eastern meditations, etc.   Yet the Human Potential Movement had no explicit patterns for guiding a person in achieving self-actualization which identified or branded the movement.

In my opinion, this non-directive approach opposing techniques created a significant problem for the movement and was one of the contributing factors for why the movement did not survive. Ultimately, the strong dislike of "techniques" as directive patterns worked against its own success.   This meant that there was no ritualized process or pattern facilitating self-actualization.

How did the non-directive approach undermine the movement? It was problematic because we need specific processes in order to translate our ideas and visions into action to unleash potentials. Without this, while the movement could inspire, it was unable to directly guide the self-actualization process. It could awaken people with visions of new possibilities, but could not predictably deliver on its promises.

I began to realize this when I asked myself, "What does the Hierarchy of Needs actually tell me to *do* to self-actualize? How does it actually guide me to experience and actualize my capabilities? Except for the generic requirement that I fulfill my lower needs, what other direction does the pyramid offer?" When I later asked many others about this, they also sensed a dead-end with the model. "How does a person self-actualize using the Needs Hierarchy?"

Rogers offered three factors for transformation—accurate empathy, unconditional positive regard, and authenticity. These factors are obviously important for the therapist. Yet *how* do we turn these traits or attitudes into specific processes or pattern? What ritualized processes can we use to guide a person in empathetic behavior? *How* do we teach and train new practitioners in effectively *performing* these concepts and principles?

And does it mean that if we are being authentic, empathetic, and giving unconditional positive regard that people will *automatically and inevitably* self-actualize and unleash their potentials? We now know that it does not. And it was this very thing that greatly troubled Maslow as noted in the chapter on Recovering Meaning (Chapter 8). The process may be organic, but it is not *that* organic that it works without our effort and discipline. Self-actualization is a chosen way of living.

Psychoanalysis had its ritualized process of the couch and free association; Transactional Analysis (TA) had its three ego-states (Parent, Adult, Child) as a dynamic visual model as well as its transaction lines and Okay/ Not Okay scripts. But the Human Potential Movement did not have any technique that people could dependably use to actualize their potentials. Retreats to sulpher hot tubs, drugs, group nudity, esoteric eastern practices were fascinating and seductive, but not easily replicable in daily life.

4) The Plethora of Techniques

It may seem contradictory at first that while there was no singular or specific technique for actualizing one's self, there were at the same time scores and scores of "techniques," or at least processes that were used. Will Schutz, who played a significant role at Esalen, wrote *Joy* in 1967 as a book that described many of the techniques. In fact, he called these techniques "human potential techniques." In the following list he included a great many things in his list and ended it with psychoanalysis of all things![4]

> Encounter, Gestalt therapy, Rolfing, transactional analysis, bioenergetics, transcendental meditation, psychosynthesis, Arica, relaxation breathing, T'ai Chi, Aikido, the Alexander technique, Feldenkrais, Trager, jogging, fasting, Yoga, Fisher-Hoffman, scientology, primal therapy, Ram Dass (LSD), est, imagery, psychodrama, rebirthing, strength bombardment technique, Gestalt hot chair technique. psychoanalysis.

In the end, not only did Rogers speak against the over-use of all of these varied techniques, but so did Maslow (1970, p. 11-12).

5) Wild and Rugged Individualism

Something else needs to be mentioned. The Human Potential Movement was as much "a child of the sixties" as were the Beatles, the Rolling Stones, the Beachboys, the counter-culture movement, the anti-war movement (the Vietnam War), and many other cultural expressions of that era in California and American culture.

And as such, *a wild individualism* within the movement, and even among the leaders, worked against the key leaders working together to create a unified vision and effectively working together. You can see this in its rawest form in Fritz Perl's "Gestalt Prayer."

> "I do my thing, and you do your thing.
> I am not in this world to live up to your expectations
> And you are not in this world to live up to mine.
> You are you and I am I,
> And if by chance we find each other, it's beautiful.
> If not, it can't be helped."

It was this kind of raw individualism that led to charges of the HPM being a monument to Narcissism and the "Me Decade" of the 1970s. As a consequence of this and some other factors, no single leader stepped into Maslow's shoes when he died in 1970. In my research I was actually shocked to find in Will Schutz's work, *Joy* (1967) and *The Human Element* (1994) that there was only a brief hand-wave to Maslow, Rogers, and May as psychologists of the Human Potential Movement.

In my research, I was shocked to find in Will Schutz's work, *Joy* (1967) and *The Human Element* (1994) that there was only a brief hand-wave as it were to Maslow, Rogers, and May as "the psychologists" of the Human Potential Movement. In fact, Schutz gave no recognition that the movement was launched a decade before he got involved or that Maslow had been modeling self-actualizers for almost 30 years.

In fact, to read Will Schutz, you would think that he invented it all! At one of my first Self-Actualization Workshops a participant was sure that Schutz was the key leader of the HPM, not Maslow. There is hardly a word about Maslow, Rogers, May, Bugental, Shostrum, or the rest of the first generation leaders in his books. It was as if it would take something away from Schutz to mention the giants upon whose shoulders he stood.

Even in reading Carl Rogers (*Becoming a Person, A Way of Being*, etc.) there is hardly a reference to Maslow. In fact, Rogers quotes ten times more often from Sigmund Freud than from Abraham Maslow. What explains this lack of reference or this inability to acknowledge sources and his seeming need to speak and act as if the new vision in psychology began with him other than the raw individualism that seemed to be rampant in that time.[5]

6) *Splintered into a Hundred Fragments*

The bottom line is that the Third Force inspired all kinds of new developments, therapies, coaching programs, and consulting processes. It gave birth to many fields and disciplines that are thriving today. And yet strangely, the majority of people in those fields are *unaware* of the role of the Human Potential Movement in their history. These include NLP, Ericksonian therapy, Brief Psychotherapy, Cognitive psychology, Reality therapy, Positive psychology, Neuro-Semantics, and many, many more.

Maslow himself actually contributed to the fragmentation of the Human Potential Movement. As a creative, never-contented, innovator, even before the Third Force had taken hold, it was Maslow himself who launched "the Fourth Force" in psychology, Transpersonal Psychology. The year was 1967.

All of the dynamic ideas about the bright side of human nature encouraged continuously learning, growing, developing, transcending, breaking through limitations, stretching to new possibilities, and actualizing talents and unique perspectives. In contrast to the older psychologies with their tendency toward a more fatalistic, deterministic, and "darker" psychology, these new models stimulated inspiring visions and processes that give more credence and practicality to the bright side.

No wonder the first two or three decades the Human Potential Movement was chaotically wild. People experimented with hypnosis, drugs, body therapies, screaming (Primal Scream), psycho-drama, family constellations, altered states, hot tubs, channeling, dream interpretations, meditations, eastern religions, LSD, and the list goes on and on.

Driving *this chaotic exploration* was the paradigm shift from a deterministic psychology to one focused on unlimited potentials, untapped possibilities, "the farther reaches of human nature," and transcending paradigms. Yet this openness also led to explorations into the paranormal, the occult, various spiritual disciplines, religious experiences, and many other fringe things. And as can be anticipated, there was much hype, a tremendous amount of overselling, and the excesses that have so often led to cults and cult-like communities.[6]

7) No Central Effective Model

Given Carl Roger's strong dislike of techniques and that Maslow created no specific process for self-actualization from his Hierarchy of Needs, I've mentioned that the movement lacked effective models for enabling people to actualize the unleashing of their potentials and so deliver on its promises.

It was further undermined by the idea that self-actualization is *an organic process which will happen naturally and inevitably.* It was this idea that led to the next one, namely, that the most that's required is to get out of the way and let it happen. The result is that this encouraged a *laize faire* leadership which mostly took a hands-off approach rather than offer direction and guidance.

So as it was left to the smaller splinter groups and individuals to come up with various techniques. And, of course, numerous processes did arise. In *Psycho-Synthesis,* Roberto Assagiloi developed an approach that included actual patterns and techniques along with visual diagrams. Unfortunately while he did visit and teach at Esalen, his work was mostly on the periphery of the movement, not its center. There was the double-chair technique of gestalt, the hot tub experiences of Esalen, the psycho-drama processes, family sculpturing, and so on. Yet rather than help, all of this diversity actually worked against finding a central self-actualization process.

One child of the human potential movement was the NLP Communication model that Richard Bandler and John Grinder created by modeling the therapeutic communication skills of Perls and Satir. Because Bandler and Grinder put themselves into the role of modelers, they focused on modeling structure, and one of their first creations consisted of modeling the structure of rapport. They detailed "rapport" to specific matching and mirroring of behaviors, gestures, tones, tempo, sensory based words, etc. Then they turned it into an empirical technique which they referred to as a "program." Using the computer metaphor of a "program" was a mistake. It offended the sensitivities of many in the Human Potential Movement and set off some of the early rhetoric in NLP against the vagueness and the non-directiveness of the helping professions, and the counter-charges of manipulation.

In spite of the strong directive approach in NLP, in 1986 Kenneth Blanchard, co-author of *The One Minute Manager* and of many other books on business and management, wrote the following in his Foreword to one of the very first books to present the basic NLP communication model, Anthony Robbin's *Unlimited Power.*

> "I think this book has the capacity to be the definitive text in the human potential movement." (p. 12)

As a child of the Human Potential Movement, NLP arose from the combined work of John Grinder using the formulations of Chomsky's Transformational Grammar and Richard Bandler to model the linguistic patterns in Fritz Perls (Gestalt Therapy) and Virginia Satir (Family Systems Therapy). They also used the formulations of General Semantics ("The map is not the territory") and the TOTE model of Miller *et al.* to create a communication model for specifying the representational steps in a strategy to detail the structure of an experience (Dilts, 1980, *NLP, Vol. I, The Structure of Subjectivity*).

What else did NLP receive from the Human Potential Movement? NLP transformed the psycho-drama of Perls and Satir (double-chair dialogues, family sculpturing, etc.) and turn them into visualization and/or conversational patterns which people could run in their minds or as therapeutic conversations. NLP modeled the language patterns which created a questioning model which became "the Meta-Model of language in therapy" (*Structure of Magic, Volume I* 1975, *Communication Magic,* 2001).

NLP also adopted the key ideas within the *Human Potential Movement* that were among the operational beliefs and assumptions of Virginia Satir, Fritz Perls, and Milton Erickson. These key ideas are today called "NLP Presuppositions." At the heart of these are the ideas that people aren't broken, but work perfectly well, that they have all the resources they need to learn and adapt. People do the best with what they have and are more than their behavior. Also, behind every behavior are positive intentions; people do things to achieve things of value to them. Etc.[7]

8) Associated with Drugs and the Counter-Culture

Because the HPM arose during the 1960s in California, it is no surprise that it became associated with the psychedelic movement. Those were the days of extensively experimenting with psychoactive drugs, cocaine and LSD for attaining altered states. Richard Alpert left Harvard, changed his name to Ross Dam, and came to Esalen specifically to explore the psychedelic effects of LSD for expanding consciousness.

This is best illustrated by the book that Stuart Miller wrote and published by Esalen, *Hot Springs* (1971). The cover of the book reads: "The escapades —sexual and spiritual— of an East Coast boy wonder bent on making it and making out in California's sensuous culture!" While the book is reportedly an account of the Esalen experience, it reads more like a cheap sex novel and not a very good one at that!

The Disappearance

So where did the Human Potential Movement go? What happened to *the Third Force* in psychology? If it disappeared, where did it go?

The answer is, I think, that it disappeared into the psychological atmosphere in a way similar that William James' psychology disappeared. As "the Father of American Psychology," and the founder of a school of psychology at the beginning of the twentieth century, William James added so much to the general field of psychology. Yet his unique contributions have been mostly lost and subsumed generally in the field of psychology.

I think the same has been happening to Maslow's psychology and paradigm shift. I think it has been absorbed into scores of sub-schools of psychology, management, leadership, and self-development, rather than continuing in an unique and distinct way as Self-Actualization Psychology.

Maslow himself was so inclusively benevolent in his attitude and approach. Yet for his own abundance and inclusive style didn't seem to be appreciated or copied. Today his "bright side" of psychology with its vision for health, excellence, and actualizing one's highest potentials is incorporated in people's thinking everywhere.

Key Points in this Chapter
*   The Human Potential Movement blossomed, flourished, and then vanished. So as a movement it did not survive. In spite of all the energy, excitement, and passion about unleashing human potential, the "movement" as it existed in public awareness collapsed and disappeared.

- To a great extent the HPM collapsed due to faults and weaknesses within. Yet we can now learn from those faults. With hindsight we can take a lesson from that history and avoid the former mistakes and so launch a new initiative of achieving human potential.

End Notes:

1. Both Maslow and Rogers attempted to deal with the vagueness as each worked to operationalize their terms and as each attempted to ground their work in science and in the scientific method. Maslow's attempt to do this is in Chapter 4 (1965).

2. Everett Shostrum in fact wrote a book with the title of *Actualizing Therapy*. See page 254 for more about this.

3. Will Schutz made "Enounter Groups" his speciality. Abraham Maslow wrote about them as a powerful tool for self-actualizing potentials.

4. Will Schutz wrote *Joy* in 1967, then rewrote it in 1989. It was published as *Joy: Twenty Years Later; Expanding Human Awareness.*

5. Rogers also hardly even mentioned Maslow in his books, let alone acknowledge his leadership role. Yet historically they co-sponsored conferences and Maslow constantly referred to Rogers in his papers and books.

6. Esalen was recognized back in the 1960s as the center of the Human Potential Movement. In 1977 Esalen went bankrupt and in its reorganization a new vision statement was created: to unite Eastern and Western methodologies.

7. The list of NLP presuppositions. No NLP book, not even my own, has even identified the source of these basic premises. I originally located them in Perls and Satir thinking they were the source. Now I know that they took them from Maslow and the Human Potential Movement.

Chapter 22

LAUNCHING A NEW

HUMAN POTENTIAL

MOVEMENT

If the first Human Potential Movement was so dynamic in its wild and chaotic explorations of *Self-Actualization Psychology,* and if we can learn from the mistakes that led to its demise, is it possible to launch a new Human Potential Movement today? While this is the primary question for this chapter, it is not the only one. Here are some others:

- Did Maslow, Rogers, *et al.* pioneer a truly legitimate psychology about the bright side of human nature that can be re-launched today?
- Can we start from their research, offer some corrections with the insights that we can gain from hindsight, and launch a new initiative for the actualizing of human potentials?
- Are the ideas that launched the third force still relevant today?
- What would it take to launch a new Human Potential Movement?

If we start from the premise that the ideas and vision of the first Human Potential Movement are relevant, the direction important, and the possibilities viable, then the question is: *How can we launch these ideas anew*? The vision of the bright side of human nature continues today to inspire and awaken people and communities. The problem is not, and has not been, the idea of unleashing human potentials. The problem has been, and continues to be the process—*the how.* In fact, the basic premises of the *Human Potential Movement* increasingly accepted by psychologists, coaches, consultants, therapists, entrepreneurs, and leaders, inventors, etc. Today these ideas are part and parcel of coaching, human resources, self-development, wealth creation, and many other fields.

Endings and Beginnings

In the last chapter the question examined was *how* could such a dynamic, exciting, paradigm changing movement that exploded on the scene in the 1960s, and that spread around the world in just a few years, disappear?

If the key factors that made the Human Potential Movement vulnerable to disillusionment was that it over-focused on *vision over process* so that it dis-valued *techniques*, over-emphasized non-directiveness, failed to make clear and specific the self-actualization process, failed to produce a clear and explicit model, suffered from the raw individualism of its leaders, suffered the fragmentation into scores of sub-groups and new fields, was too wedded to therapy, lacked practical processes, became distracted by Maslow's introduction of the Fourth Force (Transpersonal Psychology), and so on, what then? How can we address these things and relaunch self-actualization as a practical reality?

As the primary developer of *the bright side of human nature*, and the first to truly launch out in this direction, Maslow was a pioneer. Consequently, he spent a great deal of his time arguing for the need to study healthy humans and to distinguish his work from the psychotherapy of Behaviorism and Psychoanalysis. In his early years he spent tremendous energy distinguishing the lower and higher needs. He also did not want to alienate these first two forces of psychology and so he focused on showing how the new psychology integrates the previous schools simultaneously taking them to a new level.

Another factor was Maslow's early and untimely death. Because Maslow died so early (at 62) and because Rogers applied his work exclusively to therapy (Client-Centered Therapy), they did not create an actual "model" of Self-Actualization Psychology. This was the shock I experienced when I began my explorations. When I began, I assumed that they had. *Yet Maslow and his colleagues left behind no fully developed Self-Actualization model.*

Maslow's *Hierarchy of Needs* model of human needs and values illustrates his revolutionary distinction between lower and higher needs. It positions self-actualization as the highest need in the hierarchy. Yet this Hierarchy does *not* have within it a model of Self-Actualization Psychology. Sure, it assumes it, but does not model it.

Now if a dynamic paradigm-shifting movement like *the Human Potential Movement* could fade away after a few decades, then the vitality of an idea alone is insufficient to drive and sustain a movement. So what we can learn that can assist us today in launching a new Human Potential Movement?

1) Hands-on and Directive Leadership

As we step back and reflect on the first Human Potential Movement, there was a leadership problem. Maslow and Rogers were obviously the key thought leaders and the visionary leaders, yet neither of them had the personality or skills to lead the movement as administrative leaders. Maslow spent the majority of his life as a College Professor and while he had dozens of doctoral students that he mentored, his biographers noted that his style was *laissez faire* in approach and that he never mentored any of them to step up into the kind of leadership that was needed. He simply did not groom them for an active leadership.

Rogers operated from the same mind-set. So committed and focused to his idea of a *non-directive* style, as in his *non-directive* client-centered therapy, he didn't lead in that direction. In pioneering his non-directive approach he focused his teaching and leadership on therapy, research, and education.

So after Maslow's death in 1970, the Human Potential Movement lacked the pioneering and visionary leadership that launched it. Those who were forceful and direct and who identified with the movement (William Schutz, George Leonard, Michael Murphy, Richard Price, Everett Shostrum, etc.) were leaders, but led out in their own individual areas, promoting their own trainings, therapy, workshops, models, books, etc. and not the movement as a whole.

It could have fallen to Fritz Perls, but in the same year of 1970 he also died. In addition to that, he was already the leader of Gestalt Therapy. Then there was the fact that he did not get along well with Maslow, once commenting that Maslow was just "too nice of a guy." So, after his and Maslow's death, no one rose up to become the next leader of the Human Potential Movement. This left the movement leaderless.[1]

Yet every movement needs leadership if it is to continue to grow and thrive and evolve. It needs hands-on practical leaders who can make the ideas and models of the movement readily available by a large portion of the population. It needs leaders who have a specific vision about what they have, what they offer, and where they want to go. Without such leadership, a movement is not likely to survive. The same holds true for any group, company, or organization.

Along with the absolute need for a specific self-actualization process, this is perhaps the most important need for launching a new Human Potential Movement. We need leaders. In fact, we need a leadership team of men and women who share the vision and who can collaborate to such an extent that they can provide the full range of leadership functions—visionary, pioneering, thought, administrative, charismatic, marketing, and structural leadership.

2) An Explicit and Simple Model

As important as the persons leading, we also need an exceptionally clear and explicit model of self-actualization. Over the past three years, when I have asked knowledgeable people about this, "What model of Self-Actualization did the Human Potential Movement give us?" Most think hard for a few minutes and then shrug their shoulders, "There is none." Those who do mention anything, mention the Hierarchy of Needs. I then ask:

> "How is that a model of self-actualization? What specific direction does the Hierarchy provide a person for actualizing his or her potentials? How can I use it as a map to guide the unleashing of my potentials?"

And with those questions both of us shrug our shoulders in the realization that while the Needs Hierarchy is valuable in distinguishing the levels of needs, distinguishing higher from lower, positions the self-actualization needs as biological needs that emerge, it is actually not a model of self-actualization. So while it positions the self-actualization needs at the top, emerging from the gratifying of the lower needs, it does not map out how we humans actually actualize our highest and best.

Contrast that to another model which arose within the same time frame, captivating the world and which is still around, and in some places (e.g. England) actually thriving. I'm speaking about the

Transactional Analysis Model (TA). In that movement there was definitely some leadership, Eric Berne as the thought leader and Thomas Harris as the marketing and perhaps charismatic leader (*I'm Ok, You're Ok*) as well as other leaders creating the organization— the journals, the conventions, the training centers.

There was also a very clear model—the 3-ego states of Parent, Adult, and Child and the visual representation of three circles on top of each other with lines showing the transactions as well as basic guidelines for using it.

> "Don't cross ego-states. There are four life scripts, I'm Not Okay, You're Not Okay; I'm Okay, You're Not Okay; I'm Not Okay; You're Okay; I'm Okay, You're Okay."

No wonder TA took the psychological and self-development world by storm with a simple visual-digital model. And they did this as their way to popularize Psychoanalysis! Read Berne's *Games People Play* and you will find a book loaded with the abstract concepts and the jargon of psychoanalysis. It's not an easy read at all. So how did T.A. succeed as it did? It succeeded because it developed a simple and easy-to-grasp visual diagram along with a few easy-to-apply principles, and some best selling books like *I'm Okay; You're Okay.*

By contrast note what happens when we ask, "What are the actual processes used in the Human Potential Movement?" Now we have to make a list of a wide range of things from encounter groups, sensitivity training, Gestalt double-chairs, yoga, meditation, hypnosis, message, hot tubs, primal scream, psychoactive drugs (LSD), and on and on. Being as eclectic as it was, the HPM incorporated lot of things under its umbrella in doing so it lacked a simple unifying process. There was no singular process specifying how to activate and actualize human potentials.

Further working against this was the assumption about organic growth that Carl Rogers introduced. Rogers believed that growth was *organic* and it would just naturally occur. His focus, and to a good extent Maslow's, was that all we have to do is to remove the interferences. Other than that, there's nothing to do. Just get the interferences out of the way.

To launch a new Human Potential Movement today we definitely need a simple to communicate model so that people can easily understand how to unleash human potentials. If a movement is to capture people's imaginations, this is essential. We need a simple diagram that can be literally *seen*, practical guidelines so that it can be *stated* in sound bites, and practical directive processes so that people can *do* something in using the model. The more conceptual a model, the more a visual diagram is needed which can be easily replicated and practically used.

3) A Self-Organizing Attractor

Perhaps the HPM would have succeeded even with weak leadership, a non-functional diagram, the lack of a practical process, and the eclectism of scores of processes, but then Maslow himself sabotaged things.

The story is that somewhere around 1965 Maslow became more and more intrigued by the transcendence of the meta-needs (meta-values) and so he moved more and more into the realm that we typically designate as the "spiritual" realm. As a life-long avowed atheist, Maslow was looking for something. So thinking that the third force was not sufficient, he created and launched the Fourth Force in Psychology, *Transpersonal Psychology*.

It's not that much of a surprise that this had the effect of de-emphasizing the Third Force of the Human Potential Movement when that movement was still in its formative stages and when it needed lots of attention. The movement, still in its wild and chaotic days, was mostly undeveloped. There was still no model of Self-Actualization Psychology and the one person who was providing the primary visionary leadership was onto something else.

Also, with Transpersonal Psychology, Maslow unwittingly undermined the scientific validity and empiricism he had worked so hard for so many years to create. This had the effect of opening the door for dozens of things that were non-empirical and non-scientific. This also had the effect of undermining the credibility of what he had begun as it also dispersed the focus. With Transpersonal Psychology came in all kinds of new age practices from channeling, extra-sensory perception, eastern religious beliefs, etc. diverting the energy of the original vision. Because of this, many people dismissed the HPM and accused it of mysticism.

This also severely mis-directed the self-actualization movement. In fact, it contributed to the movement fractionalizing further into scores of sub-groups and fractions. If there had been a self-organizing attractor in the movement, such as *self-actualization*, it was now gone. And without a singular thing (or person) attracting and organizing the movement, the movement lost even more momentum and direction.

This suggests that to launch a new Human Potential Movement today we need *a clear and singular focus that operates as an attractor for people.* We need a central focus and emphasis that pulls the vision of the bright-side of psychology together.

To refer to the field of TA again, the attractor there was that of transactions and life scripts. These processes gave people a focused direction about what to do— rewrite the life script, straighten out the transactions, and recognize when you are operating from the different ego states. This made real Freud's original formulation of his program: "Where there is Id, let there be Ego."

What self-organizing attractor can we use for the new Self-Actualization Psychology introduced here? We can use the Meaning —Performance Axes of the Self-Actualization Quadrants. Within this attractor, we have numerous attractive ideas. Within these quadrants we have the path to the zone of self-actualization and this can operate as the heart and soul of self-actualization. Using this we can brand the new movement as, "How to get into the zone at will." This gives us the compelling idea of being able to now step in and out of the zone whenever we desire.

From there is the recognition that we can experience little everyday tastes of self-actualization in those surprising peak experiences that we can cultivate. After that is the idea of moving to peak performances and so able to seek and reach the peak of optimal performance in our area of passion. The time has now finally come for these ideas enabling us to make them our singular focus in Self-Actualization Psychology.

4) Supportive Scholarship

Even without sufficient leadership or models, the movement might have survived and continued if there had been a supportive community of scholars. But again, there was not. There could have been. Maslow did initiate the *Journal of Humanistic Psychology* (which continues to this day) and he did work in an academic setting and in 1968 he was even elected President of the American Psychological Association (APA). Yet in spite of all that, neither the

HPM nor Humanistic Psychology, nor Self-Actualization Psychology ever became incorporated as a School of Psychology.

As part of my research, I read through scores of the journals published throughout the 1980s. I was amazed at how the editors allowed, or even encouraged, writers to be what struck me as brutally critical of Maslow and Rogers. Reading some of the articles, like "The Failure of Self-Actualization Theory: A Critique of Carl Rogers and Abraham Maslow" by Leonard Geller in 1982 (volume 22, number 2), I was stunned by the viciousness of the critiques and the level of mis-representations. My sense is that these critiques worked like a cancer eating away at the life and vitality of the movement. For a new movement, that kind of critical competitiveness from within the ranks was disastrous.

By the mid-1980s, at Conferences of the Humanistic Psychologists, various writers and theoreticians were bewailing that the movement had failed and that there was not a single University with a department of Humanistic Psychology.

> "Humanistic psychology was a great experiment, but it is basically a failed experiment in that there is no humanistic school of thought in psychology, no theory that would be recognized as a philosophy of science." (Cunningham 1985, in Schulz, 1992, p. 18)

In 1982 M. Brewster Smith, another former president of the APA commented, "The 1980s find the humanistic psychology movement in decline." He said it was time to take stock and "recapture the flag of humanism in psychology." Prophetically, he wrote, "Now I claim that the movement is running out of steam . . ." And so it was. For Dr. Smith, a big part of the problem was the shift of focus to the transcendental and transpersonal. And yet that's what the Journal mostly published in those years, especially with the focus that Ken Wilbur brought to it.

Having a critical and skeptical and negative disposition seems to be one of the occupational hazards for anyone who earns an advanced university degree. With the ability to write "scholarly papers" of analysis also comes the ability to tear down and criticize. And while there's certainly a place for that, it is not in the early days of a movement. Scholars need to be able to control the negativity of their critical eye. They need to be able to turn it off when it's important to provide support.

To launch a new Human Potential Movement today we similarly need people to take up the challenge of research to make the models and processes acceptable to academia and to create the kind of quantitative and qualitative research that validates the legitimacy of the models.

On with the Launching
Given what we have learned (and can learn) from the demise of the first Human Potential Movement, to launch a new movement that avoids the mistakes and to put it on much firmer footing, what else is required?

1) Clarity
We need to clarify the specific processes by which we can facilitate ourselves and others in unleashing their potentials. We need the ability to articulate the specific mechanisms and processes by which human potentials are unleashed. We need the ability to operationalize our terms and to benchmark such terms as "potentials," "self-actualization," "peak experiences," "peak performances," etc. With this kind of clarity we will be able to distinguish what facets belong to philosophy, theology, and metaphysics and what belongs to psychology.

2) Directive and Non-Directive Balance
Given that Self-Actualization Psychology requires both directive and non-directive facilitation, as we learn the distinctions separating these, we will be able to create a healthy balance in using both directive and non-directive processes. This will allow us to invent new choices and techniques for self-actualization. We will then be able to be more directive when direction is needed and non-directive when people have sufficient inner direction.

3) Thinking and working Systemically
If we want to work systemically we have to have a systemic approach that results from thinking systemically about self-actualization. We will know that we have such when we are able to answer the question,

> "How do you know *what* to do, *when, with whom,* and *why*?"

Given that at the heart of the self-actualization vision is the belief in working holistically and systemically with people and human nature, we need a model that works with the mind-body-emotion system and how it operates within layers of contexts or systems. If our focus is on how to tap into the hidden potentials within people and coach people for behavioral, developmental, and transformative change in the unleashing of possibilities, we need to be able to specify the mechanisms governing the mind-body-emotion systems.

4) Cooperative Collaboration

If the "raw and rugged individualism" of the 1960s and 1970s, and the "Me Generation" contributed to undermining the first Human Potential Movement, then we will need to be more mindful in using and practicing the principles of self-actualization to reign in our individualism. It will be required of those in leadership to cooperate and collaborate in working together for Self-Actualization Psychology. This means acknowledging sources, playing to our strengths, and supporting each other. It means embedding our individualism within a larger frame of collaborative cooperation.

5) Separating Self-Actualization from Therapy

The first Human Potential Movement was deeply wedded to therapy. That's because it didn't separate itself from therapy, but sought to directly use it for the healing of wounds and pathology. This made it more difficult to sell it to those who didn't need therapy. Now while it is possible to apply Self-Actualization Psychology for therapy (Chapter 23), it is primarily for those who are psychologically healthy and ready for the challenge of activating their full potentials.

6) A Specific Focus

Maslow called the new Self-Actualization Psychology *psychogogy.* With a name like that, no wonder it did not take off! So while in his day there was no field for the psychologically healthy, today there is. Today the fields of coaching, sport psychology, modeling, peak performances, development and training—all of these fields focus exclusively on those who want to develop their best. And given that coaching has arisen as a field that ideally addresses this population, we now have an entirely new context for Self-Actualization Psychology (Chapter 25).

Phoenix Rises

To facilitate the launching of a new Human Potential Movement, I began delivering a series of workshops, the Self-Actualization Workshop in 2007. This Neuro-Semantic approach was designed to see if we could gather together sufficient numbers of people who might catch the vision of a re-launching and become part of a new

Human Potential Movement. For details about this, see the website, www.self-actualizing.org.

Key Points in this Chapter

- Movements, organizations, and businesses can arise, go through growth stages, and then either die or evolve is to new forms. It takes much more than a great idea to launch and sustain a viable movement. It takes a great idea plus effective leadership, a sense of direction, lots of people pulling together, management of the community to maintain the focus, collaborating of many others to support it, and a constant renewal of the vision and purpose.

- Today, I believe in the bright side of human nature, modeling it, and developing more explicit processes so that we can unleash human potential more effectively because this is essential for the survival and well-being of the human race.

End Notes:

1. The tradition and rumors of the conflict and dislike between Fritz Perls and Abe Maslow are abundant. One of Fritz's many memorable quips about Abe was, "'a sugar-coated Nazi' who pandered to a happy world of optimism that did not in fact exist." (Kripal, 2007, . 157). Of course, this from a man who was known for his cruelty and obnoxiousness and who described himself as a "dirty old man." Even Gregory Bateson said that Maslow was simply "too nice" for his own tastes.

PART III:

THE

APPLICATIONS

Chapter 23

SELF-ACTUALIZATION

THERAPY

"... Every man who is kind, helpful, decent, psychologically democratic, affectionate, and warm, is a psychotherapeutic force even though a small one."

Abraham Maslow

- What is the relationship between self-actualization and therapy?
- Can the processes of self-actualization that were originally designed for psychologically healthy people be employed as therapy for wounded people?
- And if the facilitation approach of coaching is the epitomy of the self-actualization process, can it also be used in the context of therapy?

These and many other questions regularly come up whenever I present the new Neuro-Semantic approach to Self-Actualization. The reason is, in part, because we typically present such in the context of *coaching*. And in that context, I always attempt to make a clear line of demarcation between therapy and coaching.

The reason for doing this is due in part because of where the field of coaching is today (2008). Having recently emerged from a mixture of disciplines (mentoring, therapy, training, consulting, hypnosis, etc.), *coaching* is only now becoming a field and is still a long way from becoming a profession. So in contributing what we can to support that movement, in Meta-Coaching we have been defining the boundaries for Coaching in order to separate it from other disciplines and make it different from other fields.

When I made the presentation in Paris a few years ago, several people began asking questions about the possibility of doing "therapy" by using the methodology of coaching and enabling a person to self-actualize through the developmental psychology principles and the healing principles of cognitive-behavioral psychology. And of course, the short answer is, "Yes, certainly."

Facilitative Therapy
In fact, for several decades this has been a major direction in the field of psychotherapy. Beginning with the Cognitive Psychological Movement (initiated in 1956 by George Miller and Noam Chomsky), and then the Ellis – Beck forms of cognitive therapy, the Ericksonian therapies which led to Solution-Focus Therapy, Brief Psychotherapy, Narrative psychotherapy, even NLP psychotherapy (NLPt) in Europe and England, along with many others, the discipline of psychotherapy has been breaking with the past and has been increasingly moving to a more collaborative and facilitative approach. This has been blurring the traditional boundaries of therapy.

As such therapists have been setting aside the role of the expert in relation to the client, doing less diagnosis, less use of such instruments as the DSM-IV, and working more to *enable* and *empower* the client to become self-supportingly resourceful. This was the dream that Carl Rogers began in the 1950s and which he developed into the Client-Centered Therapy approach.[1]

In fact, most of the developers of the Human Potential Movement were in the field of therapy when the paradigm shift occurred as Maslow began modeling *healthy self-actualizing humans.* It was then that they began to use the principles of self-actualizing psychology in working with clients. This was not only true of Carl Rogers, but of Viktor Frankl (Logotherapy), Roberto Assagioli (Psycho-Synthesis), Rollo May (Humanistic Existentialism), William Glasser, and many others.

Maslow was the primary exception. He was not officially a therapist, but a college professor, researcher, psychologist, and life-long explorer into "the farther reaches of human nature." Yet while he was not a therapist, in his journals he described doing therapy with his students. That's why, in part, Maslow did speak and write about the relationship between self-actualization and therapy.

Basic Needs Therapy

Maslow used his meta-motivation theory of the hierarchy of needs to correlate the relationship between illness, pathology, and the experience of self-actualizing human needs. By working forward from the biological and physiological *needs* of humans, Maslow created a paradigm shift as he challenged the assumptions of the old psychologies. First he questioned the habit of comparing human needs to "the bad-animal model" of our inner nature. "What about the good animals?" he asked. "Why not identify with the higher intelligent and milder animals like deer, elephant, or dog, or chimpanzee?" He then questioned the whole idea of "instincts" in humans. While animals have instincts that are "powerful, strong, unmodifiable, uncontrollable, unsuppressible, this is not true for humans."

At best, we humans only have instinctoids which are "easily repressed, suppressed, controlled, and that can easily be masked, modified, or suppressed by habits and culture." (1954 *Personality and Motivation,* p. 80). He wrote that when we—
> ". . . recognize instinctoid needs to be not bad, but neutral or good, a thousand pseudo problems solve themselves and fade out of existence." (p. 87)

Maslow then declared that when we recognize that pleas for acceptance, love, admiration, meaning, order, etc. are legitimate demands or rights, "of the same order as complaints of hunger, thirst, cold, or pain," we accept the need to gratify them rather than frustrate them. This exerts a healthy therapeutic force. To do the opposite, to frustrate our basic needs causes illness and pathology. For Maslow "therapy" means "a pressure toward breaking controls and inhibitions" against our basic needs (1970, p. 103).

Maslow also distinguished two kinds of deprivation: an unimportant deprivation and a threatening one. In doing so he came so very close to recognizing the critical role of *meaning.* He wrote,
> "Deprivation is not psycho-pathogenic; threat is." (p. 107)

What creates the need for therapy is fundamental *threats* to our basic needs. Therefore gratifying the basic needs is a first line response and often eliminates the organizing causes that lead to neurosis.

Growth Therapy

Self-actualization, as the forward movement of human growth and development, stands in opposition to the hurt and pathology that requires healing or therapy. Anything that hurts, wounds, traumatizes, and inhibits growth creates pathology and calls for healing. Conversely, anything that facilitates the growth of actualizing one's best is therapeutic. And given that we are born without instincts and have to learn how to be human, we develop cognitive distortions and erroneous maps as we navigate our way through life. About this Maslow (1968) wrote:

> "The neurotic is not emotionally sick, he is cognitively *wrong!*" (p. 153)

Maslow even asks and answers the question about what is psycho-pathological.

> "What is psycho-pathological? Anything that disturbs or frustrates or twists the course of self-actualization. What is psychotherapy? Any means of any kind that helps to restore the person to the path of self-actualization and of development along the lines that his inner nature dictates." (p. 270)

In *The Farther Reaches of Human Nature*, Maslow (1971) describes neurosis in the following way.

> "[Neurosis] . . . is a failure of personal growth; falling short of what one could have been. Human and personal possibilities have been lost. The world has been narrowed, and so has consciousness. Capacities have been inhibited." (p. 33)

> "The people we call 'sick' are the people who are *not themselves,* the people who have built up all sorts of neurotic defenses against *being human.* Learning to break through one's repressions, to know one's self, to hear the impulse voices, to uncover the triumphant nature, to reach knowledge, insight, and the truth— these are the requirements. To become more, more actualizing, more realizing what you are in potentiality." (p. 51, italics added)

Maslow (1970, p. 242) identified that psychotherapy takes place in seven main ways and enumerated this as follows:

1) By expression: act completion, release, catharsis.
2) By basic need-gratification: giving support, reassurance, protection, love, respect.
3) By removing threat: protection, good social, political, and economic conditions.
4) By improved insight, knowledge, and understanding.
5) By suggestion or authority.
6) By direct attack on the symptoms.
7) By positive self-actualization, individuation, or growth.

What then is the relationship between self-actualization and therapy? First and foremost, the self-actualizing dynamics and processes are inherently *therapeutic* processes. They facilitate the unleashing of our fully humanness giving us an inner vitality and robustness.

Self-Actualization for the Psychologically Healthy

If self-actualization is all about becoming our potentials, if it is about finding and activating our capabilities, then coaching that level of growth and change makes perfect sense. We coach a person's self-actualization as we *awaken* him or her to the inner possibilities and then soundly challenge them to make those possibilities real in that person's everyday life.

We do this with healthy people who are ready for stretching and who are hungry for challenge. With their basic needs basically gratified, other needs arise—the need for challenge, for change, and for adventure. They want to grow, to be more, to experience more, to shake things up, to be stretched. They want to contribute, to be a part of something bigger than themselves, to contribute to the world, to make a difference socially, to experience a mission, and to leave a legacy. They grow to the place where the meta-needs kick in.

We coach the actualizing of one's most fundamental potentials by holding *a fierce existential conversation* about the things that really matter. These are the things that get to the heart of the matter.

> "What's your biggest dream? What's even bigger than that? What are you doing today about actualizing that dream? How are you holding yourself back? How are you selling yourself short? How are you locking up your potentials preventing them from fully blossoming? What's impossible that you are going to do today? How have you been playing yourself small? Are you ready to go for your highest and best?"

Of course, all of this presupposes a generous dose of ego-strength—the ability to look the facts of reality in the face without caving in. It presupposes the ability to be authentically strong and true to oneself and to not let oneself off the hook from self-responsibility. It presupposes a healthy personality. For this we need something else that Maslow described—"the observing ego is necessary for therapy" (1971, p. 63).

Therapeutic Self-Actualization

But what about people who are hurt and damaged? What about people who don't have sufficient ego-strength, self-acceptance, self-confidence, self-esteem, self-initiative, and self-responsibility? What about people who suffer from the parenting errors of parents who never darkened the door of a *Parenting 101* class?

* Can we coach the self-actualization process as a way to do therapy and facilitate therapeutic healing?
* Can we use the self-actualization models to coach people who are not yet "up to average" and fully "free to be themselves," and to resolve old traumas and distortions?

Before we can explore these questions, we need to define what we mean by "therapy." *Therapy,* which means healing, presupposes hurt, wounds, trauma, ego-defenses, etc. As such it brings up the subject of pathology—how human nature can become sick and distorted, how self-description and experience can become malformed. It also brings up the *degree and extent* of such malformations in human personality, *how much* therapy does a person need? How far is the person from becoming a psychologically healthy person?

In a general sense, anything that facilitates growth, learning, and human maturization operates as a therapeutic influence. Human kindness, acceptance, friendliness, generosity, respect, love, and the like are therapeutic forces. Healthy communication that's open, honest, and transparent is therapeutic. So also are supportive relationships that provide care, understanding, genuineness, listening, etc. In this, there are lots of therapeutic influences that we can activate and provide without being a trained therapist. Maslow spoke to this in *Motivation and Personality* (1954):

> "Accepting this, it is our clear conviction that not only is every good human being potentially an unconscious therapist, but also we must accept the conclusion that we should approve of this, encourage it, teach it. Let people realize

clearly that every time they threaten someone or humiliate or hurt unnecessarily or dominate or reject another human being, they become forces for the creation of psycho-pathology, even if these be small forces. Let them recognize also that every man who is kind, helpful, decent, psychologically democratic, affectionate, and warm, is a psycho-therapeutic force even though a small one." (p. 254)

The Therapeutic Discipline

Yet this differs from the actual discipline, science, and art of therapy. Psychotherapy, as a profession, arose at the end of the nineteenth century as a supplementary force to the medical profession. As medicine had been making tremendous strides to heal and cure physical aliments at that time, therapy at the same time was seeking to heal and cure mental-emotional and personal-interpersonal aliments. It sought to deal with the pathologies of the soul (*psyche*) and at first to address the disorders that made people unable to cope with reality, who were unable to get along with others, to work, or to even endure themselves.

From the perspective of Self-Actualization Psychology, *therapy* is for people in whom the natural growth tendency has been blocked or interfered with in some way. In some way or other, the organic developmental process of growing into a healthy, autonomous, authentic, self-actualizing person has been blocked. The person is stuck. Perhaps he is "living in the past." Perhaps she is defensive and shut down. Perhaps he is delusional. Perhaps she is trying to "finish" some "old business" that she deems unfinished.

Whatever the block, the interference, or distortion of the pathology, the person is not "okay," not "up to average," not in the present, not open, response-able, or empowered, and doesn't have the ego-strength to get beyond the block without some assistance. The person feels insecure and so uses the defense mechanisms to defend against reality and the escape mechanisms to escape it. This, of course, is a general description. With every person we will find different degrees of hurt and trauma.

This explains the need for a competent and qualified therapist. What's needed is someone who understands normal human development, who can identify where the client is in the process, and who can create a relational context for the person. This context is the creation of a therapeutic relationship wherein the person can experience the acceptance, understanding, and non-judgment that was missing from parents, relearn better thinking, emoting, and coping patterns, reverse cognitive distortions, and open up to courageously try out new ways of responding.

That's why therapy almost inevitably tends to activate the transference of the client's original feelings about parents and authority figures to the therapist. Failure to recognize this, as well as the "power" differential between therapist and client, the possibility of counter-transference, and one's skill set for working with various levels of dysfunction and personality disordering are essential skills for a psychotherapist. Accordingly, the governments in most nations and states have established a set of criteria of study, experience, and testing to determine competency for therapists.

The Therapeutic Relationship
What we have discovered over the more than a hundred years of psychotherapy is that *it is not the theory that makes the most difference, but the relationship.* It is the therapeutic relationship that seems to provide the central and most essential healing aspects that result in therapy.

This relationship can take three very different forms. The quality of the relationship can be:
> 1) Authoritarian or dominant-subordinate.
> 2) Democratic or equalitarian.
> 3) Laissez-faire or aloof.

Maslow noted that what the person in therapy needs is what he or she has never received in a straight-forward way—they need the protection, love, respect, etc. that they have not receive. And while many look upon entering the therapeutic relationship as weird, abnormal, sick, unusual, an unfortunate necessity, that very attitude creates the biggest barrier to receiving help. Entering any beneficial relationship like marriage, friendship, partnership, friendship, etc. should be viewed as healthy and desirable (1970, p. 252).

Actualizing Therapy
With all of this in mind, let's return to our original question, "Can we use the coaching methodology in doing therapy with someone?" The answer is yes. Everett Shostrom, in fact, wrote a book on this very subject, *Actualizing Therapy* (1976). Shostrom's work focuses entirely on using the ideas and premises of *Self-Actualizing*

Psychology in the context of therapy.

What are some of the differences in a self-actualizing therapy? First it reframes pathology as "attempts at self-actualizing." Shostrom:

> "It does explain much pathological behavior as abortive attempts at actualizing. It joins a theory of function with one of malfunction. Psychopathology may be described in terms of limited or distorted attempts to actualize. When the actualizing person can feel that he is separate and autonomous and at the same time rhythmically able to be angry and loving, strong and weak interpersonally, he can avoid the control and rigidification that ends in neuroses or psychoses." (102)

We provide a much more positive frame-of-reference when we frame pathology, not as an evil in itself, but as a wrong-headed attempt at trying to self-actualize. And simultaneously we eliminate any need for the client to hate, feel anger, or feel guilty about those attempts. Following Maslow who framed neurosis as a failure of growth, Shostrom said this means we can frame what has been labeled sickness as *creativity*.

> "Perhaps psychology needs new therapeutic methods that do not diagnose sickness but that really appreciate the creativity involved in pathological attempts to survive in the world. Perhaps therapists need to say, 'Man, that was really ingenious,' rather than, 'Man, you are really sick.'" (102)

A shift in one's frame of reference like this can begin to enable a person to shift from merely surviving and getting along to actualizing his or her best. In this, therapy itself can begin to awaken in people a much larger vision for their human nature and human life.

> "Therapy is a process that moves a person outward from a basically *survival* frame of reference to a basically *actualizing* frame, but the therapist must appreciate the actualizing involved in all survival behavior. Laing's (1965, 1967) point that we can learn a great deal from the special strategies of psychotic persons, which they invent in order to live in an unlivable world is relevant." (103)

Finally, Colin Wilson (1972) in *New Pathways in Psychology*, in his biography of Maslow, said that the ideal way to cure neurosis is to evoke a powerful sense of meaning (p. 176). And this, of course, is one of the key concepts in the Meaning/ Performance axes.

In Self-Actualization Psychology, one tool or process that is highly therapeutic is the Crucible. In this Neuro-Semantic process we bring together seven elements of transformative change so that we can let old meanings that are outdated and ineffective or toxic and dis-empowering melt down. The Crucible burns the dross off as it refines one's powers so that out of it arises a new casting of meaning.[3]

Key Points in this Chapter

- The overall design of *Self-Actualization Psychology* is to describe the bright side of human nature as it develops over our lifespan. It describes human nature as we unfold and develop, find and activate our talents, turn our talents into skills, and increasingly unleash more and more potentials. As such, Self-Actualization Psychology inherently contains a therapeutic model.

- *Self-Actualization Psychology* also identifies many of the ways that development is arrested through interferences and hurts. So while the model focuses primarily on psychologically healthy people, and maps out the farther reaches of human nature, within it we can identify many of the therapeutic steps for undoing the damage and getting on the pathway to self-actualization.

End Notes:

1. If you want to examine a whole book on the 14 "personality disorders" of the DSM-IV, see our book *The Structure of Personality*. It offers a therapeutic facilitative approach using NLP and Neuro-Semantics.

2. Maslow wrote an entire chapter on this, Chapter 15 in *Motivation and Personality* is titled, "Psychotherapy, Health, and Motivation."

3. For more about the crucible, see *Unleashed* (2007), chapter 10. Also an entire day of the Ultimate Self-Actualization Workshop is devoted to experiencing the Crucible as a change process for unlearning.

Chapter 24

COMMUNITIES OF

SELF-ACTUALIZERS

"The main function of a healthy culture . . .
the fostering of universal self-actualization."
(1968, p. 159)

". . . Human nature is extremely malleable in the sense that it is
easy for culture and environment to kill off altogether or to
diminish genetic potential . . ." (1970, p. xviii)

"Self-actualizing people are not well adjusted . . . they get along
. . . but they resist enculturation." (1970, p. 171)

D oes self-actualization apply in social contexts? Does *Self-Actualization Psychology* translate over to groups of people? Does it translate to companies, communities, and to businesses? Could we translate it to countries and nations?

- If you can actualize your highest and best as a single individual, what happens when you and twenty others do so?
- What happens, or could happen, if a thousand self-actualizing people got together?
- Could a million self-actualizing people create a community, a business, or a government? Since people as individual human beings can develop self-actualizing lives, what about their group experience as a people?
- What about the existence of self-actualizing companies and communities? What would a self-actualizing company be like?
- How would a group of people dedicated to the principles of self-actualization operate?

- How would their community differ from the way communities arise and develop who don't believe in and operate in a supportive way of bringing out the best in every person?

Simply because *self* is within the term "self-actualization" does not make it exclusive to individuals, it is also for groups. It is for companies, communities, families, nations, etc. For self-actualizing individuals to unite together to create a movement, a community, a company, or a nation, they will create a union around the principles of *Self-Actualizing Psychology.* Operating from the bright-side of human nature, they will assume that people want to grow, assume new responsibilities, stretch to new levels of performance, take pride in learning, developing, and achieving. They will assume that people want to make a difference, create and experience meaning in their activities, career, and relationships and that given an appropriate environment, they can create new empowering contexts to farther each person's self-actualization.

They will also assume that as people gratify the lower needs with true and adequate satisfiers and move beyond them to the higher, they will develop a whole new form of motivation. They will move from deficiency motivation to abundance motivation—the motivation of *being* their best selves and *expressing* that best self. This will enable them to be less competitive with others, more collaborative, more of a team member, and more supportive.

Given all of that, what if we allowed ourselves to begin to *imagine what a self-actualizing company or community would be like.* If you find that difficult to imagine, it is probably because your references regarding people trying to get along in a supportive and cooperative way are not-so-encouraging. As people, we do not have a great track record of cooperating, collaborating, and playing well together.

A company of self-actualizing people would not be a top-down, command-and-control hierarchy. It would be much more democratic. It would support people learning, recovering from mistakes, interacting with others, exploring possibilities, and creating together a flexible and learning organization.[1]

The Good Conditions for Social Self-Actualization
Maslow, especially in his work on business and management (*Maslow on Management*), addressed a lot of these questions as he

spoke about translating the ideas of self-actualization to human cultures and businesses. To that end he spoke about the necessary *conditions*, the "good conditions" that correlate with a group of people self-actualizing together.

Yet what about these good conditions? What does that mean? And, are good conditions a guarantee that everyone will self-actualize? In *The farther reaches of human nature,* Maslow (1971) wrote:

> "It is now quite clear that the actualization of the highest human potentials is possible — on a mass basis—only under "good conditions. . . . Or more directly, good human beings will generally need a good society in which to grow. That society is good which fosters the fullest development of human potentials, of the fullest degree of humanness." (p. 7)

What are the good conditions that make self-actualization possible? And how many of these good conditions are required in order to begin, or continue, the self-actualizing process? First, we need the freedoms of democracy for the freedom of thought and freedom of speech. We need the ability and opportunity to explore new possibilities by using the marketplace of supply and demand to determine in the values in our groups and the basis for our financial structures. We need the good conditions of having lower needs (survival, safety, social, self needs) basically gratified to free us so we can explore order, excellence, love, contribution, beauty, music, mathematics, and all of the other things (the B-values) that create meaningful significance in our lives.

These are the minimal requirements. And because of this, we need to encourage cultural and social reforms that enable people to experience the basic freedoms and to create a good life with the basic goods of life— food, water, shelter, warmth, safety, security, etc.

People living on the edge of survival, safety, social connection, and even self-regard are far more likely to be endangered by exploitation. A society that does not make the basic goods available to all of its people will not be a "good" society for self-actualization. Where there is inequality, disenfransizement, poverty, destructive drugs, corrupt police, judges, and government, there will be a dark hole in that society, a cancer in its growth and development. In itself, this will be a meta-pathology at the cultural level. It will be a sickness, a psychological sickness, that will infect and influence everyone in that society.

A society can only be "good" —good for the self-actualization of its people and itself—if it is organized, structured, governed, and led by the principles of equality for all and opportunity for all to fulfill their needs for survival, safety, social connection, and self-value. Where there are toxic influences like poverty, insecurity, crime, conflicts, fighting, disrespect, classifying, prejudice, racism, etc., these will hold back, interfere and undermine self-actualization of individuals and communities.

> "The good and healthy society would then be defined as the one that permitted man's highest purposes to emerge by satisfying all his basic needs." (1970, p. 58)

For Maslow, this is one of the truly "Big Problems" in our world. How do we create better human beings? Writing during the cold war, he noted the need for this was the very survival of the human race. He said that if we don't learn how to create better humans, we will be wiped out. (1971, p. 18).

Who is the good person? In terms of *Self-Actualization Psychology* the good person is the self-evolving person, the responsible-*for* himself-and-his-own-growth, and responsible-*to*-others, the awakened person who is self-accepting, and compassionately caring about others. It is the internally creative person who asks questions, gets the facets, and thinks synergetically. It is the person who operates as a therapeutic-force-of-one in the world. Without people who are healthy enough and strong enough, social reforms will not work or at least will not last.

Beyond Good Conditions
So what kind of world do we need for self-actualizing people to grow and thrive in? Maslow wrote,

> "Improving individual health is one approach to making a better world." (1968, p. 6)

Yet good conditions, in and of themselves, are not enough. Merely having the time, money, energy, and intention to self-actualize does not automatically lead to or "cause" a person to self-actualize. There are plenty of people with the financial and time resources who do *not* self-actualize, and who have no intention of doing so. There are also those who, when given the time, space, and money for self-actualization, use such resources for the very opposite. They use it for taking advantage of others, engaging in crime, hurting people. As Maslow came to realize this, he wrote,

> "The big point is not to think that good conditions inevitably make all human beings into growing, self-actualizing people. The little bit of larceny and sadism and all the other sins which you can find in practically any human being may be called forth by these 'good conditions' when the person is trusted and put completely on his own honor."

What does this mean for building self-actualization communities and companies? It means that without *self-responsibility* to undergird self-management, people will not be on their best or do what's noble. Give a person "good conditions" who is not able to control his or her own thinking, emoting, valuing, believing, acting, etc. and you could just as well create a criminal, even a sociopath. The mere fact of the external conditions that are "good," i.e., democratic, full of resources (e.g., time, money, energy, health, etc.) does not make self-actualization inevitable. Inner conditions of the person are also required.

Every group, society, and business can be characterized as either fostering or hindering the self-actualization of people. If it works *for* self-actualization it is a "good" culture and if it works *against* people self-actualizing, it is a "bad" culture.

The Required Inside Conditions
Here's something counter-intuitive. While self-actualization is an inside job which is expressed outerly, it starts with gratifying the basic needs. So here we need an environment sufficiently developed to provide that. We also need some internal good conditions—those inner conditions required for self-actualization in people. After all, ultimately self-actualization is something chosen, envisioned, and personally experienced. It arises through the mindful effort of those who develop to that stage of maturity.

So what are the necessary internal good conditions? Self-responsibility, self-empowerment, vision of the possibilities beyond wealth and fame, self-efficacy, inner self-freedom to choose, the elimination of semantic blocks, the reduction of semantic reactions, semantic relaxation, the balanced of over-loading semantically, proactivity, courage, and so on.

Maslow also spoke to this:

> "One characteristic of good conditions that are emerging is that good conditions can have a bad, even catastrophic effect

on a certain small proportion of the population. Freedom and trust given to authoritarians will simply bring out bad behavior in these people. Freedom and permissiveness and responsibility will make really dependent and passive people collapse in anxiety and fear." (235)

How about that? *Good conditions can have bad effects.* It can even have catastrophic effects. Amazing, is it not? Give some people (i.e., authoritarians, fanatics, "true believers") the conditions that are "good" and useful for self-actualization and it can sometimes bring out the worst in them! Give it to people who are ill-intentioned, undeveloped, under-developed, stuck in an unresourceful state, traumatized, personality divided, dependent, passive, etc., and good conditions can actually make things worse.

Here is a dilemma to address. After we identify and develop the conditions that are good for calling forth the self-actualizing vision and process, with some people it will evoke the opposite. In this we cannot rely exclusively upon external social engineering, politics, etc. We also have to work to build and engineer internal attitudes and resources, to change and transform belief frames so that people develop a new inner game to play. When we have good conditions of inner resources as well as outer, then and only then can we realistically expect that people and group will actualize their highest and best.

Economics and Meta-Rewards

Given all of that, what does self-actualization say about economic theory? How does it relate to economics? Or, how do we pay someone for work or a job when it is a self-actualizing job?

First, we can now ask if the facets of work within a company will help human nature grow healthily to its fullest stature? (1968, p. 220). This includes the kinds of work, the kinds of management, and the kinds of reward in terms of pay and meta-pay.

When we apply *Self-Actualization Psychology* to organizations, companies, and businesses we can determine whether the conditions serve or limit people. Synergic conditions of what's good for individual and good for society or business describe the *eupsychian* (prounce: yew-sign-kay-an) conditions of work, enlightened work. They are good for both the health and the prosperity of the person and the organization.

We now know that money and economic rewards are not enough. After a certain level of financial renumeration, more money has less and less effect on motivation, satisfaction, joy, or well-being. Pay itself needs to shift upward so that we look for various forms of meta-pay—acknowledgment, praise, time for creativity, association, responsibility, status, etc.[1]

Today's Paradigm of Companies and Communities	A Self-Actualizing Company or Community
Authoritarian	Collaborative, Democratic
Bureaucratic, bureaucracy	Representational
People told what to do	People have a voice
Command and control	Dialogue
Told where to fit in	Supporting discovery
	Team spirit, choice
	Responsibility and buy-in
Conformity	creativity, risk taking
Fear	Room for exploration
	Fun, excitement

Assumptions:

Theory X	*Theory Y*
People are lazy, hate work	People want to be involved and challenged
Making things stay the same	Ever-changing marketplace
	Anticipating trends
Status, rank	Respect for all persons
Money	Meta-Pay
Dependent, passive	Proactive, responsible
Unthinking	Honor of the job
Obedient, compliant	Mutual accountability
People avoid responsibility	People prefer responsibility
People prefer to be directed	People prefer self-direction
People are not creative	People are creative

Culture

Maslow said that the authentic person is one who resists enculturation and so transcends culture (1968, p. 12). As such, self-actualizers are not "well-adjusted" in the naive sense of receiving complete approval and identification with their culture. Maslow noted that self-actualizers resist enculturation and that they are "members at large of the human species" (1970, p. 174).

So while a culture does not create the human being, culture is absolutely necessary to actualize what's within us as human beings (1968, p. 161)

> ". . . a culture is a *sine qua non* for the actualization of humanness itself, e.g., language, abstract thought, ability to love; but these exist as potentialities in human germ plasm prior to culture." (211)

This in Self-Actualization Psychology enables us to create a comparative sociology. We can now speak about good or bad cultures and evaluate such in terms of whether the culture supports and facilitates human growth, maturity, and development, or whether it works against such. We can even set up measures regarding the extent and degree that a culture supports individuals and groups to actualize their higher potentials.

> "The better culture gratifies all basic human needs and permits self-actualization." (1968, p. 211)

The paradox is that we absolutely need culture as we begin. Culture is the womb or matrix within which our humanness is given birth. It "cultivates" our mind, emotions, speech, and behaviors so that we can enter that culture's universe of meaning. Yet as time progresses and we grow up, another developmental task arises—to individuals from our culture, to become our unique self, to find and develop our talents and skills, and to hear our impulse voices. In this step we learn to view our culture as just one among many human experiences and ways of being human. To self-actualize we now have to transcend our culture, to wear it lightly, and to evaluate our culture by the standards of self-actualization.

Culture is needed and yet it can also be a problem. Maslow noted repeatedly how the self-actualization drive is—

> ". . . very easily drowned out by habit, by wrong cultural attitudes toward them, by traumatic episodes, by erroneous education." (1968, p. 164)

Maslow noted that research indicated that attempting to teach people to be "unprejudiced" doesn't work very well. But conversely, as people self-actualize and become better human beings, they just naturally drop prejudices. Being "unprejudiced" flies off as a spark off the wheel, as an epiphenomenon, as a byproduct of becoming a better human being (1971, pp. 71-72).

Social Conflict

While Maslow's exploration of self-actualization originated in his curiosity about Wertheimer and Benedict, what set him on the course to developing his first model was World War II. It began with his inner questions about war, human nature, and human motivations. Why do conflicts erupt into armed fighting? What motivates this evil? Why are people not able to get along? For Maslow, these questions reached a zenith when America entered into war against Hitler and his cruel tyranny in Europe. It began with Maslow being unable to join the army because of his age. So he asked, "What can I do to contribute?"

He finally decided that the way he could best contribute was to create *a model of human motivation that leaders, could use to understand human motivation.* Yet this did not come out of the blue. For years Maslow had been studying motivation and human nature. His first studies involved working with Harlow and his chimpanezes. There he learned about their intelligence and gentleness. His studies in psychology until then had implied the "bad animal" model of instincts focusing especially on aggressive, competition, and survival of the fittest. What he discovered was that the higher an animal on the evolutionary scale, the more intelligent, gentle, and less violent. He also studied female sexuality and the role of sex for dominance.

From these studies, he was prepared for exploring human "instincts," drives, needs, and motivation. Out of that research, Maslow wrote his classic work which put his name on the international scene, *Motivation and Personality* (1954).

So what did Maslow discover about why people so often do not get along with each other very well? Why do we human beings get into so many conflicts with each other, behave poorly, and create the worst of human evils? Where is the source of our aggressive behaviors? Why do we get so competitive, form packs and tribes, dehumanize others as sub-human, and then seek to hurt and destroy them?

The common theory in that day from many philosophers and psychologists was the Freudian idea that people are animals. They are just evolved aggressive competitors who partake of all of the worst qualities of the most brutal animals. This is the theory of human nature as "red and bloody, a cruel claw of aggressive impulses."

Maslow disagreed. The problem is not that we have an aggressive nature that's innately destructive, hurtful, and evil which therefore needs to be controlled. We become aggressive and do "evil" things when our basic needs are *not* gratified. That's when we can become desperate. As we feel hurt and distressed, deficiency drives us to become aggressively reactive. And if we live in this kind of condition for long so that it becomes chronic, it then distorts and disorders personality.

In this model, "evil," reactiveness, and aggression make sense when viewed as signs of unsatisfied basic needs or distorted and neurotic needs. The problem lies not in our needs, not in the fact that we have biological drives and requirements, but in how we cope with our needs. It lies in the lack of gratification of our lower needs and the distortion of unfulfilled needs. This lies at the heart of the process creating what we call human evil and psycho-pathology.

Human aggressiveness then is *not* a sign that we are innately bad or evil. Human nature is not inherently dangerous and aggressive. This is a sign that one or more of our core needs have not been adequately satisfied and that we are simply reacting from a state of hurt and pain created by deficiency. At the level of the lower levels, lack evokes a sense of threat. Give a person safety and security, love and affection, trust and affirmation, self-value and dignity and then stand back. Watch that person blossom! Watch new properties, talents, skills, visions, and values emerge. Watch that person's attitude, values, and social relations change.

How do we explain the presence of evil in people? While the term "evil" sounds like a thing, it is not. As a nominalization, the term "evil" refers to a process. It is not something we *are* or something we *have,* it is something that we *do.* For *good* or *evil* to exist, we have to have some standards or criteria by which we can evaluate that something is good or evil to us, to our health, or to our communities. We have to have an agreed-upon criteria by which we measure something and can say that something contributes to the goodness of life, limb, finances, effectiveness, sight, etc. or that it works to our detriment.

If the relative terms *good* and *evil* speak about relative value and dis-value, life-enhancing quality of something versus the life-destructiveness quality of something, then in order to determine if something is "evil" to us or to another, we first have to identify the standard. Once we do that we can then determine the source of any particular evil.

In the old psychology paradigm, the source of evil was posited inside. "Man is evil at his core." Man is basically an animal— aggressive, anti-social, ego-centric, a taker, an evolutionary competitor striving in the drama of "the survival of the fittest." This is the Freudian and the Darwinian story. In religion, this is the old Calvinistic and Augustine story of man the wicked sinner who needs to be redeemed. These stories posit that the source of evil within.

In the paradigm shift of the bright-side psychology, Maslow framed people as inherently good, positive, healthful, gentle, and able to transcend self, to give of self, and contribute to the larger good. Humanity has a biological drive for the higher needs. That's a big perceptual shift!

So if evil does not come from within, then where does it come from? How do we explain evil in human experience? For Maslow, evil comes from above rather than below (1968, p. iv) and so has two primary sources:

1) *Deficiency.* Evil arises from the frustration of our basic needs. It is not intrinsic, it is a violent reaction against frustration of our intrinsic needs, emotions, and capacities (1968, p. 3). This makes the "evil" (hurt, pain, destructiveness) of neurosis *a deficiency disease* (1968, p. 21).

2) *Distortions.* Evil also arises from the distorted meanings which we create in our minds about our needs or a particular need. It arises from toxic or dis-empowering ideas and beliefs. Maslow mentioned another source. He said that what is actually evil is the demand for "Nirvana *Now!*" (1970, p. xxii).

Maslow said we have a two-fold nature: we have lower and higher needs. We have a creatureliness in our lower needs and a godlikeness in our higher needs—the actual and ideal. And both of these are to be integrated.

　　"Another kind of answer to the 'problem of evil' is suggested

> by the way in which our subjects [self-actualizing people]
> 'accept reality' as being-in-itself, in its own right. It is
> neither *for* man nor is it *against* him. It just is impersonally
> what it is. An earthquake which kills poses a problem of
> reconciliation only for the man who needs a personal God
> who is simultaneously all-loving, humorless, and omnipotent,
> and who created the world."

> "For the person who can perceive and accept it
> naturalistically, impersonally, and as uncreated, it presents no
> ethical problem. It was not done on purpose to annoy him.
> He shrugs his shoulders." (93)

> "Destructiveness, sadism, cruelty, malice, etc., seem so far to
> be not intrinsic but rather they seem to be violent reactions
> *against* frustration of our intrinsic needs, emotions, and
> capacities. Anger is *in itself* not evil, nor is fear, laziness, or
> even ignorance. Of course, these can and do lead to evil
> behavior, but they needn't." (1968, p. 3)

Actually what we call bad or evil is part of what's required for our
full development.

> "... the necessity of discipline, deprivation, frustration, pain,
> and tragedy ... To the extent that these experiences reveal
> and foster and fulfill our inner nature, to that extent they are
> desirable experiences. It is increasingly clear that these
> experiences have something to do with a sense of
> achievement and ego strength and therefore with the sense of
> healthy self-esteem and self-confidence. The person who
> hasn't conquered, withstood, and overcome continues to feel
> doubtful that he *could*. This is true not only for external
> dangers; it holds also for the ability to control and to delay
> one's own impulses, and therefore to be unafraid of them."
> (1968, p. 4)

The Thwarting Factor

At the heart of the source of most evil then is frustration. This led to
Maslow's *Thwarting Theory*. The frustration of our basic needs
refers to the *thwarting* of our drives, an important distinction in his
model.

> "Thwarting of unimportant desires produces no
> psychopathological results; thwarting of a basically important
> need does produce such. A conflict or a frustration is not

necessarily pathogenic. It becomes so only when it threatens or thwarts the basic needs, or partial needs that are closely related to the basic needs."

This explains a key source of why people don't get along very well, they suffer from *the ongoing thwarting* of their basic needs. This is what primarily creates aggression, anger, and often leads to violence and people hurting people. Feeling thwarted at a fundamental level people strike out in aggression. Yet even that alone is inadequate to fully explain the human aggression which we see in dictators like Hitler and that we see in current wars and conflicts around the world.

What else is there? *Meaning,* of course, and more specifically, the *distortion of meaning.* I can best illustrate this using Hitler's case. Lacking gratification of the basic need of self-respect, he became a sucker for the sick ideas about race superiority. With his unsatisfied need for self-regard, when he was exposed to the idea of Aryan superiority, he became a "true believer." He needed something to believe in to deal with his unfulfilled social and self needs. It was his sick way to feel okay about himself. Yet the longer the thwarting of that basic need went on, and the longer he fed his mind with the fanaticism, the more his neurotic obsession grew. And these became his justification for war, destruction, and annihilation. The amazing thing is that he wrote about all of these things in *Mein Kampf* and published them years before he gained the power to act on them.[2]

So today, when people just do not get along, and when there are constant fights, conflicts, mistreatment, and wars, we can expect to two things. We can expect the thwarting of some basic need. And second, we can expect that there are cognitive and semantic distortions about that need and how to gratify it. In this, we only have to look for limited beliefs and especially fanatical beliefs about having the ultimate Truth and the various justifications about imposing that upon unbelievers. And why? All of this is done to feel safe and secure, to protect one's group, or to build up oneself.

Creating a Self-Actualization World
Now if Maslow's theories on self-actualization led to this diagnosis, what is the solution? It is two-fold.

First, we need to *create the kind and quality of families, schools, businesses, communities, and governments that provides the basic human needs of survival, safety, social needs, and self needs.* In fact, the ability to adequately provide for the gratification of these needs is the first step to facilitating and creating a better world—better conditions for people to thrive and to experience their full humanity. The challenge here is to provide true satisfiers and to discourage false satisfiers. Doing that will change motivations as it enables people to move to the higher human realm of self-actualization.

The second part is tougher. *We need to create and provide the kind and quality of meanings that promote deep democracy of all peoples.* This will evoke a profound sense of equality, care, and respect in our communities, societies, and cultural institutions for all people. What mostly does damage to us, to our relationships, and that creates conflicts and wars are the meaning frames of erroneous ideas and beliefs. Here our neuro-semantic frames and responses operate as factors requiring us to become skillful in handling our own semantic states.

Self-Actualization at all Levels and Dimensions
Lasting cultural change most effectively begins at the individual level. When self-actualizing people are awakened to the higher vision of cultural change and feel a passion to make it their mission in life, they contribute to create more justice, equality, health, well-being, success of others, etc.

This is what creates a ground swell of people. And when a critical mass is reached, then the very atmosphere and attitudes of the culture start to change initiating a new geitgeist.

From working with individuals, we can then work with groups to promote self-actualization communities and businesses, self-actualization churches, schools, and governments. In the next book, *Self-Actualization Companies and Leaders,* I will focus how we can set about actually creating self-actualizing businesses.

Key Points in this Chapter
- Self-Actualization inevitably moves us beyond our self. In self-actualizing, we transcend self and ego so that we look to contribute to the larger human family. That's why self-actualizing people seek to create self-actualizing societies, companies, and businesses.

- *Self-actualization Psychology* applies socially at all levels and, in fact, enables us to determine the difference between a society that's good or bad for people becoming fully alive/ fully human.

•   A self-actualization group, business, or community organize group life to bring out the best in everybody. The group life then supports the uniqueness in people without creating a group-mind or a mindless conformity.

End Notes:

1. This chapter is just the beginning of this exploration. The next book in this series will be about *Self-Actualizing Companies and Leaders.* CEO Chip Conley of JoiedeVivre Hotels has recently published a book inj this area, *Peak: How Great Companies Get their Mojo from Maslow.*

2. See the article on the website, www.neurosemantics.com that is titled, *Games Hitler Played.*

Chapter 25

FACILITATING

AND COACHING

SELF-ACTUALIZATION

The emerging field of Coaching
is a twentieth-first century technology
for self-actualization.

- If self-actualization is growing to our full maturity and potentials, how can we *facilitate* it?
- How can we teach, coach, and train self-actualization and so facilitate the process for people to unleash their potentials?
- To what extent can we *direct* the self-actualization process?
- Are life, business, and executive coaches involved in the psycho-*actualizing* process?
- Can self-actualization be coached?

As early as 1956 Abraham Maslow was looking for a new term that would describe the profession of facilitating self-actualization in psychologically healthy people. In the end his choose *psychogogy* (the education of the psyche).[1] In spite of his good intentions, self-actualization continued in his time to be used in the therapeutic context.

By the 1990s, however, a new field began to emerge, a field that actually started with Tim Gallwey's *The Inner Game of Tennis* (1972).[2] Coaching, as a helping profession, is not therapy, training, or consulting, and yet it addresses many of the same concerns and often works with the same population. Today the field of Coaching is extending itself to many niches and goes by a wide range of terms: Business Coaching, Executive Coaching, Life Coaching, Personal Coaching, etc.

As a new emergent field specifically designed for psychologically healthy people, coaching is primarily for the purpose of facilitating self-actualization, and presents itself as a new profession actualizing the work of Maslow, Rogers, and others in the Third Force. Simultaneously the traditional people-helping professions of consulting, therapy, mentoring, teaching, and training are less adequate vessels for self-actualization since they presuppose specific expert-knowledge and skill that is offered a client. Coaching, by contrast, involves expert knowledge and skill *not* of the content of what a person wants to self-actualize, but of *the facilitation process itself.* Coaching, in fact, is the facilitative approach par excellence. So what if it turns out that *coaching* is the "technology" of self-actualization and one of the missing ingredients of the first human potential movement?

As we explore this, a key question is whether we can directly coach self-actualization. In *Unleashed,* I addressed this as I explored the vision, premises, and processes of Self-Actualization Psychology. There also I presented numerous patterns for how to unleash potentials. Now while we may at times need some therapy, training, mentoring, and consulting to actualize some new facet of ourselves, we mostly need someone who understands *Self-Actualization Psychology* and is able to simply facilitate the meaning construct, the transformation of the crucible, and the processes for entering into the zone of self-actualization.

Given this, could Coaching, as an emergent field that centrally focuses on and uses *Self-Actualization Psychology,* be a new discipline that uniquely operates with the specific techniques for facilitating self-actualization? What if the coaching approach itself is one of the missing ingredients of the first Human Potential Movement? And what if we took the process and techniques of coaching as a central way for unleashing our potentials as well as those of others?

From the theory of *Self-Actualization Psychology* we know that in order to move beyond the lower needs we must first gratify them with true satisfiers without over-loading them with *being*-level meanings. Then we can move on to the higher or meta-needs of self-actualization. This enables us to take the next step in human development, a place where we are ready to take on challenges that will actualize our highest and best.

Prior to this, we might need therapy for personal healing, training for skill information and development, and/or consulting to obtain the appropriate expert information about a given area where we want to self-actualize. Self-Actualization Psychology describes an area beyond the traditional psychologies which deal with hurt and trauma, building a sense of self and ego-strength, and satisfying deficiency needs.

Self-Actualization Psychology focuses on psychologically healthy people who are "OK," "up to average," have finished the past, and who are ready for living life to the full. So, what's beyond therapy? And who is best equipped to work with the change processes of unleashing potential for those who embrace change (rather than resist it) and who are looking for challenges to take their skills and capacities to a new level?

What if the coaching process itself is the answer to these questions about self-actualization? What if coaching is an ideal modality for facilitating the unleashing process? In asking these questions I am not saying the coaching is the only self-actualization process, only that it is clearly one process. To whatever extent this is so, then what is coaching and how does it facilitate the self-actualizing process?

Beyond Therapy to Coaching
Therapy is designed as an interaction for those who operate from *deficiency,* who lack the skill to survive and cope effectively, who *lack* safety and security, love and affection, self-esteem and self-regard. It is for those who feel an urgent need to fulfil deficiencies and to become okay. That's why becoming *okay* is the first goal of therapy. The aim is to get up to average.

The second goal is to develop sufficient ego-strength to face reality for what it *is* without caving in, reacting mindlessly, or over-reacting. The third goal is to heal any hurt or trauma of the past so a person can come into the present and to be in full sensory awareness in the moment. These are significant goals in the psychotherapeutic context and demand tremendous skill and patience in any effective practitioner.

After that, then what? Who works with clients who have moved to the level beyond the therapy level—to a level beyond gratification of deficiency needs? Who works with those who live at the level of the self-actualization and the meta-growth needs? Moving to this place a person is no longer motivated by deficiency or the need for homeostasis. A person is now motivated by an endless restlessness that embraces disequilibrium. The self-actualizing person wants more—more learning, growth, change, and discoveries.

At this level our drives change. Our urge is not to fill up what is missing, not to fix what is broken or distorted, it is *to more fully express ourselves,* our talents, values, aptitudes, passions, and interests and to awaken new talents and potentials. We want to discover our highest potentials by challenging and unleashing what is yet untapped. We want to transcend who we are today, what we know and can do today, and stretch forward to become all that we can become. In *Self-Actualization Psychology* the passion for more is not only a drive of human nature, it is a higher developmental stage. It is also built into people of all cultures and times. This is where a psycho-*actualizer* can coach us to the next level of development.

Coaching as a Meta-Discipline
Given all of this, what is coaching and how does it uniquely facilitate the unleashing of potentials? While life, business, and executive coaching is similar to sports coaching, *it is not the same.* The difference is that a sports coach is the expert in the content and so teaches, trains, motivates, and drills.

The kind of coaching that works best for self-actualization involves *stepping back to a meta-position to work with structure, processes, and contexts.* Because this process involves working from a meta-position, we describe it as *meta-coaching* to differentiate it from sports coaching. In coaching self-actualization, stepping back from content enables us to facilitate the self-actualization by activating the person's potentials. It is in stepping back as a coach that enables us to facilitate numerous self-actualizing processes.

As a meta-discipline, the coaching focuses, not on the content of a person's self-actualization, but on *the dynamic processes* involved in actualizing one's best. In Meta-Coaching we have formalized this as a systematic approach to utilize the principles and premises of Self-Actualization Psychology and to create a set of techniques for the processes that we use in unleashing.

The Prerequisite Processes of Coaching
In creating a systematic approach to Meta-Coaching I first made an analysis of coaching and then, with Michelle Duval, we identified and developed specific models to address its essence. So what is coaching and what uniquely distinguishes this domain as a profession?

In answering these questions, *we first identified what it is not.* By examining the closely-related professions, we looked for the critical differences, and especially for the core skill in each profession. Consulting, mentoring, training, and therapy represents separate and special domains governed by a core competency. Knowing these core competencies enables us to determine the boundaries of the field of coaching.

- *Consultancy*: Given that a consultant is an expert in a particular area with specialized knowledge and skills, a consultant is paid for *giving expert advice*. This is precisely what a coach does *not* do. The coach's skill differs from giving advice.

- *Mentorship*: Given that a mentor is a more experienced person in a particular area, someone who has "been there and done that," a mentor *guides* using his or her expertise in that area. This is precisely what a coach does *not* do. What a coach does differs from guiding.

- *Training*: Given that a trainer is someone who has specialized knowledge and the ability to transfer the information to others, a trainer is someone who *teaches, drills, and instructs.* Teaching is precisely what a coach does *not* do. What a coach does differs from teaching, conditioning, and drilling.

- *Therapy*: Given that a therapist or counselor is someone who focuses on healing hurts, mostly from the past and mostly with people who are stuck in deficiency needs, a therapist is someone who reparents a client, finishes psychological unfinished business, heals traumatic hurts, and gets a person up to average. This is precisely what a coach does *not* do.

What a coach does differs from working on the hurts and traumas of the past.

As we clearly differentiate what these professionals do, and their areas of expertise, is there any area left that is unique for coaching? By pushing back these areas, we notice that consulting, mentoring, training, and counseling are basically areas of *content expertise.* It may be highly directive as in therapy or training, and it may be less so, more indirect and more facilitative as in consulting and mentoring, yet the value in each is that *the professional is an expert in the content.* In each of these professions, the person knows what's best for the client and so works toward a predetermined outcome. This is precisely what a coach does *not* do.

Above and beyond everything else, *a coach is an expert in the meta-discipline of facilitating the processes of self-actualizing.* As a meta-field, coaching supports, enables, empowers, questions, and facilitates the expertise of the client. *Coaching makes the client the expert in his or her own life,* in his or her own visions, dreams, values, potentials, and passions. As an expert in the processes and the structure of the processes, the coach does not determine what the client needs or wants. In this, the coach has no predetermined agenda to impose. The coach facilitates the process of the client deciding on his or her own outcomes.

What Coaching Is
To make the meta-coaching approach truly systematic, we created an operational description of the expertise of a professional coach (psycho-*actualizer*) based on what coaching actually *is.* The following describes the essence of the coaching process: [3]

1) *A conversation that's highly focused*
   Coaching is a specialized communication and a conversation that most people seldom experience. It is a conversation that gets to the heart of things through the exploring of one's dreams, intentions, hopes, values, meanings, and identity and creating a precise description of one's desired outcome.

2) *Unconscious back-of-the-mind communication*
   Coaching is communicating with a client's whole mind, and given the special kind of self-reflexive consciousness that we humans have, coaching facilitates awareness of our higher levels of beliefs, decisions, identities, permissions, hopes, etc. —all of the things in the back of the mind. This ability to

communicate with the multiple dimensions of a person's inner communications is what makes the communication insightful and powerful. This kind of conversation makes explicit a person's highest frames for exploration and choice.

4) *Systemic awareness and ecology*

Coaching is systemic as it works holistically with the whole person. Coaching is systemic in that it works with multiple systems: it facilitates the whole mind-body-and emotion system, the relationship systems, career, health, spiritual, etc. systems. Doing this enables the coaching changes to be congruent, aligned, and ecological.

5) *Transformative change that generates new possibilities*

Coaching facilitates multi-dimensional levels of change so a client transforms in mind, heart, speech, and behavior in unleashing new potentials. Rather than therapeutic remedial change, coaching is generative and developmental change.

6) *Implemented performance*

Coaching facilitates the actualizing and embodying of meanings, ideals, goals, values, and visions to make them real in actual life. Coaching facilitates the creating of an action plan and then the measuring of one's progress to determine where a person is and the next step for development. Coaching facilitates the execution of action plans.

6) *Self-Actualization Psychology*

Coaching facilitates the unleashing of potentials as the highest level of human experience and the ultimate design in psychological health and well-being. This enables a client to activate his or her best, and to experience peak performances.

7) *Facilitation*

Ultimately coaching is facilitation as it facilitates all of these processes and others. Coaching does this to create a space of trust and rapport. This initiates the kind of personal and emotional safety so clients can more easily explore their inner nature and possibilities.

For a professional coach, these different facets represents what coaching is and calls for models so we can handle each of these facets of coaching. These are the very facets that govern how we coach the unleashing of potentials. In Meta-Coaching, our particular approach, we use the following models:

1) *A conversation that's highly focused*

We use the Neuro-Linguistic Communication model (NLP) which identifies the languages of the mind, that is, the movies that we play in the theater of our mind composed of specific sensory representational systems. From these representations arise the states that our communication creates in us and others, the relationship that develops and the level of rapport. NLP makes explicit the precision questions that facilitates clarity about what we are doing.

2) *Unconscious back-of-the-mind communication*

We use the Meta-States model of reflexivity to explore the processes governing how we create layer upon layer of frames of mind, the multi-dimensional nature of how we construct meaning and set frames in the back of our mind.

3) *Systemic awareness*[4]

We use the Matrix Model, based on the latest developments in developmental, cognitive, and behavorial psychology, offers a unified format for following the energy in a mind-body-emotion system and for quickly identifying leverage points of change.

4) *Generative and transformative change*[5]

We use the Axes of Change model as we work with self-actualizing people. Currently, this is the only generative and non-therapeutic change model in the field of coaching. Every other change model comes from therapy and typically includes resistance and relapse which indicates that the model is designed for therapy clients, not change-embracers. It is built on four axes governing how self-actualizing people and people who are basically healthy change, change-embracers transform: motivation, decision, creation, and solidification.

5) *Implemented performance*[6]

We use the Neuro-Semantic Benchmarking model to operationalize concepts about invisible processes and to create the metrics so we can measure these intangible skills and concepts. We also use the Mind-to-Muscle pattern to enable people to integrate the great ideas that they know in their heads so they become part of their muscle memory.

6) *Self-Actualization Psychology*

We use the Self-Actualization Quadrants, the Self-Actualization Matrix, and Self-Actualization Psychology as models for working with the kind of bright-side psychology and describing how self-actualization actually occurs and what unleashes human potentials.

7) *Facilitation*

We use the Neuro-Semantic Facilitation Model that identifies the process of facilitating using the seven core coaching skills as well as the nine change coaching skills and two dozen additional advance skills. We have benchmarked all of these skills to set a bar for competency and to measure them.

With this full set of seven models, a professional coach or Meta-Coach knows *what* to do *when, how* to do it, with *whom* and *why* in working with a client to facilitate his or her self-actualization. This is what gives this system its particular robustness for developing effectiveness in working with healthy people to unleash new potentials.

Key Points in this Chapter

- A current profession that is uniquely suited for facilitating the unleashing of potentials so people can self-actualize is the meta-discipline of coaching.

- As a professional modality for working with those who are change-embracers and who are looking for a challenge to take their skills, experiences, and sense of self to a new level, expertise in coaching does not focus on the *content* of the potentials we want to unleash, but upon the *processes* of how this unleashing occurs. This makes coaching inherently a *meta*-profession.

- In coaching self-actualization numerous processes play a critical role in facilitating self-actualization. These include a robust dialogue, an empathetic relationship, a reflexivity that enables us to track the spiraling of thoughts, the implementation process for executing what we know, a model for change embracers, a systems model for tracking feedback and feed forward loops, and the unleashing process that actualizes our best self.

COACHING AND META-COACHING

Coaching	*Meta-Coaching Models*	*Psychologies*
1) *Communication:* Relationship, Rapport	NLP Communication Model	Cognitive-Behavioral
2) *Unconscious and Meta-Communication* Self-Reflexivity	Meta-States Model	Cognitive, Meta-Cognitive
3) *Systemic*	The Matrix Model Matrix Business Plan	Developmental
4) *Change and Learning*	Axes of Change model	Gestalt
5) *Implemented Performance*	Benchmarking Model	Cognitive, Sports Psy.
6) Self-*Actualization* Unleash Potentials	Matrix of Self-Actualization Self-Actualization Quadrants	Systems Self-Actualization Existential psych.
7) Facilitation	The Facilitation Model	Client-Centered Therapy

---

End Notes

1. Maslow (1968), p. 46-48. He also suggested other terms such as *meta-counselor* (1971, p. 47). "I have used the words 'therapy,' 'psychotherapy,' and 'patient.' Actually I hate all these words and I hate the medical model because it suggests that the person . . . is beset by disease and illness." (1971, p. 49).

2. Timothy Gallway was one of the many seminar leaders at Esalen and presented the Inner Game there in the 1970s.

3. There's one other thing that we could add to this description: coaching is also a business. Yet this does not directly have to do with *the process of coaching* (working *in* the business), but rather about working *on* the business as a business. So above and beyond the content expertise of facilitation, coaching is a business and so requires business acumen to add value in the marketplace, to market onself effectively, and to apply coaching to oneself in terms of creating a successful and viable commercial business.

4. See *The Matrix Model* (2003).

5. See *Coaching Change,* Meta-Coaching, Volume I. (2005).

6. For more about *Meta-Coaching*, see the following websites: www.meta-coaching.org; www.metacoachfoundation.org, and www.neurosemantics.com.

SELF-ACTUALIZATION

PSYCHOLOGY

There you have it. The *Self-Actualization Psychology* that I have presented it here is based upon the brilliant pioneering work of Abraham Maslow as well as the study of psychologically health people as expanded through the work of Carl Rogers, Rollo May, Viktor Frankl, and many, many others and now updated for the twenty-first century. This represents the foundational theory and understanding that undergirds the processes of self-actualization in previous book, *Unleashed: A Guide to Your Ultimate Self-Actualization.* And while I have attempted to contribute to this kind of psychology, what I've developed here

This is, however, only the beginning. There's much more to learn, much more to develop, and especially, much more to experience. And, ultimately, that is the bottom line—*experiencing the full humanness that we all have within us and creating the best version of ourselves.*

To your highest values and best visions!

BIBLIOGRAPHY

Allport, Gordon. (1971). *Becoming: Basic considerations for a psychology of personality.* New Haven: Yale University Press.

Anderson, Walter Truett. (1983). *The upstart spring: Esalen and the American awakening.* Reading, MA: Addison-Wesley Publishing Company.

Armstrong, Lance; Jenkins, Sally. (2003). *Every second counts.* New York: Broadway Books.

Armstrong, Lance; Jenkins, Sally. (2001). *It's not about the bike.* New York: A Berkley Book.

Assagioli, Roberto. (1965). *Psychosynthesis.* New York: Hobbs, Dorman.

Association for Humanistic Psychology, website. www.ahpweb.org

Bandler, Richard; and Grinder, John. (1975). *The structure of magic, Volume I: A book about language and therapy.* Palo Alto, CA: Science & Behavior Books.

Bandler, Richard and Grinder, John. (1976). *The structure of magic, Volume II.* Palo Alto, CA: Science & Behavior Books.

Bateson, Gregory. (1972). *Steps to an ecology of mind.* New York: Ballatine.

Block, Peter. (2002). *The answer to how is Yes: Acting on what matters.* San Francisco: Berrett-Koehler Publishers. Inc.

Branden, Nathaniel. (1996). *Taking responsibility: Self-reliance and the accountable life.* New York: Fireside Book, Simon & Schuster.

Bridoux, Denis; Merlevede, Patrick; Vandamme, Rudy. (1997). *Seven steps to emotional intelligence.* Wales, UK: Crown House Publishing.

Bugental, James F.T. (1967). *Challenges of Humanistic Psychology.* New York: McGraw-Hill Company.

Bridoux, Denis; Merlevede, Patrick. (2004). *Mastering mentoring and coaching with emotional intelligence.* Wales, UK: Crown House Publishing.

Carkhuff, Robert R. (1981). *Toward Actualizing Human Potential.* Amherst, MA: Human Resource Development Press.

Chiang, Hung-Min; Maslow, Abraham H. (1969). *The Healthy Personality Readings.* D. Van Nostrand Co. New York.

Child, Irvin L. (1973). *Humanistic psychology and the research tradition: Their several virtues.* New York: John Wiley and Sons, Inc.

Chomsky, Noam. (1965). *Aspects of the theory of syntax.* Cambridge, MA: MIT Press.

Conley, Chip. (2007). *Peak: How great companies get their mojo from Maslow.* San Francisco: Jossey-Bass.

Cox, Frank. (1973). *Psychology.* Debuque, IO: William C. Brown Company Publishes.

Cunningham, S. (1985, May). Humanists celebrate gains, goals. *APA Monitor, pp.* 16, 18.

Csiksezentmihalyi, Mihaly. (1991). *Flow: The psychology of optimal experience.* New York: Harper & Row.

DeCarvalho, R. (1991). *The founders of humanistic psychology.* New York: Praeger.

Dyer, Wayne. (1980). *The Sky's the Limit.* New York: Simon and Schuster.

Ellis, Albert. (1973). *Humanistic psychology: The rational-emotive approach.* New York: Julian Press.

Ellis, Albert and Harper, Robert A. (1976). *A new guide to rational living.* Englewood Cliffs, NJ: Prentice-Hall, Inc.

Frankl, Viktor. (1959). *Man's search for meaning.* Boston: Beacon Press.

Fosdick, Harry Emerson. (1943). *On being a real person.* New York: Harper and Brothers, Publishers.

Gallwey, W. Timothy. (1974). *The Inner Game of Tennis.* NY: Random House.

Gardner, Howard. (1983). *Frames of mind: The theory of multiple intelligences.* NY: BasicBooks.

Gardner, Howard. (1983). *Multiple intelligences: The theory in practice.* NY: BasicBooks.

Giulianai, Rudolph W.; Kurson, Ken. (2002). *Leadership.* New York: Miramax Books.

Goble, Frank G. (1970). *The third force: The psychology of Abraham Maslow.* New York: Pocket Books, Simon & Schuster.

Goleman, Daniel. (1997). *Emotional intelligence: Why it can matter more than IQ.* New York: Bantam Books.

Goleman, Daniel. (2002). *Working with Emotional Intelligence.* London: Bloomsbury.

Grant, Dave. (1983). *The ultimate power.* Old Tappan, NJ: Fleming H. Revell Company.

Grinder, John; and Judith DeLozier. (1987). *Turtles all the way down: Prerequisites to personal genius.* Scotts Valley, CA: Grinder & Associates.

Glasser, William. (1976). *Positive Addiction.* New York: Harper & Row.

Guthrie, Robert T. (1971 Ed.). *Psychology in the world today: An interdisciplinary approach.* Reading, MA: Addison-Wesley Publishing Company.

Hall, Michael. (2000). *Meta-states: Managing the higher levels of your mind's reflexivity.* Clifton, CO: Neuro-Semantic Publications.

Hall, L. Michael; Bodenhamer, Bob G. (2005). *Sub-Modalities: Going Meta.* Formerly, The structure of Excellence. Clifton, CO: Neuro-Semantic Publications.

Hall, L. Michael. (2000). *Secrets of personal mastery: Advanced techniques for accessing your higher levels of consciousness.* Wales, UK: Crown House Publications.

Hall, L. Michael. (2001). *Games slim and fit people play.* Clifton, CO: Neuro-Semantic Publications.

Hall, L. Michael; Bodenhamer, Bob. (2001). *Games for mastering fear.* Clifton, CO: Neuro-Semantic Publications.

Hall, L. Michael. (2001). *Communication Magic.* Wales, UK: Crown House Publications.

Hall, L. Michael; Duval, Michelle. (2004). *Coaching Conversations: Robust Conversations that Coach for Excellence.* Clifton, CO: Neuro-Semantic Publications.

Hall, L. Michael; Duval, Michelle. (2005). *Coaching Change: For higher levels for success and transformation.* Clifton, CO: Neuro-Semantic Publications.

Hall, L. Michael. (2007). *Unleashed: A guide to your ultimate self-actualization.* Clifton, CO: Neuro-Semantic Publications.

Hardy, Christine. (1998). *Networks of meaning: A bridge between mind and matter.* Westport, CT: Praeger.

Hanna, Thomas. (1979, Editor). *Explorers of humankind.* New York: Harper & Row, Publishers.

Hoffman, Edward. (1988). *The right to be human: A biography of Abraham Maslow.* Los Angeles: Jeremy P. Tarcher.

Hoffman, Edward. (1996 Ed.). *Future visions: The unpublished papers of Abraham Maslow.* Thousand Oaks, CA: SAGE Publications.

James, William. (1890). *Principles of psychology.* Vol. 1. New York: Henry Holt Co.

Jourard, Sydney. (1971). *The Transparent Self.* NY: Van Nostrand Reinhold.

Knapp, Robert R. (1976). *Handbook for the Personal Orientation Inventory.* San Diego, CA: EdITS publishers.

Korzybski, Alfred. (1933/ 1994) *Science and sanity: An introduction to non-Aristotelian systems and general semantics,* (5th. ed.). Lakeville, CN: International Non-Aristotelian Library Publishing Co.

Kuhn, Thomas S. (1970). *The structure of scientific revolutions* (2nd ed.). Chicago: University of Chicago Press.

Kripal, Jeffrey J. (2007). *Esalen: America and the religion of no religion.* Chicago: The University of Chicago Press.

Lakoff, George; Johnson, Mark. (1980). *Metaphors we live by.* Chicago, IL: The University of Chicago Press.

Lakoff, George; Johnson, Mark. (1999). *Philosophy in the flexh: The embodied mind and its challenge to western thought.* New York: Basic Books.

Leonard, George; Murphy, Michael. (1995). *The life we are given: A long term program for realizing the potential of body, mind, heart, and soul.* New York: Penguin Putnan, Inc.

Lewis, C. S. (1943). *Mere Christianity.* New York: Collier Books, Macmillan Publishing Company.

Lowry, Richard J. (1973). *A.H. Maslow: An intellectual portrait.*

Monterey, CA: Brooks/ Cole Publishing Company.

Lowry, Richard J. (Ed., 1982). *The journals of Abraham Maslow.* Lexington, MA: The Lewis Publishing Company.

Lowry, Richard. J. (Ed. 1973). *Dominance, Self-Esteem, Self-Actualization: Germinal Papers of A.H. Maslow.* Monterey, CA: Brooks/Cole Publishing Company.

Mandela, Nelson. (1994/ 2002). *Long walk to freedom: The autobiography of Nelson Mandela.* Abacus: London England.

May, Rollo. (1969). *Love and Will.* New York: Norton.

May, Rollo. (1961). *Existential Psychology.* New York: Random House.

McConnell, James V. (1977). *Understanding human behavior.* New York: Holt, Rinehart, and Winston.

Maslow, Abraham; Mittelmann, Bela (1941). *Principles of Abnormal Psychology: The Dynamics of Psychic Illness.*

Maslow, Abraham, H. (1959, Ed.) *New knowledge in human values.* Chicago: Henry Regnery Company.

Maslow, Abraham H. (1943). "A Theory of Human Motivation," *Psychological Review*, L, pp. 370-396. American Psychological Association.

Maslow, Abraham. (1970). *Motivation and Personality.* (2nd ed.). New York: Harper & Row.

Maslow, Abraham. (1968). *Toward a Psychology of Being.* New York: Van Nostrand.

Maslow, Abraham. (1953, 1971). *The Farther Reaches of Human Nature.* New York: Viking.

Maslow, Abraham H. (1998). *Maslow on Management.* Originally, *Eupsychian Management.* New York: John Wiley & Sons, Inc.

Maslow, Abraham H.; Stephens, Deborah C., Ed. (2000). *The Maslow Business Reader.* New York: John Wiley & Sons, Inc.

Maslow, Bertha G. (1972). *Abraham H. Maslow: A Memorial Volume.* Monterey, CA: Brooks/ Cole Publishing Company.

May, Rollo. (1969). *Love and Will.* New York: Norton.

May, Rollo. (1961). *Existential Psychology.* New York: Random House.

May, Rollo; Rogers, Carl; Maslow, Abraham. (1986). *Politics and innocence: A humanistic debate.* Dallas, Texas: Saybrook Publishers.

McGregor, Douglas. (1960, 2006). *The Human side of enterprise: Annotated edition.* New York: McGraw-Hill.

McWaters, B. (Ed.) (1977). *Humanistic perspectives: current trends in psychology.* Monterey, CA: Wadsworth.

Miller, Stuart. (1971). *Hot Springs: The True Adventures of the First New York Jewish Literary Intellectual in the Human Potential Movement.* New York: Bantam.

Moss, Donald. (ed.) (1999). *Humanistic and transpersonal psychology: A historical and biographical Sourcebook.* Westport, CT.: Greenwood Press.

Myerson, Abraham. (1950). *Speaking of man.* New York: Alfred A. Knopf.

Murphy, Michael; Leonard, George. (1995). *The Life we are Given.* New York: Penguin Putnam.

Nevill, Dorothy D. (1977, Ed.). *Humanistic psychology: New frontiers.* New York: Gardner Press, Inc., Division of John Wiley & Sons, Inc.

Pearsall, Paul. (2003). *The Beethoven factor: the new positive psychology of hardiness, happiness, healing, and hope.* Charlottesville, VA: Hampton Roads Publishing.

Perls. Fritz. (1973). *The gestalt approach and eyewitness to therapy.* Palo Alto: Science and Behavior books.

Powell, S.J. John. (1969). *Why am I afraid to tell you who I am?* Niles, IL: Argus Communications.

Powell, S.J. John. (1971). *Fully alive/ fully human.* Niles, IL: Argus Communications.

Rogers, Carl R. (1951). *Client-centered therapy.* Boston: Houghton Mifflin.

Rogers, Carl R. (1972). *On Becoming a Person: A therapist's view of psychotherapy.* Boston, MA: Houghton Mifflin.

Rogers, Carl R. (1980). *A way of being.* Boston: Houghton Mifflin.

Satir, Virginia. (1972). *Peoplemaking.* Palo Alto, CA: Science and

Behavior Books.

Schneider, Kirk J.; Bugental, James F.; Pierson, J. Fraser. (2001). *The handbook of humanistic psychology: Leading edges in theory, research, and practice.* Thousand Oaks, CA: Sage Publications.

Schutz, William C. (1967). *Joy: Expanding human awareness.* New York: Grove Press, Inc.

Schutz, Will. (1979, 1982). *Profound Simplicity: Learning Concepts.* San Diego, CA: University Associates, Inc.

Schutz, Will. (1994). *The Human Element: Productivity, Self-Esteem and the Bottom Line.* San Francisco: Jossey-Bass: A Wiley Company.

Seligman, Martin, E.P. (1975). *Helplessness: On depression, development, and death.* San Francisco: Freeman.

Seligman, Martin E.P. (1991). *Learned optimism.* New York: Alfred A. Knopf.

Seligman, Martin E.P; Csiksezentmihalyi, Mihaly. (2000, Jan.). *Positive Psychology: An Introduction.* American Psychologist, American Psychological Association, Inc.

Sheldon, Kennon M.; King, Laura. (2001, March). *Why Positive Psychology is Necessary.* American Psychologist, American Psychological Association, Inc.

Schultz, Duane P.; Schultz, Sydney Ellen. (1992). *A history of modern psychology.* (Fifth Edition). New York: Harcourt Brace Jovanovich College Publishers.

Shostrom, E.L. (1963). *Personal Orientation Inventory.* San Diego, CA: EdITS/ Educational & Industrial Testing Service.

Shostrom, E.L. (1974). *Manual for the Personal Orientation Inventory.* San Diego, CA: EdITS/ Educational & Industrial Testing Service.

Shostrom, E.L. (1976). *Actualizing Therapy: Foundations for a Scientific Ethic.* San Diego, CA: EdITS.

Tageson, C. William. (1982). *Humanistic psychology: A synthesis.* Homewood, IL: The Dorsey Press.

Tillich, Paul. (1932). *The courage to be.* New Haven, CT: Yale University Press.

Tournier, Paul. (1957). *The meaning of persons.* New York: Perennial

Library, Harper and Row Publishers.

Wachowski, Larry; Wachowski, Andy. (2000). Screenplay: *The art of the matrix*. New York: Village Roadshow Films.

Welch, I. David; Tate, George A.; Medeiros, Donald C. (1987). *Self-Actualization: An annotate bibliography of theory and research.* New York: Garland Publishing, Inc.

Wilber, Ken. (1996). *A brief history of everything.* Boston, MA: Shambhala Publications.

Wilson, Colin. (1972). *New Pathways in Psychology: Maslow and the Post-Freudian Revolution.* New York: Taplinger Publishing Company.

INDEX

L. Michael Hall, Ph.D.
Neuro-Semantics®
P.O. Box 8
Clifton, Colorado 81520 USA
(970) 523-7877

www.self-actualizing.com   www.neurosemantics.com
www.neuro-semantics-training.com   www.meta-coaching.org

L. Michael Hall is a visionary leader in the area of personal development, empowerment, and self-actualization. Founding the field of Neuro-Semantics with the Meta-States model in 1994, Dr. Hall has created numerous models and hundreds of patterns—all designed to enable people to facilitate their own self-actualization.

Michael is an entrepreneur, author, researcher, and international trainer. His doctorate is in the Cognitive-Behavioral sciences from Union Institute University. For almost two decades he had a private practice as a psychotherapist and was licensed as a professional counselor (LPC) in the state of Colorado.

Dr. Hall found NLP in 1986 and studied it in trainings with Richard Bandler, afterwards writing several books for him. Later when modeling resilience, he developed the Meta-States model (1994). That led to the beginning of his international trainings. In 1996 he co-created the first Society of Neuro-Semantics with Dr. Bob Bodenhamer, now *The International Society of Neuro-Semantics* (ISNS).

As a prolific writer, Michael has written more than 35 books, many best sellers in the field of NLP. While Dr. Hall first applied NLP to coaching in 1991, it wasn't until 2001 that he began creating the beginnings of Neuro-Semantic Coaching, then with Michelle Duval, they co-created Meta-Coaching Training System.

Dr. Hall, as primarily a modeler of positive psychological experiences, and has modeled resilience, meta-cognition, leadership, coaching, accelerated learning, and so on.

ISNS: International Society of Neuro-Semantics. L. Michael Hall and Bobby G., Bodenhamer trademarked both Meta-States and Neuro-Semantics in 1996 and began the first *Institute of Neuro-Semantics*.

LIST OF BOOKS

Meta-States Books

Secrets of Personal Mastery	$25
Meta-States	$25
Dragon Slaying	$25
The Matrix Model	$25
NLP: Going Meta	$25
Meta-States Magic (spiral)	$30
States of Equilibrium:	$35

Frame Games Series

Winning the Inner Game	$25
(Previously, Frame Games)	
Games Slim People Play	$20
Games for Mastering Fear	$20
Games Business Experts Play	$35
Games Great Lovers Play	$25

NLP Books

MovieMind	$20
User's Manual –Vol. I	$45
User's Manual – Vol II	$55
The Source Book of Magic	$25
Source Book, Vol. II (spiral)	$30
Mind-Lines:	$25
The Spirit of NLP	$25
Figuring Out People	$30
Meta-Detective Board Game	$39
($53 with *Figuring Out People*)	
Sub-Modalities Going Meta	$25
Time-Line: Adventures	$25
Communication Magic	$25
Becoming More Ferocious	$25
The Structure of Personality	$50

Self-Actualization Books

Vol I Coaching Change	$25
Vol II Coaching Conversations	$25
III: *Unleashed:* Self-Actualiz.	$25
IV: Self-Actualization Psychology	$29
V: Achieving Peak Performance	$35
(Spiral Limited Edition)	

Application Books:

Instant Relaxation	$18
Propulsion Systems	$25
The Bateson Report	$10
Persuasion Engineering Simplified	$ 8
Patterns for Renewing Mind	$25
Languaging	$25

Other Books that are Available

Beyond Selling	$25
Selling with Integrity	$25
Core Transformation	$20
Selling w. Integrity	$25
Doing it with Pete	$17
Apocalypse Then	$10
Motivation	$ 8
Emotions	$ 8
Speak Up, Clear, Kind	$ 8

Training Manuals $35
(Spiral books)

Stroke of Genius series
Learning Genius
Selling Genius
Writing Genius (Prolific Writing)
Wealth Genius
Business Genius

Winning the Inner Game series
Winning Inner Game Workshop
Games Fit and Slim People Play
Games For Mastering Fear

Advanced Flexibility
Defusing Hotheads
Instant Relaxation Workshop
Advanced Modeling
Cultural Modeling
Meta-NLP: Practitioner Manual
Meta-Masters: Master Practitioner
APG: Accessing Personal Genius
Or, Coaching Genius
LPG: Living Personal Genius
Coaching Essentials (NLP Intro.)
Emotional Mastery

Self-Actualization series
Self-Actualization Workshop
Creativity and Innovation

NSP
Neuro-Semantic Publications

P.O. Box 8
Clifton, Colorado 81520—0008
(970) 523-7877
(970) 523-5790 fax